SOUTHERN GARDENING
An Environmentally Sensitive Approach

Marie Harrison

Pineapple Press, Inc.
Sarasota, Florida

Inquiries should be addressed to:

Pineapple Press, Inc.
P.O. Box 3889
Sarasota, Florida 34230

www.pineapplepress.com

Library of Congress Cataloging-in-Publication Data

Harrison, Marie, 1942-
Southern gardening : an environmentally sensitive approach / by Marie Harrison.
p. cm.
ISBN 1-56164-329-7 (pbk.)
1. Landscape plants—Southern States. 2. Landscape gardening—Southern States. 3. Gardening—Environmental aspects—Southern States. I. Title.

SB407.H2825 2005
635.9'0975—dc22   2004025874

13-digit ISBN 978-1-56164-329-5

First Edition
10 9 8 7 6 5 4 3 2 1

Design by Shé Heaton
Printed in the United States of America

Map on page xiv courtesy of U.S. National Arboretum, USDA-ARS

CONTENTS

I Plants for the Environmentally Sensitive Landscape

Groundcovers and Lawn Alternatives

Trees and Shrubs

Hardy Plants for Winter and Early Spring

II   The Environmentally Sensitive Landscape, Some Considerations

INTRODUCTION

To him who in the love of nature holds
Communion with her visible forms, she speaks
A various language; for his gayer hours
She has a voice of gladness, and a smile
And eloquence of beauty; and she glides
Into his darker musings, with a mild
And healing sympathy that steals away
Their sharpness ere he is aware.

From "Thanatopsis" by William Cullen Bryant

In *Southern Gardening*, I continue to tell about my lifelong love affair with gardening to all who will listen. The plants, flowers, and critters that populate my garden are the vehicles through which I share my passion, and my books are my attempt to share this passion.

In many ways, this book is a companion and extension of my first book, *Gardening in the Coastal South*. Neither of my books is intended to be a lengthy epistle in which every plant that could possibly be grown in the South is discussed at length. What they do include is many plants with which I have had success and that have proven track records in the gardens across the South.

Included in this book are some dependable groundcovers that add interest and dimension to Southern landscapes. A section has been devoted to maintaining healthy turf and possibly revising some of our lawn-care practices so that negative impact on the environment is minimal. Some hard-working trees and shrubs are suggested as well as some easy-care annuals and perennials for all seasons.

Since we are all connected, yard-to-yard, community-to-community, and town-to-town, we become increasingly aware that how we manage our gardens affects the health of the planet. Enlisting the aid of beneficial creatures, common-sense plant selection, wise water use, and choosing the least toxic method to control harmful pests are techniques that help us be "garden friendly." Recognizing, avoiding, and eradicating exotic, invasive plants that grow on our properties and proliferate in our natural areas becomes essential if we are to continue to have a habitable place in which to live.

A month-by-month gardening guide will help seasoned gardeners and novices alike. Newcomers to the South will find this section particularly useful. After realizing that lilacs and peonies don't do too well for us, most transplanted gardeners settle down and seek out the beautiful plants that will excel in Southern gardens.

Through it all, for the diehard gardeners among us, the garden remains an integral and necessary part of our lives. It is a place of beauty, a place of peace and rejuvenation, and for many of us, it is a place of healing. We have learned that nourishment for our souls is as important as sustenance for our bodies.

It is my hope that readers will learn sound, environmentally sensitive gardening techniques and that they will learn to select plants that will make their gardening experiences more successful and rewarding. I hope they will develop a love and appreciation of gardening as a pleasurable and beneficial activity and experience the joy that comes from being intimately involved in their own very personal gardens.

Marie Harrison

EXPLANATION OF DATA CHARTS

For the reader's convenience, I have included a small data chart for each plant. Data includes:

Scientific and common names: The genus and species as well as the most frequently used common names

Family: Scientific and common name of family to which the plant belongs. In some instances recent name changes necessitated the inclusion of two family names, the most recent first

Origin: Country or place of origin

Size of plant: Height and width of plant, based on averages. Actual size may vary according to planting site, area of the country, soil, fertilization, and other factors

Zones: Plant hardiness rating as defined by the United States Department of Agriculture Plant Hardiness Zone Map

Light requirements:
Sun: Full sun
Part Sun: Plant tolerates a partially sunny exposure; also indicates Part Shade
Shade: Plant is best suited to a fully shaded site

Water Use Zone: Low, Moderate, High—Based on water needs of the plant. Environmentally conscious gardeners will strive to place plants in the landscape with water use in mind. Group plants with similar needs together to make the best use of available water. Three water-use zones are suggested: *high* (regular watering), *moderate* (occasional watering), and *low* (natural rainfall). Several of these zones can be included within an individual landscape.

High water-use zones should be restricted to small, highly visible and highly maintained areas of the landscape. In moderate water-use zones, established plants are watered only when they show symptoms of moisture stress, such as wilting or changing color. In low water-use zones, plants receive no water except natural rainfall.

Exceptions to the water-use zone rule are newly planted ornamental plants and turf grasses. These plants require regular irrigation during the establishment period (8 to 10 weeks after planting), regardless of their intended water-use zones.

Soil preference: Sandy, loam, moisture retentive, neutral, acidic, alkaline, organic, wet, tolerant, or adaptable (grows well in almost any soil).

Salt tolerance: Relates to resistance and ability to grow under conditions of high winds, salt spray, alkaline soils, and infertile, sandy soils. If any of these four conditions becomes extreme, the tolerance of a given plant to salt may be affected.

Salt-tolerance ratings for plants are listed as none, slight, moderate, and high. Definitions are in line with those described by the University of Florida as follows:

None: Plants are not known to be salt tolerant. No data were available to indicate tolerance to salt.

Slight: Plants have poor salt tolerance and should be always used well back of exposed areas and be protected by buildings, fences, or plantings of more salt-tolerant species.

Moderate: Plants tolerate some salt spray but grow best when protected by buildings, fences, or plantings of more salt-tolerant species.

High: Plants are resistant to salt drift and can be used in exposed locations.

What's in a Name?

"Oh, no, you're not going to use those scientific names, are you?" gardeners sometimes ask when they visit my yard. "Can't we just say 'bleeding heart'? Must we learn to say *Clerodendron thomsoniae?*" The answer is, of course, that they can say bleeding heart, but some folks will think that they mean *Dicentra spectabilis,* which is also called bleeding heart. Two different plant species may have the same common name, and many species have more than one common name. A plant can have only one scientific name, however.

Usually two words are enough to identify a plant: genus and species. Together these two names make up a plant's scientific name, and it is recognized throughout the world. Since it contains two words, it is called a binomial. The first word in the binomial names the genus, and the second word names the species. Scientific names are always italicized because they are treated as Latin words.

The first word, "genus," refers to a group of plants that are closely related. We sometimes use the genus name as the common name. Examples are "camellia" and "phlox". In this book, all titles are common names, and other common names are listed following the title. I have not italicized the genus name if it is being used as a common name. *Camellia* sp. means "a species of Camellia" and *Camellia* spp. means "more than one species of Camellia."

The second word in the binomial is the species name, or specific epithet. The species name is sometimes a descriptive word and is never used alone. *Paniculata,* for instance, refers to flowers "in panicles." Asking for *paniculata* at a nursery would be much like asking for pink at the department store. They would ask, "A pink what?" So we must identify the plant that we want by both its names, as in *Phlox paniculata,* or a phlox that blooms in panicles.

Much confusion comes from the fact that both the genus and the species (specific epithet) are required to name a species or scientific name. *Phlox* is a genus, *paniculata* is the species (or specific epithet), and *Phlox paniculata* names a particular species of phlox. Genus name + species name = species.

Frequently a plant is a cultivar. A cultivar (cultivated variety) is one that is selected because it is significantly different from the rest of the species. This difference may be deliberately caused by man's manipulation or it may occur naturally, and this difference is passed on from generation to generation when the plants reproduce. For example, *Cercis canadensis* is our native redbud tree. *Cercis canadensis* 'Forest Pansy', however, is a cultivar that has bright purple leaves in spring and is quite different from the species. Usually the cultivar name is an English word, so it is not italicized, but the first letter of each word is capitalized. The cultivar name is enclosed in single quotation marks.

Many cultivars, particularly of annuals, may come in a series, or many different colors. For instance, the Profusion *Zinnia* series has cultivars named 'Profusion Rose', 'Profusion White', and 'Profusion Orange'. Finding guidelines for correct notation of series names has been very difficult. I have chosen not to put the name of the series in single quotes, but specific cultivars within the series are enclosed by single quotation marks.

Further subcategories used by botanists include subspecies (subsp.) and variety (var.). Usually one or the other is used, not both, and the abbreviation of the category is used as well. Examples are *Magnolia macrophylla* subsp. *ashei,* Ashe magnolia, and *Acer saccharum* var. *nigrum.*

Sometimes two species are crossed, producing offspring. The scientific name is then written as a formula. *Laburnum* x *watereri* is a cross between *Laburmum alpinum* and *Laburnum anagyroides.* Furthermore, two different genera (the plural of genus) may be crossed. In this case a capital X is placed before the name of the plant. Leyland Cypress is X *Cupressocyparis leylandii.* It is the child of *Cupressus macrocarpa* and *Chamaecyparis nookatensis.*

It is easy to understand why scientific names are very important. Common names are fine for everyday conversation, but if we ask the nursery to order a plant for us, it is a different story. If we simply ask for *Phlox,* we might get *Phlox paniculata, Phlox subulata, Phlox divaricata,* or any of several other species of phlox. To be sure that we get the plant we want, we must use the scientific name.

So say "bleeding heart" if you wish when you are talking about a plant that is within eyesight. If you decide to place an order, however, you will most likely want to specify either *Clerodendron thomsoniae* or *Dicentra spectabilis.* A rose is a rose is a rose (maybe), but a bleeding heart may or may not be the bleeding heart you have in mind.

Acknowledgments

Thanks to
- friends Vivian Justice and Leona Venettozzi who read through the first draft of this book and suggested changes that made it better.
- the editors at Pineapple Press who waded through the manuscript and made it smoother and more readable.
- readers far and wide who continue to read my articles and give positive feedback that keeps me writing.
- my Mississippi family (three sisters and three brothers), who grew up alongside me and understand me better than anyone else in the world.
- my immediate family for support in all of my endeavors.
- Amiable Spouse, my anchor and enabler.

Illustrated by
Joe Stoy
Marie Harrison
Jay Harrison (Amiable Spouse's son)
John W. Harrison, Jr. (Amiable Spouse)
Christina Livingston (Daughter)

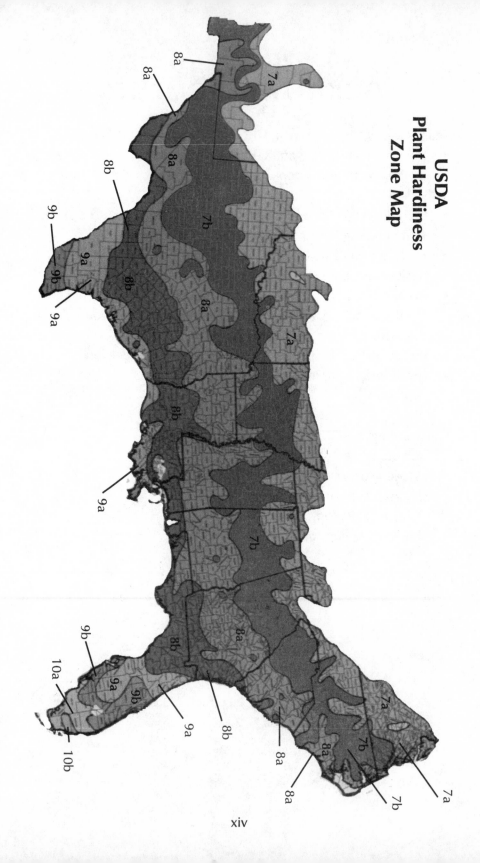

**USDA
Plant Hardiness
Zone Map**

I

Plants for the Environmentally Sensitive Landscape

1

GROUNDCOVERS AND
LAWN ALTERNATIVES

Studies show that tough, adaptable ground-covers are usually more environmentally friendly than lawn grasses. Often these other groundcovers require less water, fertilizer, and maintenance.

Many kinds of plants may be used as groundcovers. Especially effective are low-growing plants that give a flat or two-dimensional look to the landscape. Plants that spread by underground parts, such as rhizomes, stolons, and runners, establish easily. Many plants root at stem nodes when they come in contact with the soil. They are often chosen for groundcover use because they can cover ground quickly.

Groundcovers are particularly effective in areas where lawn grasses will not grow—perhaps under the deep shade of trees, on dry rocky ground, or maybe even in a damp hollow. Planted on steeply sloping places where mowing would be difficult or even dangerous, groundcovers are much more practical than lawns.

From the standpoint of landscape design, groundcovers can add unity in a way that few other plants can. When planted at the bases of trees and shrubs in a shady border, groundcovers unite the varied

3

plants and make everything seem to belong together—to be a part of the same whole. Evergreen groundcovers are especially effective in the winter when they border a tan, dormant winter lawn, adding blooms and color to what might otherwise be a humdrum landscape.

Besides, lawns are just so predictable. Simply doing something different can add interest. Groundcovers have different textures and shades of green. Furthermore, grass and other plants that are normally considered groundcovers are not the only option. Sometimes stone pavers, garden beds, or native grasses and wildflowers might add a completely new dimension.

As with all plants, groundcovers should be selected that will suit the site. Soil, light, moisture, and drainage must be considered, as well as the plant's height, hardiness, color, ability to cover, appearance, and cost. Freedom from pests and diseases or other ailments should, of course, be considered so that the groundcover itself will not become a maintenance problem.

Preparation should begin by removing any weeds or other plants in the area where a groundcover is desired. Unwanted plants can be dug, pulled, or otherwise removed by hand, or they can be treated with herbicides. Two or three treatments might be necessary to kill stubborn weeds.

Next, the soil should be prepared. Till or dig the area four to six inches deep where groundcover is to be added and add plenty of organic matter, such as peat moss, leaf mold, or ground bark. Purchase the plants needed, or look around the neighborhood. Often neighbors have enough to share, and plants just might be free for the asking. Install the plants in a gridlike pattern, and place mulch lightly between plants to retain moisture and discourage weeds. Remove weeds religiously, for once they become established they are almost impossible to remove.

Please understand that I have nothing against a grass lawn. Few surfaces make a better play area for children. Grass around the entry keeps sand from being tracked into the house, and no mice or snakes are usually found hiding behind the blades of grass. However, if you've been having difficulty keeping grass growing in a certain place, try one of the many adaptable groundcovers that grow well in the South.

Study your yard and determine the conditions that exist in the area where you wish to establish a groundcover. Is it shady, sunny, sandy, wet, or dry? Then look at the groundcovers discussed in this book and try to select one that will excel in the area you have chosen. Pertinent facts are arranged for your convenience at the beginning of each section to assist with your selections.

Arborvitae Fern (also Club Moss, Spike Moss)
Selaginella braunii
Family: Selaginellaceae (Spike Moss family)
Origin: China
Size: 18 inches and slowly spreading
Zones: 6–10
Light: Shade, Part Shade
Water: Moderate
Soil: Organic, well-drained
Salt Tolerance: Poor

We diehard gardeners are obsessive collectors. We visit every nursery possible, and we look at plants—some familiar and some unfamiliar. While we can't possibly buy everything we see that is different, we're apt to walk away with something not yet tried—some challenge, some experiment.

At one nursery at some point in time, I picked up a little plant called arborvitae fern (*Selaginella braunii*). I took a chance and bought it because I liked the way it looked in the pot. The label indicated that it would be happy in part shade, so I placed it in a woodsy spot that gets a bit of morning sun. It liked the place I picked for it—right by a path so that it could be easily seen and watered during periods of drought. It multiplied happily and in a pleasant manner—slowly, and not at all in an unwelcome or invasive way.

After several years, it spread out and covered an area of about five square feet. It is now a 12- to 18-inch-tall mound of dense, scalelike foliage that completely covers the ground. It is easy to see why its common name is arborvitae fern, because the scaly foliage resembles that of arborvitae or cedar. Yellow-green fronds of finely dissected foliage look delicate, but in fact the plant is a sturdy, well-suited workhorse. I have even shared a few clumps with special friends who appreciate pretty things in the garden.

Actually, *Selaginella* is not a fern at all. It is a prehistoric fern relative called club moss or spike moss. Though not true ferns, club mosses are vascular plants and produce spores, so they are often called ferns. Several different varieties of arborvitae fern exist. Most grow wild in tropical America and Asia, but some come from China, Japan, North America, South Africa, and Australia. Recently I bought a container of peacock fern (*Selaginella uncinata*). This diminutive club moss is noted for its iridescent blue color and is hardy in Zones 6 to 10. It grows three to six inches tall and is semievergreen. The bluish-green, iridescent leaves spread flat over the ground, and foliage turns a dark rose to rust color during the winter months. *Selaginella kraussiana* (spreading club moss or trailing spike moss) is another charming species. 'Aurea' is a cultivar that grows about one inch tall and keeps its bright yellow-green color year-round.

Most of the club mosses are hardy in the South. Grown for their pretty, scalelike foliage, they have many uses in landscaping. In addition to making a beautiful groundcover, they may be effectively grown in hanging baskets or containers where their attractiveness can be best appreciated. Propagation of the club mosses is easy. They may be divided at any time of year and planted into prepared soil. Cuttings taken and inserted into moist soil will produce roots quickly.

All this just goes to show that at times it pays to take some risks. Sometimes you get a winner, like arborvitae fern.

Asiatic Jasmine (also Little-leaf Jasmine, Dwarf Jasmine)

Trachelospermum asiaticum
Family: Apocynaceae (Dogbane family)
Origin: Southeast Asia
Size: 12 inches and spreading
Zones: 7b–10
Light: Sun or Shade
Water: Low
Soil: Tolerant
Salt Tolerance: Moderate

A few years ago Mrs. Betty Burr, a fellow Master Gardener, and her dear husband Robert moved into a new house. The existing landscape did not suit them at all, so Betty proceded to make some changes. She drew her plan on paper and set about installing the new landscape with the help of her yard crew. Mr. Robert just looked on and smiled as Betty went about her tasks, for he knew that it would look good when she finished. After all, he had seen her perform her magic many times before.

First Betty marked out the areas where she wanted tough, low-maintenance groundcovers. "I was tired of so much grass," she explained. "When Robert and I moved into the house, the large yard was covered with fence-to-fence lawn. I wanted something more interesting."

One of the groundcovers that Betty chose to replace some of the lawn was Asiatic jasmine. She purchased hundreds of four-inch pots and had the crew plant them about a foot apart. Within six months, the area was completely filled in. What a difference this groundcover made to the attractiveness of the land-scape!

Asiatic jasmine is a vine that is frequently used as a groundcover in the South. It is best used in areas where people do not walk, and it should be in an area that is maintained on a regular basis. Because it will spread and cover turf areas and sidewalks, it must be kept in bounds by edging, and infrequent mowing is beneficial.

Now you're thinking, "Well, maybe groundcover maintenance is not as carefree as I thought." Take into consideration, however, that the jasmine requires a fraction of the upkeep required by lawns. It performs well in both shade and sun and provides an evergreen surface year-round, even when most of our Southern lawns are brown and dormant. Few diseases bother this hardy groundcover. Occasionally leaf spots caused by various fungi may occur, but damage is usually not significant. Minimal fertilizer is required. During establishment, three or four applications of fertilizer may be made during the year at a rate of one pound of nitrogen per 1,000 square feet. After they are established, plants should be fertilized yearly in early spring. No irrigation other than normal rainfall is needed after establishment. Of course, in the event of extreme drought, a monthly irrigation will be beneficial.

A once-a-year mowing in late winter or very early spring, just as new growth begins, will limit the height of the jasmine and promote a more uniform appearance. Also, it will allow more air movement and minimize the risk of disease during rainy periods or if it is watered regularly with an overhead sprinkler. The mowing will, of course, remove most of the green foliage, but it will quickly recover. Weeds may be removed by hand. Though it is tolerant of Round Up herbicide when it is not actively growing, weeds are not usually a problem once it is established.

Mr. Robert is not with us any more. Mrs. Betty, though, continues her interest in her landscape and its care. Driving by her house is especially pleasurable. Her landscape is a showcase of flowering shrubs, perennials, and other plants. Not the least of its attractiveness is due to the effective use of Asiatic jasmine as a groundcover.

Border Grass [Color 1] (also Liriope, Lilyturf)

Liriope spp.
Family: Liliaceae (Lily family)
Origin: China and Japan
Size: 12–24 inches and spreading
Zones: 7–11
Light: Sun or Shade
Water: Low to Moderate
Soil: Tolerant
Salt Tolerance: Excellent

Liriope is one of the plants that epitomizes the South. Like the state-ly magnolia, Spanish moss–draped live oak, or crape myrtle, it is prominent in landscapes throughout the South. It is used so frequent-ly that it seems like one of our natives, but it hails from China and Japan. Since its introduction into our country about 200 years ago, its popularity has not waned. We frequently see it used as a ground-cover or as a border for walkways or flowerbeds. It is a great edging or shape-defining plant for large landscape areas, and because of its dense root mass, it is an excellent choice for stabilizing soil and con-trolling erosion on sloping terrain.

Just to set the record straight, liriope is not a grass at all but is a member of the lily family. Many people call it "border grass" or "lily-turf." I have frequently called it monkey grass, but that designation is also used when referring to mondo grass.

The two most frequently seen species of liriope are *Liriope mus-cari* and *L. spicata*. While the two look much the same, it is impor-tant to recognize the differences when choosing one for the land-scape. *L. muscari* is a clumping grass that slowly increases in width. It is an excellent choice to border a flowerbed or walkway. *L. spica-ta*, on the other hand, spreads aggressively by underground runners. It may be the best choice if a rapidly spreading groundcover is need-ed. Though it is more competitive against other weeds and grasses once established, it is less sun tolerant than *L. muscari*.

Liriope has stood the test of time for several reasons. It is amaz-ingly tough. It will grow in deep shade or full sun, in sand or clay. The heat and humidity of the South are much to its liking, and it tol-erates drought and salt spray. Flowers are produced most freely in sunny locations, but foliage probably looks best when some protection from the sun is provided. About the only thing that it cannot endure is standing water, or "wet feet."

Border grass is most attractive if some care is given to its appearance. In late February or before growth begins in the spring, it should be cut back to prevent last year's growth from forming unattractive brown "skirts" around the new clumps. This is most easily accomplished by mowing with the lawnmower set on its highest cutting height. To avoid fungal diseases, be sure not to overwater. Follow the recommended practice of watering early in the day so that foliage will have time to dry before evening.

Several cultivars of *Liriope muscari* are available. 'Silvery Sunproof', 'Majestic', 'Evergreen Giant', 'Gold Band', and others offer choices of green or beautifully variegated leaves from 12 to 24 inches tall. *Liriope spicata*, or spreading lilyturf, grows from 10 to 15 inches tall and may be variegated or green. Both species send up lavender, purple, or white flower spikes followed by clusters of bluish-black berrylike fruits in July and August.

Gardeners may look at border grass now with a new appreciation and recognize in it a tough, reliable plant that adds immeasurably to Southern landscapes.

Cast Iron Plant (also Aspidistra, Barroom Plant)
Aspidistra elatior
Family: Liliaceae (Lily family)
Origin: Eastern Asia, China
Size: 2–3 feet, very slowly spreading
Zones: 7–11
Light: Shade
Water: Moderate
Soil: Organic, well-drained preferred
Salt Tolerance: Moderate

Aspidistra has been a dependable presence in Southern gardens since its introduction. Brought from China in 1824, it was used chiefly as a parlor plant. Tolerant of low light and smoky interiors, it was dubbed "the barroom plant" since it was one of the few plants that could withstand such conditions. Freezing temperatures did not bother it, and the ups and downs of Victorian parlors with uneven heat had little effect.

Today aspidistra is a favorite landscape plant in the South. Planted beneath live oaks draped in Spanish moss, it is in its element. Glossy, dark-green leaves two to three feet long and six to eight inches wide adorn shady spots in many yards. It is a favorite of floral designers. Wired and curved into various shapes, stripped, torn, cut, dried, painted, or used in its naturally existing form, it has few equals in the floral design world. Japanese designers are particularly careful to notice whether  leaves are right-handed or left-handed, as that is an important design consideration for them.

Native to China, Japan, and Vietnam, aspidistra is a member of the lily family. Inconspicuous blooms are seldom visible since they are produced near the ground. Cultivars with various leaf patterns are available. One cultivar has a bold yellow stripe down its center. Another is spotted or heavily mottled, much resembling the Milky Way, for which it is named. Sizes range from diminutive to quite large.

By far the most common form is the plain green barroom, or cast iron plant. Correctly placed in the landscape, it is a delight. Incorrectly placed, however, it can be an eyesore. In bright sunlight, leaves turn a sickly yellow-green. Strong winds and rain shred the foliage and leave it tattered and torn. To keep aspidistra looking its best, remove old or ragged leaves once a year or so. If scale insects infest them, spray with horticultural oil according to label directions.

Aspidistra is at its best in deep shade. Though it is drought tolerant and lives through the most abject neglect, it thrives under somewhat better circumstances. Give cast iron plant deep shade, moist soil, an occasional top dressing of compost or balanced fertilizer, and it will reward you with beautiful, dark green strappy leaves that shine like a freshly oiled gun stock.

Division is the best way to propagate aspidistra. From an established clump, cut away a vigorous section of rhizome with an actively growing tip, or dig the entire clump and separate it by pulling apart or cutting with a sharp knife. Plant it in a container or freshly prepared shady bed. New divisions take a while to settle in, but established plantings multiply at a moderate rate because, eventually, many growing points are produced.

When planted in the right place and given minimal care, aspidistra will provide years of dependable green in Southern gardens. New cultivars make them even more interesting. Take a new look at this old favorite. You might like what you see.

Emerald Feather Calathea

Calathea louisae
Family: Marantaceae (Prayer Plant family)
Origin: Tropical Americas
Size: 2 feet, slowly spreading
Zones: 8–11
Light: Shade to Part Shade
Water: Moderate
Soil: Adaptable
Salt Tolerance: Very Low/None

We gardeners always like to share news of plants that grow well in our gardens—particularly those that give us pleasure or are unusual or different. I have just such a plant that grows under the Nuttall oak in my garden. Getting an exact handle on its identification has been hard, but I think I have it figured out now.

I have had this beautiful groundcover plant for several years. When I bought it, the name on its tag was "*Ctenanthe.*" As sometimes happens, I can't remember where I bought the plant, but I only bought one—in spite of my admonitions to others to always buy three or some uneven number of plants for the landscape. Experts contend that uneven numbers are more pleasing to the human eye.

Luckily, the little plant flourished, and now it covers an area  about four feet square. Of course, that is what all gardeners hope will happen eventually, especially if the plant turns out to be a winner. If we just have patience, one little plant rewards us with more of its kind and we learn that purchasing three was not necessary in the first place.

Recently I saw a few pots of it at a local garden center. "There's my wonderful *Ctenanthe*," I thought. Upon close inspection, I noticed that it was labeled *Calathea louisae.*

Research on the Internet aided my identification efforts. I found that the plant was a *Calathea*, but I also found that the closely related species of *Maranta*, *Ctenanthe*, and *Stromanthe* are often confused. No matter. We won't worry about such fine details as long as we can identify the plant and know where one can be obtained.

Leaves of emerald feather calathea are held aloft on long stems. While each leaf and stem together measures almost two feet, they do not appear that tall in the landscape. The foot-tall stems rise vertically, but the bold leaves, somewhere in the neighborhood of nine inches long by four inches wide, are held horizontally so that each one presents its best pose to the viewer.

The top side of the glossy foliage is dark green with light green splotches along the midrib, and the leaves are purple underneath. The pointed, roughly oval-shaped leaves sport attractive wavy edges. Growing tightly and closely together, the plants successfully outgrow any other plants that attempt to invade their space.

During the summer, spiky small white flowers appear. While they are attractive enough, they are fairly inconspicuous, and one almost has to peek underneath the leaves to find them. Technically, the flowers arise from bracts, or modified leaves, with a flower or flower cluster in the axils. Most gardeners do not worry with such fine distinctions. If something appears that is showy or different from the leaves, we usually just call it a flower.

I highly recommend emerald feather calathea to anyone in the Deep South who is looking for a different and attractive groundcover for a shady area. Research indicates that it is hardy in USDA Zones 8 to 11. Do not be surprised when the first frost kills *Calathea louisae* to the ground. Mulch it with a protective cover of pine needles or other light organic materials, and it will return next spring, eager to do its pretty thing in a shady nook in your garden.

Care of this plant has been minimal. I have watered it during periods of dry weather, and I suppose I must have fertilized it lightly at some time during its life—though I don't get to it every spring. A caterpillar or some other critter occasionally chews a few holes in the leaves, but I have not attempted to control them, for the damage they do is tolerable and the plants are still attractive.

Do not be misled into the notion that all *Calatheas* are equally hardy. The family includes many tropical plants native to Brazil and tropical America. While not all of them are hardy, most have colorful foliage and are highly desirable houseplants.

Ask for *Calathea louisae* at your favorite garden center. If they do not have it in stock, many of them will order it for you. It's worth searching for.

Holly Fern [Color 2]

Cyrtomium falcatum
Family: Aspidiaceae (Wood Fern family)
Origin: Asia
Size: 2–3 feet by 2–3 feet
Zones: 7–11
Light: Shade
Water: Average
Soil: Organic, acid
Salt Tolerance: Moderate

Most folks in the South know holly fern. It is as well suited to our gardens as live oaks and magnolias. However, since it hails from Asia, South Africa, and Polynesia, we cannot claim it as one of our natives. Hardy from Zones 6 to 10, it can withstand temperatures as low as 14°F.

Holly fern is an excellent choice for a potted specimen in a shaded corner. It tucks nicely into pockets of soil in rock gardens and is a good groundcover in shady or woodland locations. It makes an excellent understory plant beneath old reclaimed plants like camellia, sweet olive, holly, and other large shrubs that have had their lower branches removed.

Holly fern is exceedingly well mannered in the garden. Its growth rate is moderate, and plants do not usually need to be divided, although old, established clumps can be divided if desired. Lustrous, stiff, erect-to-arching fronds radiate out from the center of the plants to form attractive clumps. Individual fronds grow from 20 to 30 inches long and up to eight inches wide. Plants grow two to three feet high and spread to cover an area about three feet wide.

Leaves of holly fern are thicker than other ferns, so they stand up to coastal breezes without tattering. Moderate salt tolerance makes it very useful for those who garden near bodies of salt water. Partial to full shade suits holly fern best, and it will truly shine in loose, fertile, moist soil with high organic matter content. Follow a regular watering schedule during the first growing season to establish a deep, extensive root system. Fertilize in late winter with a general all-purpose garden fertilizer. Its appearance is enhanced if browning fronds are removed from time to time. Winter-damaged fronds can be cut back before new spring growth begins.

Like some other ferns, holly fern is attractive in floral designs. However, as with other ferns, caution is advised. Once I made a very special design for my niece's wedding. I chose holly fern for the line material and wired it into an attractive S-curve. I chose a suitably tall, slender container and then added flowers to follow the curve. It was quite beautiful, and everyone made admiring comments. I became concerned, however, when I noticed that the linen cloth underneath the design seemed to be getting dirty. I brushed at it, and to my dismay, it smeared and messed up the beautifully starched and ironed tablecloth.

I had forgotten that ferns have sori (clusters of spore cases) on the backs of their leaves. When the spores are ripe, the sori shatter and spores are scattered from here to kingdom come. Well, kingdom came right on top of my table. Chalk it up to experience. Now when I use ferns in designs, I check the backs of the fronds. If the sori are dark, they are about ready to pop. As long as they are green, they can safely be used in floral designs.

Cultivars of holly fern include 'Butterfieldii', with deeply serrated leaf margins; 'Compactum', with leaves shorter than the species; and 'Rochfordianum', which has hollylike leaves with coarsely fringed margins. Look in area garden centers for this useful plant. Buy several and plant them in broad sweeps, or cover the ground underneath a shady tree. However you choose to use holly fern, it will add grace and beauty to its place in the landscape.

Japanese Sedge

Carex morrowii
Family: Cyperaceae (Sedge family)
Origin: Japan
Size: 10–12 inches and slowly clumping
Zones: 5–9
Light: Part Shade
Water: Moderate
Soil: Organic, well-drained
Salt Tolerance: Poor

The catalog said: "*Carex morrowii aurea* 'Variegata'. Japanese Sedge. Graceful swirls of handsomely variegated leaves, green with a central yellow stripe, form neat, rounded clumps, and are fully evergreen in the South, partially so in more northerly areas. 10 to 12 inches tall and easily grown. Zones 5 to 9. One-quart container. Each $12.95." Of course, I wanted it! [Color 3]

This kind of dilemma crops up every year when the garden catalogs arrive. I spend hours looking through them all and choosing a few new things for my garden. Every year, of course, I want way too many things, and have to pare down my list to fit my budget.

Several years ago, I finally settled on a few new things from Wayside Gardens. One was the Japanese sedge. I sent off for just one of them because, when you try new things like this, you never know if it's going to work for you or not. I've placed many orders for plants that I just had to have. Some worked, some didn't. Nothing ventured, nothing gained. It doesn't take long for the money to stack up on a catalog order. Anyway, I always reason to myself that if it does well, it will spread and soon I can divide it. If I lose it, I won't worry because not too much money was invested.

The venture with the Japanese sedge was successful. It flourished in the partly shady place that I chose for it in the back yard. I planted it in enriched soil and it was watered regularly by the sprinkler system. Within a couple of years it had grown into a clump big enough to dig and divide into three plants. I planted them, and soon I was able to divide again. Now I have an area large enough to make an impact in the backyard landscape and to perform in the way that I had envisioned.

This clumping sedge grows about 12 inches tall. If you didn't know the difference, you would think that it was a small ornamental grass, and although it is about the size of liriope or mondo, it is distinctively different. Sedges are grasslike plants, but they have triangular stems. Brownish insignificant flowers emerge in late spring. During the winter the plant may look a bit tattered, but if it is trimmed in early spring, new foliage emerges and it's all fresh and new again. If I don't get around to trimming it, it still looks great by the time the new leaves emerge. The old ones seem to die down or melt away, and the planting looks none the worse for wear.

This sedge works well at the foreground of my shady backyard bed. Behind it are various ferns and hostas, and in the summer, caladiums join the group. It has been one of those nice plants that does exactly what you intended it to do. Never is it obtrusive or jarring in the landscape, and all the plants around it show to greatest advantage. It is a foil for the brightly colored caladiums and provides an interesting contrast in texture with the ferns and bold-leafed hostas. Its color contrasts pleasantly with lawn in front of it, and its short stature makes it perfect for the front of this bed.

Carex morrowii is native to woods in the low mountains in Japan. It is adaptable to a wide range of soils and has been pest free in my garden. Several cultivars are in the trade. 'Goldband', 'Silver Sceptre', and 'Ice Dance' are offered. Wayside Gardens has another sedge called *Carex stricta* 'Bowles Golden'. Even though this is a different species of sedge, I must try it, too. I guess I have the same kind of attitude about plants that Daddy had about his medicines. He thought that if a small dose did a little good, then a big dose would surely cure whatever ailed him. Well, that sedge did a great deal of good in my landscape, so I guess another kind might really spruce it up.

Leatherleaf Fern (also Leather Fern, Iron Fern)

Rumohra adiantiformis
Family: Aspidiaceae (Wood Fern family)
Origin: Australia
Size: 1–3 feet by 4–5 feet
Zones: 8–11
Light: Shade
Water: Medium
Soil: Moist, well-drained
Salt Tolerance: Poor

Every time I walk through the covered entry that connects the house and garage, a beautiful sea of green greets me. This little atrium area was hard to landscape in the beginning. First of all, it is only 12 feet by 20 feet, and a path through it to the backyard was required. That ruled out anything like a tree or large shrub. Second, it is shady for most of the day, so that further limited my options.

I began to research plants that would thrive in this spot. My Extension Horticulture Agent, Larry Williams, keeps preaching that we would have fewer landscape problems if we followed the "right plant, right place" rule. So I have tried to do that, and it has paid off in terms of plant health and maintenance.

I had other criteria, too. I wanted plants that I could use in floral designs, and I wanted them close at hand. What better place than right outside my back door? Leatherleaf fern is the dominant cut foliage used by many florists, and it is equally useful for those of us who enjoy arranging bouquets for the house. Generally, the strong, flexible stems last for about 14 days in water. The flowers in a design turn brown long before this long-lasting greenery does.

Leatherleaf fern is evergreen, and though it may be marginally hardy in our area, in the protected location between my house and garage, it remains green most years. As a matter of fact, I have never lost this fern to cold weather, no matter where in the landscape it was planted. At about 25°F it gets killed back to the ground but returns with renewed vigor each spring.

The bold, leathery fronds are triangular-shaped and top out at about three feet. Clumps spread by rusty red, aboveground stolons. Dense mats of lacy foliage about four or five feet wide are formed. Though it has shown no tendency toward invasiveness, this spreading habit makes it an ideal groundcover for shady places, and it is handy to share with friends or to pot up for plant sales.

Gardeners everywhere in the Deep South should be able to grow this highly adaptable fern, provided they have a shady place. Though it does best in highly organic, acid soil, it tolerates both clay and sand and is moderately drought tolerant. The natural dark green color is easy to maintain if it is fertilized in the spring and watered during periods of drought.

If you decide to add leatherleaf fern to your landscape, be sure to find a suitably shady place, add a bit of compost or other organic material to the soil if needed, and plant individual plants 24 to 36 inches apart. Keep away from beachfront or other places where plants may be exposed to salt, for they are not salt tolerant. Water regularly until established, and then water as needed during dry spells.

Several other ferns might be considered for Southern landscapes. Some are autumn fern (*Dryopteris erythrosora*), lady fern (*Athyrium filix-femina*), hayscented fern (*Dennstaedtia punctilobula*), cinnamon fern (*Osmunda cinnamomea*), Christmas or tassel fern (*Polystichum acrostichoides*), and royal fern (*Osmunda regalis*).

The beautiful sea of green provided by ferns and other green plants is a testament to the fact that we do not have to have flowers everywhere. Sometimes just green is all that is needed, and it somehow pleases the eye and soothes the spirit. The green of the earth and the blue of the sky—the Creator had a good eye when He chose the dominant colors of our planet. We won't go wrong if we follow His examples.

Mondo Grass [Color 4] (also Dwarf Lily Turf, Snakebeard)

Ophiopogon japonicus
Family: Liliaceae (Lily family)
Origin: Korea, Japan
Size: 1–24 inches and spreading
Zones: 5–10
Light: Part Sun to Shade
Water: Adaptable to wet or dry
Soil: Adaptable
Salt Tolerance: Good

Mondo grass is a commonly used groundcover throughout the South. Also known as snakebeard, it is hardy from USDA Zones 5 to 10. Though it is often confused with liriope, or border grass, there are several differences. While liriope demands soil that drains well and even tolerates dry shade, mondo grass can grow in standing water. More often than not, the flowers of mondo grass are hidden below the grass, while those of liriope are held well above the foliage and add significant color to the landscape. Blades of mondo grass are thinner than those of liriope, and mondo grass is generally less sun tolerant.

Ophiopogon is one of more than 30 species, about four of which are commonly grown in our gardens. They do best in part shade to shade. Tuberous roots and underground stolons make them very useful groundcovers. All will spread, some more vigorously than others, and leaves vary in height from tiny plants about an inch in height to larger plants more than two feet tall. White to lilac flowers are followed by pea-sized fruits that will easily germinate if planted as soon as they are ripe. Like most seedlings, however, there will be considerable variations.

Ophiopogon japonicus, or common mondo grass, forms clumps of dark green, needlelike foliage. Leaves are 12 to 15 inches long, and the plant spreads rapidly, making it a good choice for covering large, shady areas. *O. japonicus* 'Silver Mist' is a showy, variegated cultivar with white and green, needlelike leaves about ten inches long.

Dwarf mondo grass (*O. japonicus* var. *nanus* or 'Nanus'), is dark green with leaves about three inches long. Super dwarf mondo grass (*O. japonicus* 'Gyoku-ryu' or 'Kyoto Dwarf') is a recent introduction from Japan. Tiny, compact tufts of dark green leaves less than one and one-half inches tall spread slowly. Gardeners quickly discovered its usefulness between stepping-stones or pavers and in bonsai arrangements.

The popular species *O. planiscapus* has several cultivars with very dark purple to black leaves that are catching on in Southern gardens. It is best grown as a novelty grasslike groundcover, and it is used for border edging, in rock gardens, or in containers. It is most effective in the landscape when highlighted with plants of contrasting colors, such as yellow-leafed hostas, gold moss sedum, or dwarf variegated mondo grass. Popular cultivars are 'Arabiscus', 'Black Knight', 'Niger', and 'Nigrescens'.

Another frequently seen member of the clan is *O. jaburan* 'Variegatus', commonly called Aztec grass. *O. jaburan* 'Evergreen Giant' has coarse, solid green leaves 18 to 36 inches long. Because this species is a larger, clumping-type grass, it is effective when planted en masse to provide depth and variability to landscapes.

Choose one or more of these high-performance mondo grasses for your yard. They thrive in the South every bit as well as lightning bugs and green tree frogs, and they are just as pleasing in Southern gardens.

Muhly Grass [Color 5]
(also Pink Muhly, Hairgrass, Hair-awn Muhly)
Muhlenbergia capillaris
Family: Poaceae (Grass family)
Origin: U.S. Native
Size: 1–5 feet by 2–3 feet
Zones: 6–11
Light: Sun
Water: Low, drought tolerant
Soil: Sandy, well-drained
Salt Tolerance: Good

Gardeners have a way of keeping up with what's growing around the neighborhood, especially in the yards of their friends who are also avid gardeners. True to nature, I noticed an interesting grass in a landscape down the street. I kept an eye on the low-growing, rather inconspicuous mounds on a slope in front of a house. I thought it was probably wiregrass. I kept watching it suspiciously, though, because it didn't quite look like the familiar wiregrass that I had seen growing in area woods. One day I was walking down the street just as the first rays of the sun spilled across the bay. Early shafts of light were just touching the rise of land bordering the water. As I rounded a corner, I saw in this early sunlight a cotton-candy mass of wispy, pinkish-red blooms that seemed lit from within. They waved in the slightest breeze. I was captivated. The grass that had been nondescript all summer had transformed itself into a thing of exceeding loveliness.

I asked my neighbor what it was, and she replied, "Oh, it's muhly grass." This bit of information needed some research. I learned that the Latin name is *Muhlenbergia capillaris*, and it is commonly called pink muhly, hairgrass, or hair-awn muhly. It is native to dry woods, sandhills, savannahs, bogs, and coastal swales in the eastern half of North America in Zones 6 to 11. That means, of course, that it is adaptable to a wide range of soils and will grow well in almost any place in the South.

Muhly grass is a clumping (bunch) grass. Consequently, gardeners do not worry about it running about the landscape via underground rhizomes or runners. Thin, tubelike leaves fan out from the bottom of the clump to make a feathery mound about a foot tall. In late fall, the blooms increase the height by a foot or so. In nature, these thin plumes range in color from white and pink to red and purple. Some of the reds have obviously been selected and propagated for nursery stock, and now this beautiful grass can be purchased at almost any garden center.

Muhly grass may be planted in a perennial or annual border, and it serves well as a groundcover even when it is not blooming. It is highly drought and salt tolerant and may be planted on the sugar sand of beach dunes, in open meadowlike situations, or in street medians and roadsides.

The University of Florida recommends planting clumps a minimum of two feet apart and watering regularly until established. The perennial grass should be cut back in February, and a new growth of fresh green grass will follow. The show put on by the blooms is short—less than a month in late fall/early winter. However, it is one of those spectacular plants that effectively and beautifully marks the comings and goings of the seasons. And it's one that I want in my yard. I'll be on the lookout for this adaptable, low-maintenance, native grass.

ORNAMENTAL GRASSES

Daddy was the one with whom I always talked flowers. He'd ask, "Have you seen the crape myrtles? Did you see the purple one?" or "How did your amaryllises do this year?" They were all sources of beauty and pleasure to him, as they are to me. He was the one who came home with flats of annuals to border the walks. Mother was more concerned about feeding her seven children.

One day I mentioned to Daddy that the broomsedge that grows in the fields around home was being planted in my part of the country in people's yards. "Why would they do that?" he wanted to know.

"They think it's pretty," I answered. "It's called ornamental grass." Daddy had always considered it a troublesome weed in his pastures.

When I was a child, our brooms were made of this sedge. Mother always gathered a sizeable bundle whenever the old broom wore out. She'd gather it tightly and tie it securely with twine. Then she'd shake the smithereens out of it. She'd be standing in the middle of a cloud of seeds as they floated all around in response to her shaking. For several weeks the house would have seeds floating about as we swept the floor.

This simple broomsedge has a fancy name, *Andropogon virginicus*, or broomsedge bluestem.The professors throw it around casually and the listener seldom suspects that they're talking about broomsedge. Ornamental grasses are gaining in popularity as landscape plants. The term usually refers not only to true grasses but also to sedges and rushes that are grasslike. Leona Venettozzi, noted horticulturist and teacher, reminds us, "Rushes have ridges while sedges have edges."

All grass genera have individual species adapted to a wide variety of environments. Want a plant suited for a wet place; one for desertlike conditions; one for sun, shade, hot or cold; or any combination of the aforementioned? A grass will fill the bill. Want a tall plant, a groundcover, or somewhere in between? Try an ornamental grass, for there is one just exactly the size you need. Want something purple, silver, white, green, or red? Try an ornamental grass. As a matter of fact, they are dynamic garden features that change in size, color, texture, and shape over the season. They also add movement and sound to the garden in a way that few plants can.

Grasses are annual or perennial, evergreen or deciduous, warm or cool season, and have various colors, flowering, and winter characteristics. They may be clump-forming or creeping, with mature shape and height varying greatly from one kind to another.

Short grasses are effectively massed to provide a groundcover. Medium grasses can be used to accent areas within a planting of shrubs, herbaceous perennials, or annuals. Tall grasses provide a strong vertical element in the garden and can be used to help soften the harsh vertical lines of structures.

According to horticulturist Dr. Mack Thetford from the University of Florida, many of the grasses are drought tolerant. Water promotes growth, not survival. At the University of Florida trial gardens in Milton, Florida, the major difference between those that received regular irrigation and those that did not was the size of the plants. Those that were well watered grew much larger than those under drought conditions, but they did not live any longer. Very few plants were lost due to drought.

Plants need to be pruned around the last of February to early March. Hedge trimmers work fine. Most grasses should be cut back to within 6 to 12 inches of the ground. At this time of year, the growth response is rapid, and new growth quickly follows the pruning.

Keep your eyes open at the garden centers next spring, or check out the catalog offerings. You may find an ornamental grass that suits your landscaping needs.

GROUNDCOVERS FOR HOT, SUNNY PLACES

Everybody has a hot, dry, sunny place where nothing will grow. Many have not realized, however, that such a place has the potential of being one of the most attractive, maintenance-free areas of the landscape. With just a few drought-tolerant stronghearts, dry areas can be made to shine. Furthermore, gardeners are learning that water for tending landscapes is limited. A growing population and recent droughts have severely strained our already limited water resources. Water rationing may become a way of life. We may be forced to find drought-tolerant alternatives for some of our water-guzzling ornamental plants and lawns that we have depended on for years. Groundcovers that can perform in the landscape without large amounts of water may be part of the solution.

Several plants have served admirably in a hot, sunny area in my yard. Lavender cotton (*Santolina chamaecyparissus*) is a gray-leafed herb that does full duty out by the street where it is dependent on nature's water. A green form (*S. rosmarinifolia*) is also available. Both grow about nine inches tall and make well-mannered, mounded plants about two feet in diameter. Their fragrance and rough, narrow leaves make them a pleasant addition to the garden. Stems may be dried and used in dried wreaths and other floral crafts.

Another species that excels in the hot sunny area by the street is *Thymus praecox*. This tiny, creeping thyme does tough duty in the hottest, driest part of the landscape. Hugging the ground at a mere inch tall, it has gradually spread to fill an area about two feet square. I keep pulling up other plants nearby and encouraging it to continue its mannerly growth.

Another creeping thyme (*Thymus serpyllum* 'Coccineus') grows nearby. Reaching three or four inches tall, it has been growing and sporting its tiny rose-colored blossoms for about ten years. These pint-sized thymes are often planted between stepping-stones along a pathway. Placed so, they emit a pleasant thyme scent when they are stepped on. They are perfect at the front edge of the border where they form an evergreen groundcover of tiny leaves. Leaves of these creeping thymes may be used for seasoning and in potpourri.

Most folks are familiar with portulaca or moss rose [Color 6] (*Portulaca grandiflora*). It thrives in intense sunlight and high temperatures and is not fussy about soil. Moss rose grows to about six inches high and one to two feet across. Cylindrical, pointed, one-inch leaves trail along the ground on branched, reddish stems. Roselike flowers about one inch wide bloom in red, pink, orange, yellow, white, pastels, and bicolors.

Purslane [Color 7] (*Portulaca oleracea*) is another high performer. Unlike the pointed leaves of moss rose, purslane has broad, plump foliage. Once it is in the garden it reseeds and becomes almost weedy. As one might expect, the seedlings that come up are not the hybrid varieties that were originally purchased. They are the common yellow and orange kinds that grow in such places as ditches and sidewalk cracks. Many people have learned that these leaves are tasty and nourishing in salads, soups, and scrambled eggs, so they let them grow and enjoy not only their culinary benefits but the sheer profusion of their blossoms as well.

Sun rose (*Aptenia cordifolia*) is a beautiful little drought-tolerant succulent that hugs the ground and grows two or three inches tall. Inch-long, glossy leaves set off frilly little flowers that bloom in the bright sun. Sun rose is available in gold, rose, and white. One plant spreads to fill an area three or four feet square. Though not reliably hardy in all parts of the South, the plant is easily rooted from stem cuttings. I always root a few and put them in the greenhouse during the winter just to be sure that I don't lose it.

Try a few of these sun-loving, drought-tolerant groundcovers in a suitable area of your landscape. You may be surprised at how beautiful that section of your yard will become!

OTHER GROUNDCOVERS TO TRY

Strawberry begonia (*Saxifraga stolonifera*) is used in many gardens. Probably it started growing in a hanging basket but later surprised the gardener by escaping and spreading over the ground. It has proven to be quite hardy throughout the South.

Several dwarf or prostrate junipers make effective groundcovers. Most of them tolerate hot sun and poor, dry soil. Good performers are cultivars of creeping juniper (*Juniperus horizontalis*), shore juniper (*Juniperus conferta*), and select cultivars of Chinese juniper (*J. chinensis*) such as 'San Jose' and var. sargentii 'Compacta'.

Several flowering perennials might serve as groundcovers in appropriate places. For a sunny area try moss verbena (*Verbena tenuisecta*) like that seen along our highways. It provides a carpet of magenta flowers all summer and is perennial in the middle and lower South. Some succulent plants, such as hens and chickens (*Sempervivum tectorum*), provide interest. In partial shade, moss phlox (*Phlox subulata*) and woodland phlox (*P. divaricata*) are good choices.

LAWNS AND THEIR CARE

There's something about a soft patch of grass lawn that just feels right to many people. For Amiable Spouse and me, it's the place where we have our "tea party" each afternoon and watch the birds and butterflies that appear to enjoy the surroundings as much as we do. Missy, our miniature pinscher, sniffs out every corner, hoping to flush out a lizard or other intriguing critter. Granddaughter Emily thinks that running barefoot across the lawn at Mimi and Papa's house is a delightful thing to do, and grandson Maxwell and Papa find many occasions to toss a ball across the length of it or wrestle and tumble from one end of it to the other.

A beautiful lawn improves landscape aesthetics and enhances property value. Not only does the fine-textured groundcover add to the beauty of the area, but it also purifies air and moderates temperatures. It is a great soil stabilizer and serves to remove toxins from water that percolates through it.

In spite of all these advantages, maintaining a lawn with an acceptable appearance is a challenge in the hot, humid climate of the South. Calls to the extension offices are predominantly about lawn care. It seems that a great deal must be learned in order to care for a lawn and keep it looking good. Certain cultural practices make a huge difference in the quality of turf grasses. These cultural practices relate to watering, fertilizing, and mowing.

Watering

The University of Florida recommends that all types of turf grasses be watered only as needed. Indicators of need include the following: leaf blades that fold along the midrib (like a book closing), footprints that remain compressed for more than a few seconds, and a grayish cast over the surface of the lawn. When one or more of these indicators are present, the lawn should be watered until one-half to one inch of water has been uniformly applied. The ground should be soaked to the depth one can reasonably expect the roots to grow. Such deep, infrequent watering promotes root growth, which is the basis of a healthy lawn.

Irrigation is best done in the early morning hours while the ground is still wet with dew. Many of the fungi and diseases that attack turf grasses need several hours of wet leaf surface in order to multiply. In our humid climate, every drying hour is important.

Feeding

"Lean and mean" seems to be the formula for healthy turf. According to Dr. Bryan Unruh, turf researcher at the University of Florida's research facility in Milton, Florida, fertilizer is required in relatively low amounts. Too much fertilizer causes excessive shoot growth; poor root, rhizome, and stolon growth; higher incidences of disease and pest problems; reduced carbohydrate reserves; and poor tolerance to heat, cold, drought, traffic, and other stresses. It also causes degradation of the environment from the leaching of nutrients that can end up in our groundwater.

With all these drawbacks, it seems tempting not to fertilize at all. Dr. Unruh is quick to point out, however, that some fertilizer is necessary. Proper timing is essential. Applying fertilizer before the grass turns green in spring is a waste of money and fertilizer. Fertilizing after September may cause new growth that can easily be damaged by frost or cold weather.

Different grasses have different fertilizer needs. Centipedegrass, Bahiagrass, and carpetgrass are low fertility grasses. They will grow better and have fewer problems when fertilized only once or twice per year—once after green-up and possibly a second application during the summer. St. Augustinegrass might also get by on one spring application, but it is more common to apply a second application during the summer. Bermudagrass and zoysiagrass will require fertilizer applications two or three times over the growing season.

Which fertilizer should be chosen? The result of a soil analysis is the best indicator of nutrient needs. In the absence of a soil test, use fertilizer with a 3-1-2 or 4-1-2 ratio of nitrogen, phosphorus, and potassium, such as 12-4-8 or 16-4-8. Apply no more than one pound of nitrogen per 1,000 square feet per application and be sure that the fertilizer you choose has slow release nitrogen. When balanced fertilizers with numbers like 10-10-10 are repeatedly applied, phosphorus and potassium may build to toxic levels.

Many times retailers recommend an application of winterizer for Southern lawns. Research shows that this application of fertilizer is not necessary and may even do more harm than good, especially if the fertilizer has a high amount of nitrogen. Nitrogen stimulates new growth that can be damaged by early frosts. A better option is to let the grass go dormant when it is ready.

Mowing

Proper mowing is essential to a healthy turf. Improper mowing, combined with excessive water or fertilization can cause grass to develop thatch, a thick, spongy mat of runners and clippings above the soil surface that has not decomposed. It is just the sort of place where chinch bugs and turf caterpillars like to set up housekeeping. Thatch also ties up insecticides and fertilizers and makes them less effective.

Lawns should be mowed frequently enough so that no more than one-third of the grass blade is removed at each mowing. Mowing high improves the health of the lawn since roots grow directly in proportion to blade length. Removing only a little of the top places less stress on the grass, and the shade produced by the taller grass makes it more difficult for weed seeds to germinate. Optimal mowing height depends on the type of grass. (See sidebar.) Be sure that the mower blade is sharp, and never mow when the grass is wet.

Clippings should be left on the lawn if possible. They quickly decompose and return nutrients to the soil. Contrary to some opinions, clippings do not cause a buildup of thatch. Popular mulching mowers grind the clippings into particles that practically disappear into the lawn. Other types leave trails of larger clippings, but they can quickly be spread evenly over the area with a soft rake.

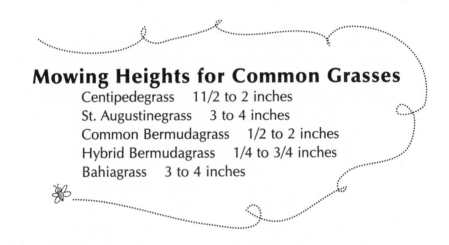

Mowing Heights for Common Grasses

Centipedegrass   1 1/2 to 2 inches
St. Augustinegrass   3 to 4 inches
Common Bermudagrass   1/2 to 2 inches
Hybrid Bermudagrass   1/4 to 3/4 inches
Bahiagrass   3 to 4 inches

Pests and Diseases

It should be obvious by now that good cultural practices encourage a healthy lawn that chokes out weeds and is strong enough to withstand most damage done by insects. Sometimes, however, in spite of their best efforts, most homeowners must deal with insects and diseases in the lawn. The best course of action in such cases is to get advice at a reputable garden center or from the extension agency. Weed and insect management has become a very precise science that in most cases requires identification of the offender, after which specific controls can be recommended.

Other Options

It is becoming more and more apparent to many people that the typical American lawn is on a kind of artificial life support. Many homeowners are taking a second look at these high-maintenance resource users. Some people are starting to minimize or even eliminate their lawns altogether.

Charla Stevens of Niceville, Florida, has just said no to insecticide use in her garden, but having some lawn is very important to her. She has opted to use parasitic nematodes for control of mole crickets, fleas, and other lawn pests. These nematodes are natural enemies of some of the damaging insect pests and are harmless to nontarget organisms. "I've had to lower my expectations just a bit," Charla said. "However, my lawn and garden are certainly acceptable, and I feel really good that I'm not poisoning the birds and wildlife."

Laurie Mackey, an Okaloosa County Master Gardener, has also taken giant steps toward making her yard an environmentally safe haven for her family and the critters that choose to share their space. "To begin with," Laurie said, "Patrick and I wanted to minimize the impact of our landscape on the environment. We chose to plant very small patches of grass. We thought about a landscape with no lawn, but found that it not only adds a pleasant softness but also has a very functional use near our house."

Much of the natural landscape was left intact near the waterfront edge of the Mackey property. Such dependable standbys as *Sabal minor*, titi, groundsel, wax myrtle, saw palmetto, and many other well-established native plants already existed there. Closer to the house, Laurie added more native plants as well as a wide variety of well-adapted exotics, such as crape myrtles and roses. In many places low-maintenance groundcovers were installed, and a water garden, complete with exotic water lilies, graces the grounds. "With such a variety of plants, I suppose the insects just stay confused," says Laurie. "There's not really enough of one kind of plant to cause a population explosion, and I have so many birds and beneficial insects that pests rarely get a chance to inflict much damage."

Valparaiso residents Carolynn and Tom Leach have chosen a different approach. "We could not possibly care for a lawn," declared Carolynn. "We choose to spend much of our time traveling, and caring for a lawn is not one of our priorities." Nevertheless, their garden was a very popular stop during a recent tour of gardens. The use of many native plants and low-maintenance groundcovers, and extensive use of mulching materials such as fallen pine needles and oak leaves, enable them to travel and come home to a yard that looks almost as good as it did when they left it. "We just have to pick up a few sticks and twigs that have fallen, maybe pull a few weeds that have decided to move in, and then we carry on as usual," said Tom.

The trick, then, is for each of us to decide just how important it is to have large expanses of lawn. If having a beautiful lawn is very important, then we must expend the necessary funds and effort to maintain it at an acceptable level of attractiveness and in a way that will have the least negative impact on the environment. If, however, we have become discouraged in our lawn-keeping efforts or disenchanted by wide sweeps of lawn, perhaps it is time to reconsider. Many options exist. Maybe it's time to choose a lawn that's right for you!

TREES AND SHRUBS

BENEFITS OF TREES

Trees and shrubs are the major components of most landscapes. Once planted, many of them are with us for the rest of our lives. It stands to reason that we would give a great deal of thought to their selection and care.

Arbor Day is a special time when we celebrate trees and what they mean to our lives. Florida celebrates Arbor Day on the third Friday in January. National Arbor Day is observed on the last Friday in April, but each state chooses its date determined by the best tree planting time for that state. In the United States, Arbor Day varies from January through May. A tree planted near the selected date has time to establish a good root system. It can better support the foliage that leafs out in spring, thus enabling the tree to photosynthesize more efficiently and in general get off to a better start than trees planted during the summer.

Of course, most people know the many benefits trees bring to our lives. We know, for instance, that trees shade our homes, filter the air, and provide homes for wildlife. We know that they add beauty to our lives, provide us with life-supporting oxygen, and are the building material of most of our homes and furniture. Well-placed trees can reduce summer air-conditioning costs from 15 to 35 percent or more. They also help control soil erosion, moderate temperature, and muffle noises. Many everyday products contain chemicals and other components of trees. Some part of a tree is used in tires, paint, adhesives, cereals, chewing gum, hair spray, mouthwash, shampoo, toothpaste, and even Twinkies. We eat their fruit and extract energy from them. Some trees even provide important medicines.

Trees can remove pollutants from soil through a process called phytoremediation. More and more frequently, trees are being used to treat municipal and industrial wastewater. A hybrid poplar, for instance, can treat a minimum of 25 gallons of polluted soil water each day during the growing season.

Did you know, however, that trees have a significant psychological impact and that they influence the physical health and well-being of people? In one study of hospital patients, those who could see trees outside their windows needed less pain medication and recovered faster than those who could see no trees. Did you know that heart rates of people who live among trees are lower than those who have no trees around them? Trees make people feel comfortable and calm. Researchers have found that children with Attention Deficit Hyperactivity Disorder (ADHD) were able to concentrate better, complete tasks, and do a better job of following directions after playing in natural settings.

Measuring the value of a tree is difficult. You can measure the noise a tree filters out, or the cooling effect of its shade. You can estimate its real estate value, and determine the volume of pollutants it removes or oxygen it adds to the air. However, when you lose a tree, you lose more than these measurable components. You also lose the psychological, sentimental, historic, and social value that is impossible to measure. Life is simply better in tree-filled neighborhoods. Homes stand nestled in quiet green. Birds' songs fill the air and bring delight to daily routine. These are more than enough reasons for everyone who has space to plant a tree.

The University of Florida suggests very specific procedures for planting container-grown trees. Dig the planting hole about one and one-half times the diameter of the root ball (wider if the soil is wet or compacted) and not quite as deep as the container is tall. Place the plant in the hole, and be sure the top of the root ball is just a bit higher than the surrounding soil surface. As you fill in around the ball, slice the shovel down into the loose soil several times and water thoroughly to remove air pockets. Do not mound soil over the roots, but form a saucerlike catchment basin around the edge of the root ball with mulch to facilitate watering. Mulch with a three- to four-inch layer of organic material to buffer soil temperature, reduce weed competition, and conserve moisture. Do not cover the root ball with mulch, but apply it all around the root ball and out far enough so that the area under the dripline is mulched. Retain the mulch out to the dripline, and remember that this area will increase as the tree grows.

Amending the soil by adding organic matter is not recommended when planting trees in the landscape. Researchers at the University of Florida have found that this practice may actually hamper tree growth by keeping the roots from spreading out into the native soil. However, watering is extremely important. The newly planted tree should be kept moist until the plant is well established. During the first week, small trees should be watered daily, then every other day for the next four to six weeks. From seven to twelve weeks, the tree should be watered once a week. Watering until the root ball and surrounding soils are thoroughly wet at each irrigation is recommended. This will encourage deep root systems. Fertilization should begin a few months after planting. A light application of slow-release fertilizer is recommended.

Now that the benefits of trees and the procedures for planting are understood, one can begin to think about which trees to select. Picking the right tree for the right spot is the first order of business. Know the ultimate size of the tree you select and be sure it has enough room to grow. Avoid planting too close to the house, sidewalk, driveway, neighbor, or underneath power lines. Select deciduous trees for planting on the southern and western side of the house to block the hot sun in summer but permit its warming rays in winter.

So many choices exist that I get excited just thinking about them. I realize at times like this that I would really like several acres of property—not just a suburban lot. Then I could plant all of the wonderful trees that I so admire. Planting trees is something that someone with my limited abilities can do to make a difference to people in future generations.

Five Fabulous Trees

People sometimes ask me to suggest a suitable tree for their landscapes. Often they want a large, deciduous landscape tree. Trees in this category grow from 50 to 90 feet tall or more. I recommend them for home landscapes if there is sufficient room for a tree of this size. All of them outlive humans and provide beauty and shelter for future generations.

Bald Cypress

Taxodium distichum
Family: Taxodiaceae (Cypress family)
Origin: USA
Size: 50–70 feet by 20–30 feet
Zones: 4–9
Light: Sun
Water: Moderate; tolerates very wet and very dry soils
Soil: Tolerant, prefers slightly acid, moist
Salt Tolerance: Moderate

Surely one of our most beautiful trees is the bald cypress (*Taxodium distichum*). This native sends up the scenic cypress knees that are such a familiar sight in our swamps. However, these knees occur only near water, so the tree does well in normal landscape situations. It  is called "bald" because it is one of the few deciduous conifers. In the fall, soft, rust-colored leaves carpet the ground. In spring, pale green, lacy new ones emerge. I often remark to Amiable Spouse that they seem soft enough for a pillow. Pale green cones about one inch in diameter are borne close to the branches. In the winter landscape, the pyramidal profile, symmetrical branching, and striated reddish-brown bark add interest. It is particularly resistant to wind and is rarely overturned by hurricanes.

Southern Magnolia (also Bull Bay)
Magnolia grandiflora
Family: Magnoliaceae (Magnolia family)
Origin: Southern USA to Texas
Size: 60–90 feet by 30–50 feet
Zones: 7–9
Light: Sun/Part Sun
Water: Moderate
Soil: Prefers rich, porous, acid, well-drained
Salt Tolerance: Moderate

No doubt one of my favorite trees for a large yard or landscape is the southern magnolia (*Magnolia grandiflora*). Showy white flowers appear throughout the spring and summer. Reddish-brown, conelike structures two to four inches long develop after the flowers. From these, bright red kidney-shaped seeds hang from threads in autumn.

Even though I do not have a magnolia in my present yard, I admire them around the neighborhood and on the grounds of large estates that dot the South. Growing from 60 to 90 feet tall, they definitely need a large space. The best way to grow the magnolia if space permits is to let the limbs grow to the ground and hide the leaves that fall and seem to take forever to decompose. If you do decide to remove the lower limbs, or if they shed naturally in shady places, do not expect to grow grass or anything else underneath it. Dense shade and a competitive root system make the ground underneath it unsuitable for underplanting.

Leave the natural mulch under the tree and supplement it with pine needles or other natural materials. Otherwise you may be doomed to raking the yard every other day or so.

Magnolia is Mississippi's state tree and Louisiana's state flower. It is native on the coastal plain from North Carolina, south to central Florida, and west to the eastern part of Texas. From the gardener's point of view, the tree is an environmentally friendly choice. Never have I known anyone who sprayed a magnolia for pests. In addition, it provides good foraging places for birds if leaves and flower debris are left in place.

Even though the flower of the magnolia is one of the most beautiful, it is not very practical in floral designs. Its flowers are not long lasting, and even touching the delicate blossom will cause a brown spot to appear. Brides who insist on using them know to wait until the morning of the wedding to collect flowers. Stamens fall from the flower easily and mar the tablecloth or whatever else is underneath it.

The leaves and cones, however, are a different matter. They are both popular in floral designs and other decorations during the holiday season. The leaves with their dark green, lustrous upper sides and lighter green or rusty undersides add boldness and structure to many a holiday display.

Many cultivars of southern magnolia exist. 'Little Gem' is more suited to small properties. In 20 years it can possibly grow to 20 feet high and 10 feet wide. 'Edith Bogue' extends the magnolia's hardiness range, for it can be grown farther north than many other cultivars. According to Michael Dirr, author of *Manual of Woody Landscape Plants*, well over 100 cultivars exist.

Red Maple (also Swamp Maple, Scarlet Maple)

Acer rubrum
Family: Aceraceae (Maple family)
Origin: USA; Florida west to Texas
Size: 40–60 feet by 30–60 feet
Zones: 3–9
Light: Sun/Part Sun
Water: Any. Tolerates extremely dry to extremely wet sites
Soil: Moist, well-drained, acid
Salt Tolerance: Slight

The red maple (*Acer rubrum*) is another excellent selection for a large property. Its red colors are evident in one way or another throughout the year. Ruby-red flowers and scarlet winged seeds are one of the most beautiful sights in the late winter and early spring landscape. In

summer the red leaf stalks shimmer in the sunlight, and fall sees a pageant of red, yellow, apricot, and orange as the trees put on their fall dresses. Many cultivars of red maple are available. Michael Dirr lists 35 cultivars in his book. Highly recommended for dependable red fall color in the South is a cultivar called 'October Glory'. Be sure to place this beautiful tree where wide-ranging surface roots will not pose a problem to drainage lines.

Blackgum (also Black Tupelo, Tupelo, Sour Gum)
> *Nyssa sylvatica*
> Family: Nyssaceae (Tupelo family)
> Origin: USA–Maine, Ontario, Michigan and south to Florida
> and Texas
> Size: 30–60 feet by 20–30 feet
> Zones: 3–9
> Light: Sun/Part Sun
> Water: Moderate
> Soil: Prefers moist but well-drained
> Salt Tolerance: Moderate

I also enjoy the fall colors of my blackgum (*Nyssa sylvatica*). It is still a little tree, but I spot large specimens in the woods. Recognizing it is easy because lower limbs are held at ninety-degree angles from the trunk. All during the summer, a solid red leaf  can usually be found somewhere on the tree. As fall draws near, more and more red leaves are evident. Finally, when fall arrives, the black gum produces some of our most dependable color. Mine is situated in plain view of the sidewalk leading to the house. All summer and fall I am treated to a parade of color.

Nuttall Oak

Quercus nuttallii
Family: Fagaceae (Beech family)
Origin: USA–Bottom lands of Southern Coastal Plains
Size: 40–60 feet by 25–30 feet
Zones: 5–9
Light: Sun
Water: Moderate/High
Soil: Prefers wet, acid. Good choice for poorly drained area
Salt Tolerance: Slight

Another favorite is the Nuttall oak (*Quercus nuttallii*) that I bought at a local nursery several years ago when it was a four-foot sapling. Now it is a pretty, pyramidal tree about 30 feet tall. It has deeply lobed leaves like most of the red oak group, and it colors up in shades of red and yellow for a show before its leaves fall to the ground. I expect this oak to outlive me and provide summer shade on the south side of my house for many years to come.

Abelia (also Glossy Abelia)

Abelia x grandiflora
Family: Caprifoliaceae (Honeysuckle family)
Origin: Hybridized in Italy
Size: 3–6 feet by 3–6 feet
Zones: 5–9
Light: Sun/Part Sun
Water: Moderate/Low
Soil: Well-drained
Salt Tolerance: None

Some mornings when I'm on my best behavior, I walk a couple of miles for exercise, general health, and because it makes me feel good. Furthermore, these morning walks give me an opportunity to see plants and flowers blooming around the neighborhood. On several mornings one summer, I walked by a yard that had a beautiful small tree blooming at the corner of the house. The flowers were white and clustered together so that they were quite visible from the street. I knew that it was not a crape myrtle, but I could not for the life of me figure out what it was.

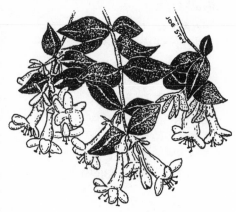

One morning in a brave move on my part, I simply entered the yard for a closer look. Amiable Spouse always hangs back on such excursions. He cautions that one day I'm going to get shot. I knew, however, that the house was the home of one of my garden club friends, so I was not afraid. Much to my surprise, at close range I discovered that this small tree was glossy abelia.

Abelia x grandiflora might be a good choice for gardens needing moderately salt-tolerant plants. The most common hybrid, often called glossy abelia, is evergreen to semi-evergreen. Small, funnel-shaped, white flowers flushed with pink are borne in profusion for most of the summer. Leaves are a lustrous dark green in summer, turning to shades of bronzy red in fall. New growth is mostly red. In most of Florida it is evergreen, though it is semi-evergreen in the upper reaches of its range (to Zone 5).

Those of us who were born and raised in the South remember the glossy abelia in our grandparents' and parents' yards. This dependable, old-time favorite is often grown as a clipped hedge, but to many it is more beautiful when allowed to grow into its naturally rounded, fountainlike form. Arching branches spread out to form a dense, rounded shrub that usually tops out at six feet tall and wide. However, the small tree at my friend's house was closer to eight or ten feet tall. Lower growing varieties exist that may be better suited to smaller landscapes. 'Francis Mason' grows three to four feet tall and has pink flowers and new leaves that are rich yellow. 'Prostrata' reaches about one and a half to two feet tall, is more compact, and has smaller leaves that turn purple-green in winter. 'Sherwood' tops out at three to four feet tall with a bit wider spread. It is a good plant for massing in sun or partial shade. 'Edward Goucher' averages five by five feet at maturity and bears clear pink flowers.

Glossy abelia is easily maintained. It has no serious pests and requires only occasional pruning to keep it attractive. Hard pruning in late winter will rejuvenate old plants. Flowers are produced on new wood, so they will flower the same year after drastic winter pruning. If the natural fountain shape is wanted, old canes should be pruned from the center of the plant at ground level.

Drought tolerance is also a winning feature of this shrub. On a vacant lot behind my house, one grows and blooms dependably every summer with nary a drop of irrigation water. I promise myself each time I notice it among the overgrown weeds, briars, and yaupons on the vacant lot that I will take a cutting and try to get it started in a dry spot in my landscape. I will increase my chances of seeing more butterflies and hummingbirds, for they are frequent visitors. Until now, it has only been a good intention.

American Holly

Ilex opaca
Family: Aquifoliaceae (Holly family)
Origin: USA
Size: 30–60 feet by 18–35 feet
Zones: 5–9
Light: Sun/ Part Sun
Water: Low (Drought Tolerant)
Soil: Well-drained
Salt Tolerance: Moderate

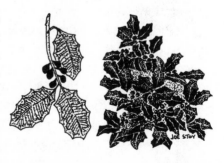

Cousin Harold has a place in the country. He asked me to suggest some plants that would fit into his landscape. I have suggested several natives that will blend in wonderfully with his wooded property. One that I suggested is American holly. Growing to 50 feet, the evergreen leaves have sharp-pointed tips and spiny-toothed margins. Pale trunks stand out in the landscape on single or multi-trunked specimens. Yellowish-white, small flowers bloom in spring and provide an early source of nectar for bees, ants, wasps, and night-flying moths. If the tree is a female and a male tree is nearby for pollination, bright red, orange, or sometimes yellow berries shine in the winter woods. These colorful berries are eaten by at least 18 species of birds, including the mourning dove, wild turkey, northern bobwhite, and many songbirds. Henry's elfin butterfly and the striped hairstreak lay their eggs on American holly, for it is their larval food plant. In addition, some mammals, including opossums and raccoons, eat holly berries. Cattle and deer have been known to browse the foliage.

Though the largest trees are found in rich, slightly acidic bottomlands, they are adapted to a wide variety of conditions. They can be found on sand hills, gravely soils farther inland, or thin mountain soils up to an elevation of about 3,000 feet. Truly a plant for the humid Southeast, *Ilex opaca* is hardy in Zones 6 to 9 and grows in acid soil that ranges from rich to poor or wet to dry. Salt tolerance makes it desirable for those who live near bodies of salt water or where saltwater intrusion might occur.

In nature, native plants grow in plant communities or associations. American holly is at home under native canopy trees in the company of musclewood, pawpaw, sourgum, flowering dogwood, titi, redbay, sweetbay, hawthorn,blueberry, and huckleberry. In home landscapes, it is best planted at the edge of woodlands or in a place where some protection is offered from the worst of summer's sun. A naturally mulched area some distance from the house might be best. The spiny leaves carpet the ground underneath and make walking barefoot beneath it an impossibility.

The ornamental value of this holly makes it a favorite for holiday decorations. Glossy, red berries and leathery, sturdy leaves make it outstanding in floral designs, wreaths, and other holiday accents. In most floral designers' gardens, a holly can be found that is pruned each winter around Christmas time.

Ilex opaca is not our only native holly. Deciduous holly natives include possum haw (*I. decidua*), Sarvis holly, (*I. amelanchier*) and winterberry or black alder (*I. verticillata*). Yaupon (*I. vomitoria*), gallberry (*I. glabra*), myrtle holly (*I. myrtifolia*), and dahoon holly (*I. cassine*) are some of the evergreen hollies.

To add to the confusion, hybrids of *Ilex opaca* and *I. cassine* have been developed. This group contains some of our most useful landscape subjects, and includes such well-known names as 'Savannah',

'Fosteri', and 'East Palatka'. One Internet mail-order source (Windrose Nursery), lists 39 cultivars of American holly with sizes ranging from the one-foot 'Maryland Dwarf' to the 40-foot 'Merry Christmas'. Wow! That's a lot of choices—at least, I thought so until I looked in Dirr's *Manual*. According to him, over 1,000 named cultivars exist!

With all of these selections, a holly can surely be found that will perfectly fit Harold's property, or mine or yours, for that matter. Dirr recommends choosing one of the superior cultivars instead of a seedling and reminds us that a male is necessary among the females for good berry production. Select one of these adaptable trees for your landscape, and every day will be a holly-day!

Century Plant (also Agave, Maguey)

Agave americana
Family: Agavaceae (Agave family)
Origin: Mexico, USA
Size: 6–8 feet by 8–10 feet
Zones: 8b–11
Light: Sun
Water: Low
Soil: Well-drained
Salt Tolerance: High

A friend called me one day and exclaimed, "Marie, there's something down on Valparaiso Boulevard that you've just got to see!" Then came e-mails from other folks telling me about a rare phenomenon that was taking place at the time. Several century plants were in bloom around town. It was enough to cause quite a stir.

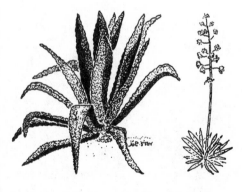

For most of its life the century plant is a large rosette of blue-green, stiff, sword-shaped foliage. Each leaf can grow up to six feet long and ten inches wide, so its statement in the landscape is quite dramatic even before the bloom is produced. When the bloom does come—as it does after ten or more years (not a century as some sup-pose)—it is an amazing thing. The flower spike emerges from the center of the plant and elongates and thrusts skyward at the rate of one to two feet a day. Finally, it reaches a lofty height of 15 to 40 feet. The treelike flower stalk regales those who are lucky enough to wit-ness the scene. Individual yellow to white six-petaled flowers grow in clusters that face upward at the ends of horizontal branches.

The sad part of this drama is that after the blooms fade, the plant dies. It is not a time for despair, however, for dozens of pups or baby agaves are waiting underneath the mother plant and are ready to be planted in containers and shared with friends (or enemies, as the case may be).

Agaves are armed and dangerous. Spines arm the edges of each leaf, and a long, sharp, terminal spine grows at each leaf tip. Needless to say, this is not a plant to place near foot traffic. If plant-ed underneath a window, however, it would surely work better than a watchdog at foiling the attempts of thieves or other brigands who might attempt an unwelcome entry.

Maintenance is usually minimal. Removal of the lower leaves is sometimes necessary and can be a difficult proposition. Sometimes the sharp spines at the tips of the leaves are removed to protect peo-ple and pets. Removal of the entire dead plant after blooming is quite an undertaking, and the garbage crew may take offense for some time.

If, however, a plant is needed that will tolerate drought, salty conditions, constant wind, and occasional sand blasting, then an agave might fill the bill. In some parts of the South, cold tempera-tures might occasionally nip them, but they are hardy to the low teens.

In the landscape, agave makes a striking specimen or accent plant. Since it requires excellent drainage, it is at home in sandy soils or in rock gardens. If you choose to plant an agave in your landscape remember to give it plenty of room. It grows six to eight feet tall and spreads eight to ten feet. That means that at least a 12-foot diameter circle would be necessary in order to have room to pass by it on all sides. Common sense would dictate that it be planted where it is to stay, because moving it is a daunting task.

Gardeners may choose from among several different cultivars. *Agave americana* 'Marginata' has yellow-edged leaves, and

'Mediopicta' has a broad yellow band running down the middle of each leaf. Other species can also be found, such as *Agave vilmoriniana*, *A. picta*, and *A. filifera*. Some of these do not grow as large as our native *Agave americana*, and many of them are not as hardy.

The Mexican Indians who lived in the Sonoran Desert used the leaves to make a ropelike fiber called sisal, and they could separate the fibers into translucent sheets, which were used as paper. Most people are probably more familiar with the plant's use in making tequila. Actually the real elixir is made from the fermented hearts of the blue agave (*Agave tequilana*).

Agaves are often available where houseplants are sold. Sometimes they are lumped in with succulents. Of course, one might also beg a pup from a friend or neighbor.

Chaste Tree (also Monk's Pepper, Hemp Tree, Chasteberry)

Vitex agnus-castus
Family: Verbenaceae (Verbena family)
Origin: Europe, Asia
Size: 15–20 feet by 15–20 feet
Zones: 6–10
Light: Sun/Part Sun
Water: Low
Soil: Well-drained
Salt Tolerance: Moderate

For several years I have noticed a small tree at the church down the street. Each year it blooms spikes of lavender flowers three to six inches long that pierce the air from the ends of each branch and give it an interesting bristly outline. Of course, such intriguing appearances always attract my attention and persuade me to examine each minute detail and record it on film, lest I forget.

Leaves are distinctive because each leaflet is attached to a common point with five to seven fingerlike leaflets (palmately compound). They are dark grayish-green on top and lighter and hairy underneath. When brushed against or bruised, they give off a sharp, aromatic scent.

A friend down the street has a lovely specimen with pink flowers. In addition to the species that bloom lilac flowers, cultivars such as 'Alba', 'Colonial Blue', 'Rosea', and 'Silver Spire' offer flowers with white, blue, or pink flowers. *Vitex negundo* and *V. rotundifolia* are also used in landscapes, but they differ significantly from *Vitex agnus-castus.*

I still watch the chaste tree beside the church as it grows and blooms each year in May and June. Since it blooms on new growth, it will continue to flower during the summer as long as it continues to grow. Pruning off old blossoms may encourage another flush of flowers. Chaste tree is well suited to the South because it is tolerant of drought and heat, and it exhibits moderate salt tolerance. No pest or disease problems are evident on any of the trees I have observed. It is easily pruned into a shrub, or it may be limbed up and grown as a small tree.

Though chaste tree is native to Europe and Asia, it is cultivated from Texas eastward to Florida and northward to North Carolina. As a matter of fact, it has naturalized in many areas of the South. It has a medium fast growth rate and lives 20 years or more. Trees top out anywhere from 15 to 25 feet.

If you have a friend who has a chaste tree, ask for a cutting. Stick it in moist soil and expect it to root in a few weeks. Seeds can also be planted for a source of this highly adaptable tree.

The chaste tree has had a wealth of interesting uses over the years. In Rome, vestal virgins carried twigs of it as a symbol of chastity. It has been called "Monk's pepper" because of its peppery tasting seeds and reported ability to quiet the sexual appetite. It has been used for the treatment of menstrual difficulties for at least 2,500 years. In modern medicine it continues to be used as a treatment for premenstrual syndrome and other female difficulties.

For me, however, the primary use of this tree is as a specimen for the landscape. Amiable Spouse offers to make me a concoction from time to time because he knows of its therapeutic powers. I firmly refuse his offer, however. This, too, shall pass.

Common Persimmon (also American Persimmon)

Diospyros virginiana
Family: Ebenaceae (Ebony family)
Origin: Eastern USA
Size: 30–60 feet by 20–35 feet
Zones: 4–10
Light: Sun/Part Sun
Water: Adaptable
Soil: Adaptable
Salt Tolerance: High

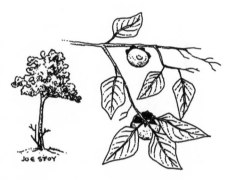

For several years I have enjoyed a common persimmon tree in my backyard. It dependably produces fruit, and even though I don't usually eat it, I enjoy using it in fall floral arrangements. In spring I enjoy its inconspicuous but delightfully fragrant three-quarter-inch, cream-colored flowers. Glossy leathery leaves make it attractive in the landscape all summer, and shades of red and yellow arrive in the fall. The only thing I ever have to do is cut an occasional sucker growing out from the roots. It was one of the things that lived here when I moved in—possibly a gift from a passing bird. It grew on its own, never demanding water, fertilizer, or spraying for this disease or that insect.

Common persimmon is dioecious, meaning that the male (staminate) and female (pistillate) flowers are borne on separate trees. My fruit-bearing tree is one of a small thicket, so some of her consorts must be male. Trees begin to produce fruit when they are about ten years old. After the fruit turns orange, and especially after a good frost, it becomes palatable. Folks use it in a variety of desserts, and it is readily eaten by birds, raccoons, deer, bear, and my resident 'possums.

Wood of the persimmon is heavy, hard, strong, and very closely grained. Because of its hardness, smoothness, and even texture, it is sometimes used in golf club heads, shoe lasts, and shuttles. Dried, roasted, ground seeds have been used as a substitute for coffee. The inner bark and unripe fruit have been used to treat fever, diarrhea, and hemorrhage. Indelible ink is made from the fruit.

Common persimmon is native to the southeastern quarter of the United States. It grows well in a tremendous range of conditions from very dry, sterile, shady woodlands to moist river bottoms to rocky hillsides. Common associates are elm, eastern redcedar, hickory, tulip poplar, oak, maple, and sycamore. At maturity its average height is 30 to 60 feet, but in rich soils it may reach up to 80 feet tall. Several cultivars are available with improved fruit size and quality.

To get a persimmon tree for the landscape, it may be easiest to start one from seed. Transplanting one from the wild would be very difficult because it has a deep taproot. To start plants from seeds, collect a few fruits when they are thoroughly ripe. Clean the flesh from the seeds and let them dry for a day or two in an airy place. Then wrap the seeds in moist peat moss or sand and place in a plastic bag and seal. Store in the vegetable bin of a refrigerator where the temperature stays about 40°F. After two to three months remove them from the refrigerator and soak for two or three days in water. Then plant in light soil and cover to a depth of about half an inch. Once the propagation process is started, do not allow the seeds to dry out, as they may lose their viability. By the following fall the seedlings should be ready to transplant into permanent places in the landscape.

It's funny how we live with something all our lives and just take if for granted. On the farm in Mississippi, common persimmon was considered a woody weed. I remember it along fence rows and in abandoned fields. Daddy used to cut them out of the pastures regularly, because he said that the fruit made the cows sick. My brothers and sisters and I used to dare each other to taste a green one. Seldom did we take the dare, because the astringent fruit would pucker our mouths for some time. Still it was lots of fun to trick some of our city cousins into taking a bite.

Only recently have I begun to value common persimmon and its contributions to my residential landscape. I guess it reminds me of home. Too, after tending to fussy flowers and plants for half a century or so, it is refreshing to have something that will grow well with no effort on my part. I just let it be, and that's exactly what it does. It just is, and I enjoy its is-ness, its beauty, and its presence—for free. Lucky me.

Coral Bean (also Cherokee Bean, Cardinal Spear)

Erythrina herbacea
Family: Fabaceae (Bean family)
Origin: SE USA and Mexico
Size: 3–4 feet by 3–4 feet
Zones: 7–10
Light: Sun/Part Sun
Water: Low/Medium
Soil: Adaptable
Salt Tolerance: High

My introduction to coral bean was not exactly pleasant. Several garden club members were working in the club's wildflower garden in Florida Park. At the head of the plot was a pretty plant; at that time I didn't know what it was. However, it was much too large to be a part of this very small garden. I decided to prune it back, so I grabbed a limb and pulled on it. As it slipped through my hands it let me know in no uncertain terms that it was armed and dangerous.

We decided that the small plot didn't need this plant or the beautyberry with which it was entwined because together the two plants took up most of the space. I asked Amiable Spouse to dig both plants up. The beautyberry came out easily in the sandy soil, but the coral bean was another matter. He dug and dug—and finally thought he had it. It proceeded to regrow almost immediately, so at the next work session, I asked him to tackle the job again. After much persistence, he removed a solid mass of root about the size of a five-gallon bucket. None of us could believe that a plant that size had such a root.

If I had known what the plant was, I might have let it stay. It is one of our beautiful native plants, and it provides nectar for butterflies and hummingbirds. On the other hand, it might have been a poor choice for a park where children play because its bright red berries are poisonous and hallucinogenic. As a matter of fact, the seeds have been used to poison rats and to paralyze fish.

Since that incident, I have learned some things about coral bean. Sometimes called Cherokee bean, this native legume provides a splash of red for a couple of months in spring when it blooms and again in autumn when the beans burst open to reveal bright red seeds. It remains attractive throughout the growing season.

In southern Florida coral bean may attain a height of 20 feet, but in areas farther north it seldom exceeds a height of eight feet because it gets killed to the ground in freezing weather. Gardeners usually remove the dead limbs. One grower noticed, however, that hummingbirds used the dead branches as perches when the plant started blooming the following spring. I suppose each of us makes a personal decision about whether or not to prune. Certainly in nature the dead branches are not removed and the new foliage grows up to cover them.

Bright red flowers are borne on narrow, leafless spikes 8 to 13 inches long that contrast sharply with the plant's green foliage. Blossoms are tubular, curvy, and grow on spikes a foot or more in length. The compound leaves are composed of three triangular-shaped leaflets six to eight inches long, and the stems are armed with short, recurved spines on the underside of each leaf.

In a recent interview, a reporter asked me about future plans for my home landscape. I told him that I wanted to make my yard more natural. I have already begun to add tough plants to my landscape— plants that will survive with minimal help from me. Many tough natives seem tailor-made for my plans. I am looking for plants that require no fertilizer, no extra water after they are established, and ones that will grow in the sandy conditions that exist in my garden. DeFuniak Springs Garden Club's annual native plant sales are a boon for my intentions, and it is here that I have found several such plants. One, of course, was a coral bean.

I placed my coral bean in a corner of the garden where I seldom go. There it keeps company with other tough natives like beautyberry, red buckeye, grancy graybeard, sparkleberry, trumpet honeysuckle, and tall pines. I expect it to thrive in this mostly sunny location. It seems a perfect choice in light of my gardening goals. I may or may not prune the dead limbs after it dies back to the ground. If I decide to prune, I will have on my toughest pair of gardening gloves.

Propagation of coral bean is not especially complicated. Collect a few seeds and sow them on top of the soil, uncovered. Check for newly sprouted plants the following spring and move them where they are wanted or pot them up for other uses. Alternatively, take a few cuttings, which root easily and may be taken after new growth turns semi-woody.

If your garden needs something for a hot, sunny spot—something that will be there whether or not you have time to tend it—think about selecting a coral bean. It thrives in both sandy soils and poorly drained clay soils. Drought and salt tolerance are additional attributes that increase its attractiveness and suitability for Southern gardens.

Coral Tree
(also Crybaby Tree, Christ's Tears, Cockspur Coral Tree)
> *Erythrina crista-galli*
> Family: Fabaceae (Bean family)
> Origin: Brazil
> Size: 15–20 feet by 15–20 feet
> Zones: 8b–10
> Light: Sun
> Water: Moderate
> Soil: Well-drained
> Salt Tolerance: Moderate

Related to the coral bean is the coral tree (*Erythrina crista-galli*). This shrub or small tree is sometimes called the crybaby tree or Christ's tears because nectar drips from the blossoms like a teardrop. Dark crimson and scarlet flowers bloom in several waves between spring and fall. It is hardy in USDA Zones 8b to 10, and likes full sun and regular to occasional water. It appreciates well-drained soil and roots easily from semi-hardwood cuttings, or it may be started from seed.

Gardenia (also Cape Jasmine)

Gardenia jasminoides
Family: Rubiaceae (Madder family)
Origin: China
Size: 3–5 feet by 3–5 feet
Zones: 8–10
Light: Part Sun
Water: Moderate
Soil: Acid, organic, well-drained
Salt Tolerance: Slight

Gardenias have been a part of our landscapes for many years. Many Southerners recognize the unmistakable fragrance and insist on growing it in their gardens. The glorious perfume makes it worth the effort.

My first memories of gardenias come from Grandmother's garden. She had a perfect set-up in her kitchen. Her dishpan was on a counter right by a window. The window and screen were attached at the top by hinges that allowed them to swing open from the bottom. Grandmother threw her dishwater and table scraps right out the window. I remember her calling, "Here, chick, chick, chick." The chickens would come running and gobble up every crumb.

Right under the window grew her gardenias, or cape jasmines, as she called them. I'm sure that she knew just what she was doing when she planted them in that particular place. She frequently tossed her soapy and slightly greasy dishwater directly on the gardenias. Never did I see the sooty mold growing on them that so frequently plagues mine. I don't remember white flies or thrips. All I remember are the creamy white flowers and the marvelous scent.

Gardenia is native to China and is hardy in Zones 8 to 10. More than 200 different species have been identified but only a few of these are regularly grown. Large-flowered cultivars like 'Mystery' and 'August Beauty' are among the most popular. *Gardenia jasminoides* 'Veitchii' grows two to four feet high and produces abundant small flowers over a long period. Dwarf cultivars like 'Radicans' and 'Prostrata' grow two to three feet high and form graceful, spreading shrubs.

Gardenias, like camellias and azaleas, are acid-loving plants. For optimal growth, they should be fertilized lightly in spring and again during the summer with a gardenia-azalea-camellia fertilizer. Lightly is the key word. Overfertilization may cause problems because gardenias are sensitive to salts in the soil. Sometimes leaf chlorosis or yellowing occurs. It can be corrected at least temporarily by acidifying the soil with elemental sulfur or applying iron to the soil or directly to the leaves in the form of a foliar spray.

Gardenias prefer well-drained soil high in organic matter. Mulch around the base of plants conserves moisture and controls weeds. They appreciate some protection from sun and thrive in much the same conditions preferred by camellias and azaleas. Lustrous dark green, leathery leaves make the plants attractive year-round. If pruning is necessary to keep the plants shapely, it should be done just after the plant has finished blooming.

Even though I greatly admire gardenias, my enjoyment of them is marred by the fact that it takes a great deal of effort to keep them looking good. Unfortunately, my shrubs are not located underneath a kitchen window where the dishwater can be handily tossed on them. Such plagues as powdery mildew, sooty mold, aphids, scale, mealybugs, white flies, thrips, and mites prove to be troublesome. The cure is, of course, spraying with a soap and oil mixture, horticultural oil, or insecticidal soap. Being sure that the soil has plenty of organic matter best controls nematodes, which also plague gardenias.

If you have a friend or neighbor who has a gardenia that you greatly admire, take a cutting in June, July, or August. It will root easily either in water or moist soil. If you choose to plant a gardenia in your landscape, be sure that you are prepared to give it a bit of extra attention. A well cared for plant is a thing of beauty. However, those of us who have little time for spraying and combating pests would probably be wise to enjoy them in the yards of our friends who have time to care for them properly, unless, of course, we have a handy place under the kitchen window like Grandmother did.

Japanese Aucuba
(also Aucuba, Japanese or Spotted Laurel, Gold Dust Plant)
Aucuba japonica
Family: Aucubaceae (Cornaceae) (Aucuba family)
Origin: Japan
Size: 3–8 feet by 3–4 feet
Zones: 8 (7b)–9
Light: Shade
Water: Moderate
Soil: Sandy loam, well-drained
Salt Tolerance: None

For several years, a gold dust plant has grown out back underneath an oak tree. There it successfully competes with the oak roots for nutrients, and it beautifies the shady spot with bright green leaves heavily speckled with gold. This beautiful plant is rather like the little girl who had a little curl right in the middle of her forehead. If you remember, when she was good she was very, very good, and when she was bad she was horrid!

If you can find a place where aucuba does well, it does exceedingly well. If, however, it starts having problems, you might as well dig it up and throw it away, for it will never be the attractive addition to the landscape that you envisioned. Gold dust plant is very picky about soil and placement. In exposed locations, it is often afflicted with leaf spots and stem dieback. Foliage will burn in the sun, and overhead watering increases problems with leaf diseases. Root rot may occur if the soil is not to its liking, and it is susceptible to damage by root knot nematodes. To help control foliar problems, provide some protection for the plants during cold winter weather. Prune out any dead branches immediately. Avoid overhead watering that may cause the foliage to remain wet for long periods of time.

Root problems may be avoided by being sure that the area is well drained and that plants are planted no deeper than the soil level in the container. Avoid places where either they or azaleas have died before. Mulch is fine, but keep it about six inches away from the main stem. Avoid excess fertilizer. Highly organic soil is the best defense against nematodes, so amend sandy soils prior to planting.

Even with the problems associated with this plant, I am going to have it if at all possible. For floral designers, it is one of the "must-have" plants. Its beautiful foliage is attractive in designs, and it is long-lived in water. As a matter of fact, if it is left in the water long enough, it sends out roots. At this time, it may be potted up and allowed to grow for a few months. Before long it will be ready for another shady place in the garden or for the next plant sale.

Aucuba japonica may be either male or female. Female plants form pretty but toxic scarlet berries if a male is nearby to pollinate them. I chose *Aucuba japonica* 'Variegata', or gold dust plant, for my yard. Others are *Aucuba japonica* 'Crassifolia', a male form with large, dark green leaves, and *A. japonica* 'Serratifolia', a green-leafed female form that produces heavy fruit if a male pollinator is nearby. Michael Dirr lists twenty-one varieties or cultivars in his book, *Manual of Woody Landscape Plants*. In my landscape, gold dust plant is grown at the rear of a shady border. Growing four to six feet tall and wide, it makes an excellent background for ferns and other shade-tolerant plants that share its space.

Aucuba japonica is truly a plant for the Deep South, because the northern edge of its cold hardiness is USDA Zone 8. It can, however, be successfully grown as a container plant and protected from cold in more northerly places.

Japanese Fatsia (also Fatsia, Japanese Aralia)
Fatsia japonica
Family: Araliaceae (Ginseng family)
Origin: Japan
Size: 6–10 feet by 6–10 feet
Zones: 8–10
Light: Shade/Part Sun
Water: Moderate
Soil: Moist, well-drained
Salt Tolerance: Moderate

When I first started floral design classes, I paid close attention to the plant materials the teachers used. I wanted some of the plants in my yard, for having a good selection of plant materials from which to

choose means a great deal to floral designers.

Japanese fatsia has been one
of my favorites. Bold, glossy,
deeply lobed, evergreen leaves
eight to ten inches across and just
a bit shorter in length lend a tropical look to the landscape. For
designs, just one leaf is often all
that is needed to add a touch of
boldness and distinction. The edges can be trimmed or cut into interesting circular shapes, and they are long lasting in water.

Creamy-white flowers bloom in winter. They are visually significant, as many of the one-inch, circular flower clusters are produced
on stems held well above the foliage. As the flowers mature, clusters
of round, berrylike fruits about one-eighth of an inch in diameter are
produced; first green and then turning black.

If fatsia is to do its best, it should be planted in loose, well-
drained, moist, slightly acid soil. Partial or full shade, especially during afternoon, is necessary. Even winter sun and wind can cause
injury. Growth is slow at first, but once it becomes established, it
grows more rapidly.

Fatsia is hardy in USDA Zones 8 to 10. Folks farther north sometimes grow it in containers and move it to protected places during
the winter. A fair performance can be expected when it is grown as
an indoor houseplant, but care must be taken in this situation to provide it with bright light but no direct sun. Even then it appreciates a
vacation outdoors during the summer.

Fatsia can grow six to ten feet high and wide. Old specimens up
to 15 feet tall have been seen, but such size is rare. Often tall stalks
will arise above the plant, and they will be leafless except at the very
tops of the stems. Improve the looks of such overgrown plants by cutting the longest stems off at ground level. New, young plants are
always at the base waiting for their spot in the limelight. Have several pots of soil on hand, however. Cut the long stems into sections
about eight inches in length and stick in moist soil. The cuttings will
root and make excellent offerings for the next plant sale.

Seeds collected and planted at just the right time germinate
quickly. Collect the black seeds when they are ripe. Remove the

pulp, and plant the seeds in a mixture of moist peat moss and sand. Keep them damp until germination occurs and then pot up the tiny seedlings in four-inch pots and let them grow until they are large enough to be put in a permanent place.

Gardeners may choose from several cultivars. 'Moseri' is more compact than the species. 'Aurea' has golden variegated leaves, and 'Variegata' has white variegation patterns dispersed over the leaf. Though this species is generally trouble-free, I did get an infestation of scale insects one summer and fall. I managed to get them under control by spraying with ultrafine horticultural oil.

So there you go. Another good plant—if you give some attention to its cultural needs.

Leatherleaf Mahonia (also Oregon Grape Holly)

Mahonia bealei
Family: Berberidaceae (Barberry family)
Origin: China
Size: 4–10 feet by 3–4 feet
Zones: 6–9
Light: Shade/Part Sun
Water: Moderate
Soil: Well-drained
Salt Tolerance: Moderate

Amiable Spouse and I built a covered walkway to connect the house and garage. We added a tall fence to shield the walkway from public view. I worried about it for a time because I was afraid I would have difficulty finding plants that would grow well in so much shade. I needn't have worried, though, because I found a few plants that actually flourish in this environment. One of them is leatherleaf mahonia. Because it offers something interesting all year long, I have particularly enjoyed it in this prominent location.

More than 70 species and probably an equal number of hybrids and cultivars of mahonia exist worldwide. A native of China, it is widely grown in the South from Zones 6b to 9a. Dense, three- to six-inch-long spikes of yellow flowers begin blooming in January. They arise from the top of the plant and are held at a perfect height for viewing up close and enjoying their delicious fragrance. Pendulous masses of bluish-purple fruits about the size of small grapes follow the flowers. In fall the plants take on a reddish color, and occasionally a solid red leaf will appear. Tough, leathery, compound leaves are borne in horizontal tiers up each unbranched stalk. Spines along the margin of each leaflet make it a poor choice for planting in places where people may brush against them.

I do not worry about mahonia when a freeze or frost threatens because temperatures in the South are not likely to fall low enough to cause damage. Even the flowers are frost-tolerant to about 24°F. Because the flowers open over a one- to three-week period, they recover nicely from a freeze. These plants are equally at home in our summer heat.

The distinctive sculptural form of the shrub combines well with rich browns of stonework and wood. An interesting and exotic effect results when used with contemporary structures. Plants are effective grouped in masses. They may be used as a backdrop for low shrubs, and they are equally suited for use as specimen plants. On the north side of a house, in woodlands, or under tall trees are good places for mahonia as long as the soil is moist and well drained. In ideal conditions a clump may eventually spread up to eight feet wide. Complete fertilizer may be sprinkled around the base of established plants in late winter.

Seeds or cuttings can be used to propagate leatherleaf mahonia. No stratification (storing of seeds in a chilled moist environment or material in order to induce germination) is needed, so seeds may be planted immediately when they are extracted from ripe fruits. The gardener, however, will have to watch closely and get the ripened fruit before the birds make off with it. Part of the enjoyment is watching the mockingbirds scold and dive at the squirrels that also relish the fruit.

Sometimes old stems may grow six or more feet tall and become leggy and top heavy. The appearance can be improved by removing about one-third of the tallest canes at ground level. New stems will grow from the base. Old, nonproductive canes should be removed in winter. The mahonia growing in my yard has been remarkably disease-

and insect-free. Moderate salt tolerance makes it an excellent choice for coastal gardens. Even though I have never noticed any propensity for invasiveness in my Florida garden nor seen any mention of such a tendency in the literature for Florida, check to be sure that it is not invasive where you live. In Tennessee it is on the list of Invasive Exotic Pest Plants. It is listed as Rank 2, which is defined as "an exotic plant species that possesses characteristics of invasive species but are not presently considered to spread as easily into native plant communities as those species listed as Rank 1." By all means, avoid this plant if it is prone to causing problems in your area.

Loquat (also Japanese Plum)

Eriobotrya japonica
Family: Rosaceae (Rose family)
Origin: Japan
Size: 15–30 feet by 15–35 feet
Zones: 8–10
Light: Sun/Part Sun
Water: Moderate
Soil: Well-drained
Salt Tolerance: Moderate

One of my most treasured small trees is loquat. Native to Japan, this evergreen fruit tree is a member of the rose family. Hardiness in USDA Zones 8 to 10 makes it a good choice for the Deep South. Commonly called Japanese plum, it produces creamy-white, pleasantly fragrant flowers that bloom between November and January. After blooming, edible one-to two-inch, oval-shaped orange or yellow fruits are produced. The showy plums are attractive to wildlife and make a tasty snack for humans, as well. Blossoms are also attractive to bees. This was proven quite conclusively when bees followed the garden club's Christmas float one year to sample the nectar of the loquat blossoms that were used as decorations.

Although loquat may grow 20 to 30 feet high and 30 to 35 feet wide, more frequently it stays within the 15-foot-tall range. This stature makes it useful as a street tree in areas where overhead space is limited. Because of its salt tolerance, it is frequently chosen for locations near bodies of saltwater or where saltwater intrusion might become a problem. As with many salt-tolerant plants, it is also drought-tolerant.

The evergreen tree is valued especially for its lustrous, dark green foliage with rusty, wooly undersides. Variable in size, but ranging from six to nine inches long and three to four inches wide, the coarsely toothed, wrinkled leaves with strongly set midribs and parallel veins are extraordinarily attractive.

Japanese plum is handsome in the landscape. Pleasing textural contrasts are achieved by placing this coarse-leafed plant next to more narrow-leafed shrubs such as juniper or Japanese yew. The dark leaves make a perfect background for flowering plants, and it mixes well in a shrub border. It stands alone, too, as an impressive specimen plant.

Though I enjoy loquat in the landscape, I must admit to an ulterior motive for including it in my yard. Long-lasting leaves and flowers make it ideal as transition material in floral designs. Not only is foliage useful fresh, but it can be dried. Preserved in glycerin, it lasts for many years and may be kept indefinitely. Luckily, the tree tolerates pruning. Otherwise, we floral designers might be out of luck!

The fruit of the loquat is quite tasty. It peels easily and the seeds are readily removed. A friend reports that she peels, seeds, and then dehydrates the fruit in her food dehydrator. To use it, she re-hydrates it in orange juice with other dried fruit. Wine made from the fruit is a tasty addition to her pear-mincemeat pie. In pie, it tastes a bit like peaches. She reports that jam made from loquat is a bit bland, so she recommends livening it up with another fruit. However, another friend reports that loquat is the source of her family's favorite jam.

Seeds often sprout under established trees, so getting a young plant from a friend is an easy way to get a start. Cuttings may be taken in June and July and placed in soil until they are rooted. Available cultivars include 'Golden Nugget', 'Champagne', 'MacBeth', and 'Thales'. 'Variegata' has leaves variegated with white and is rather attractive. While seedlings make good ornamental plants, fruit quality is unpredictable. If fruit is definitely wanted, look for one of the grafted cultivars.

Grow loquat in full sun. Mulch well out from the trunk to prevent mechanical damage to the thin bark. Overwatering and overfertilizing are two practices that may contribute to root rot and increased sensitivity to fire blight disease that can infect loquats. To reduce problems, provide good air circulation, plant in well-drained soil, and keep away from other fire blight hosts, such as Pyracantha and pears.

To preserve plants in glycerin, mix one part glycerin to three parts water. Split or hammer the stems of woody plants and place them in a few inches of the solution. Let the stems stand until they have absorbed as much of the solution as possible and are pliable. This usually takes two to three weeks. Preserved leaves will turn a dark, rich brown suitable for many arrangements.

Red Buckeye (also Scarlet Buckeye)

Aesculus pavia
Family: Sapindaceae (Hippocastanaceae) (Horse Chestnut family)
Origin: SE USA
Size: 15–20 feet by 15–25 feet
Zones: 5–9
Light: Part Sun
Water: Moderate
Soil: Moist, well-drained
Salt Tolerance: Slight/Moderate

Early in February my red buckeye starts leafing out. It's one of the first things to emerge in spring. What a welcome sight the dark green leaves are! And how beautiful they are with their dark red petioles (leaf stalks) and central veins. I shudder to think what may happen in years when a really hard freeze comes along just as the leaves flush out. They appear so fresh and tender and delicate, and so vulnerable to the vagaries of late winter weather. I guess they know what they're doing though, for they are one of our natives and have grown for centuries regardless of what nature sent their way.

Long before I tire of admiring the newly emerged leaves, three-to six-inch-long panicles (elongated clusters) of bright red flowers bloom at the tips of the branches. I am not the only admirer of the flowers, for early-returning hummingbirds routinely stop by for a sip of nectar. Some references suggest that the red buckeye is dependent on hummingbirds for pollination.

Identification of this plant is easy, since no other plant in our area even remotely resembles it. Kurz and Godfrey in *Trees of Northern Florida* say, "No other tree of our range has opposite, palmately compound leaves with five to seven pinnately-veined leaflets." Upon close inspection, I found leaves with three and four leaflets. Five-leaflet leaves are by far the most common.

Red buckeye is at home in rich deciduous woodlands, low mixed hammocks, and river banks throughout the South. In our area it usually remains a shrub or small tree not more than five feet tall. According to Rogers and Rogers in *Woody Ornamentals for Deep South Gardens*, one at Eden State Park in Point Washington, Florida, is about 12 feet tall. Farther north it may reach 25 feet tall.

Its native range extends from coastal North Carolina all the way into Texas and throughout most of the southeastern part of the United States. It can be found in USDA Zones 5 to 9. It does best in moist, well-drained soil and partial sun, although it will flower in shade. Moderate tolerance to salt makes it a good choice for coastal areas. No pests or diseases are of major concern.

Red buckeye can be used as a novelty patio tree or as part of a shrubbery border. Branches develop near the ground, but they can be removed for a more treelike appearance if desired. Leaves fall as early as late September, and they offer no appreciable fall interest. However, the bright brown or tan bark of the tree will attract attention in winter.

Years ago my brothers back home in Mississippi carried the fruit of this tree in their pockets. They believed that the buckeye seed brought them luck. They thought that it resembled a buck's eyes, and I suppose that's how it got its name. Amiable Spouse says that it is a good worry stone. The covering is hard and smooth, so rubbing it gives a soothing sensation. The round, one- to two-inch brown seeds attract squirrels and mammals but are toxic to humans. Planted in moist soil, they will germinate easily and plants will begin flowering after about three years.

A few cultivars of buckeye can be found. 'Atrosanquinea' has deeper red flowers, and 'Humilis' is a low or more prostrate shrub with red flowers in small clusters. Variation in the species is tremendous, and some plants even have yellow or white flowers. Other species of buckeye are Ohio buckeye (*Aesculus glabra*), bottlebrush buckeye (*A. parviflora*), and painted buckeye (*A. sylvatica*).

Keep your eyes peeled in spring for bright spots of red in the woods. You may be a lucky person who actually gets to see this beautiful native in bloom.

Sassafras

Sassafras albidum
Family: Lauraceae (Laurel family)
Origin: USA, Mexico, Guatemala
Size: 30–60 feet by 25–40 feet
Zones: 5–8
Light: Sun/ Part Sun
Water: Low
Soil: Dry, sandy
Salt Tolerance: Slight/None

Walking along the bayside road of my hometown in the Florida Panhandle is always pleasurable. On one side of the street is Tom's Bayou with its ever-engrossing stretch of water. One has only to be there to be privileged to the sight of brown pelicans flying so close to the water that their wings seem to skim the surface. At other times dolphins cavort just offshore, or mullet jump to elude an unseen predator—or maybe just because they can. Woodpeckers call to each other from tall pines, and myriad birds chase insects or each other. Folks walk along and absorb the glory of it all. They notice the bright, billowing masses of thunderheads towering skyward and floating along on darkened bases. Or maybe high cirrus mares' tails feather the powder blue of the sky. It's a beautiful world.

On the other side of the road are the houses that people have built so that they can see first-hand the loveliness that nature freely gives. Occasionally a small piece of land can be seen that for some reason has escaped being chosen for one of these homes. It's a vacant lot, and no doubt its days are numbered. It is here, however, that rare glimpses of native plants can be found that have escaped the axe or the bulldozer.

It is on one of these lots that I see and enjoy sassafras (*Sassafras albidum*). I always look for it, and it is easily identified by its combination of plain, mitten-shaped, and three-lobed leaves. It's hard to resist breaking off a piece of the stem because I know that the leaves are fragrant. It is an eye-catcher in fall when its leaves change from shades of yellow to deep orange to scarlet and purple.

I remember drinking sassafras tea when I was a child. Mother boiled the roots and poured up a tea that we drank—not for any purpose that I can remember, but just to see how it tasted. Luckily we didn't drink much of it. Once it was used to flavor root beer, and it was recommended as a stimulant, febrifuge, antispasmodic, and even a cure for syphilis. Unfortunately, safrole, a constituent of sassafras oil, has been identified as a carcinogen, and the Food and Drug Administration has outlawed the sale of flavorings containing sassafras root. Although we do not drink the tea or flavor dishes with the roots any more, they are reportedly safe for external use. The root bark has antiseptic properties, making it effective for treating wounds and sores. It has been used for relief from the itching of poison oak and poison ivy.

Sassafras is a good choice for planting at the corner of a meadow, at the edge of the woods, or in naturalized areas in home landscapes. Usually it occurs in thickets where it grows about 20 feet high. It can be trained as a specimen, however, that grows 40 to 90 feet high. Its native range is in thin woods and old fields in the eastern United States from Zones 5 to 8 and in the mountains of southern Mexico and Guatemala. Companion plants include common persimmon, post oak, red maple, sparkleberry, and American holly. Such consorts indicate its liking for dry, acid soil.

Dark blue fruit is produced on a red stalk by female trees. These fruits are favorites of the robin, kingbird, catbird, brown thrasher, pileated woodpecker, and others. Leaves are hosts to spicebush swallowtail butterflies, and humans use them as filé in gumbo. Wood is used as a building material. I was surprised to learn that the interior of my brother's home in Mississippi is paneled with sassafras.

Sassafras is hard to dig and transplant from the wild because of a deep taproot. It can be purchased in containers, or new plants may be started from seed. This method of propagation is easiest after seeds are put through a special treatment called stratification. To stratify, put seeds in a plastic bag in damp sand or peat moss and place in a refrigerator for about four months. After that time, seeds can be planted in a container in regular potting soil. When seedlings are big enough to transplant, plant them in the desired places in the landscape.

I was lucky to find sassafras for sale at DeFuniak Springs Garden Club's native plant sale. I planted it near the edge of the woods. After establishment, I expect it to get along on its own with whatever conditions nature provides. Won't that be nice for a change?

Saw Palmetto

Serenoa repens
Family: Arecaceae (Palm family)
Origin: SE USA
Size: 3–10 feet by 3–8 feet
Zones: 8–11
Light: Sun/ Part Sun
Water: Low
Soil: Adaptable
Salt Tolerance: High

Sometimes we gardeners in the Deep South fail to appreciate such commonplace plants as saw palmetto. We see it every day and take it for granted. Sometimes we may be forced to take notice of it, especially if it is in a place where we don't want it and attempt to remove it. Then we find more than we bargained for because the trunk often runs several feet underneath the soil surface. Sometimes heavy equipment is needed to remove it.

Recently, though, some enlightened folks recognized palmetto as a beautiful little palm richly deserving a place in the ornamental landscape. I recently noticed an area where saw palmettos, together with various hollies, wax myrtles, and other native plants had been planted to serve as a screen between the highway and homes in a subdivision. In several cities, they are widely used in median plantings. More and more homeowners and businesses are leaving existing saw palmettos in the landscape instead of having them removed.

Why this sudden change of heart? Saw palmetto is, of course, a native plant. It occurs naturally on the coastal plain from South Carolina to southeastern Louisiana. Its habitat ranges from seaside sand dunes to dry scrub, even occurring in moist forests, pine flatwoods, and wetlands. In certain southeastern pine forests, it is the dominant ground cover, sometimes covering hundreds of acres. Since it is so well adapted in nature, it thrives in home landscapes with no supplemental water or fertilizer once it is established.

Although saw palmetto forms suckers, it does not transplant well. However, propagation from seed is easy. Seeds are best sown as soon as they are ripe. Then they germinate freely. Stored seeds are more difficult, and must be presoaked for 24 hours in warm water before they are planted. When seedlings are large enough to handle, they should be potted up in individual pots and grown in a protected place for two winters. After that, they can be planted in a permanent place in the landscape.

Floral designers always know a ready source for saw palmetto, for it is one of their favorite and most frequently used plant materials. It is easily wired into curves, and it is excellent line material. Many designers dry it and paint it whatever color they wish for their designs, but it dries naturally to a soft, light green. Usually it can be purchased in floral supply stores, but those of us in this part of the world can simply go out and cut what we need. The berries and blossoms, too, are excellent floral design materials.

Native Americans have long consumed the fruit and harvested honey made from the flowers. The palm heart or terminal bud makes an excellent salad or cooked vegetable. My friend Mary Ann would quickly point out that saw palmetto is important to butterflies, and is host to the monk or Cuban skipper, the palmetto arpo skipper, and the palmetto-borer moth. It provides excellent cover for wildlife, and the fruit is eaten by several bird species and by raccoons.

All parts of the plant are reputed to have certain health properties. Extracts from the fruit of this palm are being used to treat prostate cancer. Saw palmetto has been used as an appetite stimulant, to treat thyroid deficiencies, and as an expectorant and inhalant for bronchitis, asthma, and colds. Some proponents claim that it treats urinary tract disorders, acts as an anti-inflammatory agent, and stimulates hair growth in men.

Much study needs to be done to test the validity of these health claims. Few people would take any herb or medication indiscriminately or without the advice of a health care provider. It is not the purpose of this article to support or refute these claims. I merely wish to point out that saw palmetto is another of our beautiful natives that fits well in most home landscapes. Why buy some exotic plant from Japan or China when such a beautiful plant grows at our doorsteps?

Sparkleberry (also Woody Huckleberry, Farkleberry)

Vaccinium arboreum
Family: Ericaceae (Heath family)
Origin: SE USA
Size: 6–33 feet by 4–15 feet
Zones: 7–10
Light: Sun/Part Sun
Water: Low
Soil: Adaptable
Salt Tolerance: Moderate

Several years ago when I married Amiable Spouse and moved into our present house, I was struck by the diversity of plants that existed on the property. Never a landscape critic himself, A. Spouse felt that he had done well if the green lawn matter (not necessarily grass) in the yard was mowed occasionally and the pine needles raked once a year or so. He tried to keep the cherry laurels and other plants beat back a bit to retain some open spaces. He did pretty well, too, and had a yard that met his needs, expectations, and ability to maintain.

Several hale and hardy plants had managed to grow to considerable stature. He liked them, but took no special effort to see to their welfare. One of my favorites was a plant called sparkleberry, also known as woody huckleberry or farkleberry (*Vaccinium arboreum*).

This tree ranges from Virginia and North Carolina to central Florida, southern Illinois, and Texas. Trees may grow to about 33 feet on favorable sites and are attractive year-round. Showy white to pink flowers are produced in abundance during the spring. This tree's kinship with others of the blueberry group is evident in flowers that hang down from the stems in typical blueberry fashion. The quarter-inch-diameter, black, persistent fruit is attractive to wildlife but not very tasty for humans.

One thing that makes this small tree a good landscape subject is its ability to survive in adverse conditions. Take A. Spouse's yard as an example. He didn't know anything about improving soil. No watering system was installed, but maybe he had a sprinkler to attach to a hose that he used infrequently. Trees that lived on the property did so with no human assistance. In fact, sparkleberry grows on sand dunes, hammocks, dry sterile hillsides, in rocky woods, abandoned fields, and meadows. It occurs also on moist sites such as wet bottomlands and along creek banks. Understanding why it is common throughout much of the Coastal Plain is easy. Hardly a situation exists where sparkleberry will not grow satisfactorily.

Sparkleberry is important to wildlife. White-tailed deer browse them in many areas, and several species of hares and rabbits feed on the leaves and twigs. Fruits and flowers provide spring and summer food for bobwhite quail, black bear, and many species of birds. In my yard I have seen brown thrashers, tufted titmice, and mocking-birds feeding on the fruit. The flowers are attractive to various bees, and the leaves are the larval plant for Henry's elfin butterfly. Many butterflies enjoy nectar from the flowers.

Sparkleberry can be used as rootstock for some edible blueberries such as highbush blueberry (*Vaccinium corymbosum*). The resulting cultivars are well suited to droughty upland sites with soils that have a relatively high pH. This allows people who could not ordinarily grow blueberries a better chance for success.

Such hardy and well-adapted plants as sparkleberry are the ones that I want for my landscape. They're beautiful, carefree, and environmentally friendly.

A Story of Mighty and Minnie Pine

"Oh, it's fall," rejoiced Mighty Pine. "My old needles are falling. It's about time, too, because the ground around my feet is getting quite bare. A new cinnamon-brown needle carpet is just what I need. It will cover the weeds now gaining a foothold and competing with me for moisture and nutrients. My roots will be kept warm in winter and cool in summer. Birds will scratch around looking for worms that flourish in my natural mulch. Oh, what a lovely season is the fall!"

Mighty Pine's happiness reverberates through the crisp autumn day as his needles begin fulfilling their appointed task. Suddenly, his feeling of well-being screeches to a halt. Mr. Homeowner One, intent on making his yard the showplace of the neighborhood, gets busy with his rake. "What is he doing?" Mighty Pine wonders. "Taking my needles away? Piling them at the curb? Where are they going? What's happening to my beautiful needle carpet?"

Meanwhile, down the street a few houses away, another scene is taking place. Mr. Homeowner Two knows that the needles are valuable. He is raking them into a pile around the trunk of Minnie Pine. Higher and higher the pile becomes. Finally, a perfectly shaped cone skirts Minnie's trunk.

"Oh, no, what's this?" wails Minnie. "So much mulch will rot my trunk! Insects and diseases will invade my weakened tissue! Oh, please, Mr. Homeowner Two, spread the needles evenly out to my drip line! Remove them from my trunk! Oh, my days are numbered!"

The Good Lord had an excellent plan when he created trees. He gave them leaves or needles and all the mechanisms they need to live healthily ever after. We all know the story. Sun shines on the green leaves, photosynthesis takes place, and the tree makes its own food. Leaves drop to the ground to protect the roots. Eventually they break down and become a part of the soil— just the kind preferred by the tree. He had it all figured out.

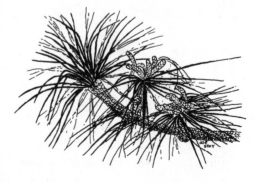

We, being human, decide to alter His plan. We want a pretty, manicured yard, so we interfere and interrupt the cycle. We rake the leaves. Not to worry. Next spring we'll fertilize the tree—with chemical fertilizers, of course. Those that leach into neighboring bodies of water. Those that pollute the earth.

And we go our merry way.

THE TALE OF MAJESTIC OAK

Once in the heart of the Vale of Paradise there lived a majestic oak. Squirrels and birds scurried and flitted among its branches and made their homes in its shelter. Soon a man came to live in the shade cast by the great oak. His children played beneath its branches, and it continued to grow in grace and strength. It towered to the sky. All was well in Paradise.

Now the mighty tree is gone—cut down and shredded into mulch. Its death seemed sudden, but we later residents of Paradise know that it took many years for the giant oak to expire. Only in the cutting down process did we learn what had happened.

Long ago, power company employees lopped off some limbs that interfered with a power line that was being installed for the man. At the time, the power company workers followed the accepted practice of the day and cut the limbs flush with the trunk. Little did they know that their cuts inflicted such damage that the tree would never recover. In the great live oak, rot and disease progressed from the cuts straight to its heart. Death was imminent.

The tree would still be alive and well if proper pruning cuts had been made. Research has conclusively shown that cuts made flush with the trunk of a tree actually remove part of the trunk. Decay sets in, causing the eventual death of the tree.

Proper pruning cuts of large branches require three separate cuts. The first cut is made on the lower side of the branch about 15 inches away from the trunk and as far up through the branch as possible before the branch weight begins to bind the saw. The second cut is made downward from the top of the branch about 18 inches from the main trunk, which causes the limb to split cleanly between the two cuts without tearing the bark. The remaining stub is easily supported while it is cut from the tree.

Removal of the stub is often the killing blow. Before making this last pruning cut, one should find the branch bark ridge. It is usually rough and always darker than the surrounding bark and is obvious on most species. Next, locate the branch collar, which is the swelling beneath a branch. The final cut should begin just outside the branch bark ridge at the top of the branch. From there it should angle to just outside the branch collar at the bottom of the branch. (See illustration.) Never make a flush cut.

Research has proven that painting wound dressing on the cut is not a desirable practice. Often, when exposed to the sun and weather, the protective coating cracks, allowing moisture to enter and accumulate in pockets between the wood and the wound covering. This situation may be more inviting to wood decay organisms than one with no wound dressing.

Correct pruning cuts begin on the outside of the branch bark ridge. Do not cut into the branch collar. It is trunk wood and the trunk can decay if this tissue is damaged.

If the power company's young men of many years ago had known about proper limb removal, the mighty oak would still be standing. How I miss it! Paradise is still here, but it has been diminished. Only a stump remains where glory once lived.

TREE DISEASES

Dr. Ed Barnard of the University of Florida Plant Pathology Department taught one of the most interesting seminars that I attended at a Master Gardeners' Conference in Gainesville. The topic of his session was "Tree Diseases—Bane, Boon, or Both?" Some interesting ideas came out of his presentation. He says that a perfectly healthy, disease-free tree is something of a rarity. Some pathogens live in trees on bark and leaf tissues at all times. They become operative only after a stimulus mobilizes them. Old age, severe weather events, fire, insect activity, or manipulations by man are outside forces that may cause native pathogens to respond. Usually, however, the tree and its pathogens coexist peacefully.

True, some pathogens cause the loss of entire species of trees, such as Dutch elm disease and chestnut blight. Dr. Barnard noted, however, that these two diseases were imported into our country where no natural defenses existed. They swept through forests of trees and decimated them because there was no natural control.

To answer the question that was the topic of the seminar, Dr. Barnard concluded that it all depends, and that tree diseases have to be evaluated in context. What is good for one situation might be bad for another. He pointed out heart rot in old pines that creates nesting habitat for the endangered red-cockaded woodpecker. Is that good or bad? Many examples were given, and we began to see that many diseases we consider bad are in fact part of nature. "Why," Dr. Barnard questioned, "do we feel a need to control tree diseases that are natural, cyclic, sometimes beneficial, and often senescence-related?"

Dr. Barnard pointed out that by the time the homeowner notices that a tree is in trouble it is probably too late to do anything about it. Often the problem is the result of stresses placed on the tree by the homeowner. Herbicides are regularly put on grass that grows underneath trees, though the directions plainly state that the product should not be distributed in the root zone of trees. Roots are damaged during construction. Parking under trees compacts the soil and damages roots, often causing limbs to die. Mulch may be piled up against a trunk causing it to rot. Instances have been seen where an entire tree was girdled by string trimmers or severely damaged by lawn mowers or other mechanical devices. Then the homeowner wonders why it dies.

Finally, Dr. Barnard observed, we don't want our trees to grow old. Often a tree's problem is simply that it has lived its allotted number of years and its life span is finished. In such instances nothing can be done that will make any difference.

We were cautioned not to fall victim to "tree experts" peddling quick fixes for sick trees. Usually their recommendations are neither quick nor do they fix the problem. He also pointed out that an entire industry has sprung up that is willing to sell any number of sprays and chemicals for sick trees. For them, tree diseases are definitely a boon. Some tree diseases do not need to be controlled, and others are simply beyond our control.

The overriding principle is that we should live with our trees and treat them with respect. Plant them correctly and use proven beneficial cultural practices, such as mulching correctly, watering during drought, correct pruning when necessary, and calling in the real experts or arborists when problems occur that we feel unequipped to handle. Plant trees that are suited to our climate, and think carefully before deciding to try to save a tree that seems badly diseased. With good cultural practices and no unseemly acts of nature beyond our control, most trees should last a lifetime.

OTHER TREES AND SHRUBS

Discussions about the following trees and shrubs are in my book, *Gardening in the Coastal South*:

Brugmansia and *Datura*	Angel's Trumpets
Callicarpa americana	American Beautyberry
Camellia spp.	Camellia
Chionanthus virginicus	Grancy Gray-beard, Fringe Tree
Ficus carica	Common Fig
Hibiscus mutabilis	Confederate Rose
Hibiscus syriacus	Althea, Rose of Sharon
Hydrangea macrophylla	Hydrangea
Hydrangea quercifolia	Oakleaf Hydrangea
Lagerstroemia indica	Crape Myrtle
Loropetalum chinense	Chinese Fringe, Loropetalum
Magnolia x soulangiana	Saucer Magnolia
Malvaviscus arboreus	Turk's Cap
Michelia figo	Banana Shrub
Osmanthus fragrans	Sweet Olive, Tea Olive
Rosa chinensis	China Rose

Easy-Care Plants
for Summer and Fall Color

The South is particularly blessed with a wide range of flowering annuals and perennials that color our landscapes during the summer and fall. Many tropical plants also offer opportunities for color, and they can be kept for many years if protected during our winter months.

Stars of the Summer Garden

Allamanda [Color 8] (also Golden Trumpet Vine, Yellow Allamanda)
Allamanda cathartica
Family: Apocynaceae (Dogbane family)
Origin: Brazil
Type: Vine
Size: Depends on height of supporting structure
Zones: 9b–11
Light: Sun
Water: Moderate to low
Varieties: Several cultivars
Color: Yellow
Soil: Fertile, Well-drained
Salt tolerance: Moderate/Slight

Recently on a trip to one of my favorite nurseries, I purchased my two allamandas for the year. Every year I plant two of these beautiful South

American natives on the arbor in the front yard. There they scramble to the top and bloom all summer with bold, funnel-shaped, five-lobed flowers that are slightly but distinctly twisted. Buds are reddish-brown, but large, three-inch flowers are golden yellow when fully open.

Yellow allamanda is a fast-growing vine that perfectly complements the arbor and provides a focal point in the front yard. This place suits it well because it is in full sun most of the day, and the soil is enriched and well drained. I find that the vines are basically carefree, but I remember to give them a bit of slow-release fertilizer every few months.

Although yellow is my color of choice for the front arbor, allamandas can be purchased that are rose, white or cream-colored, and a "chocolate" version is available as well. Cultivars include 'Flore Pleno', which sports golden double flowers, 'Compacta', which tops out at about two feet, 'Hendersonii', that has yellow-orange flowers tinged brown or purple in the bud form, and 'Williamsii', which has large double flowers. Bush allamanda (*Allamanda schottii*) is a shrub, and flowers are smaller but very similar to the vining species.

Allamanda is hardy in USDA Zones 9b to 11. That means, of course, that it is a tender vine that will not survive winters in the temperate South. However, it can be grown in a container and moved to a protected location during the winter months. During this time, it should be cut back hard and allowed to rest. Water sparingly during this dormant period and apply no fertilizer. About the first of April, feeding should be resumed, and the plant can be moved back to its summer place. Treated this way, the plant will last for years.

However, because in all likelihood I am becoming a bit slothful, I find it too much trouble to move them inside every winter. I plant them in the ground where they are to grow and resolve to buy new ones each spring. I could, if I wanted to, root cuttings taken from the vines after they become well established. Then I could share with friends or overwinter a few cuttings in the greenhouse.

Pruning is difficult for me to do, however, because new flowers are produced on the tips of shoots, and I know that I'm cutting off flowers each time I trim. Sometimes, however, the vine looks better with a bit of training and pruning. It tends to sprawl and grow long shoots that don't branch well. As a result, fewer flowers are produced than would be if I simply made up my mind to sacrifice a few flowers now for more flowers later.

Allamanda should be grown on some support, such as a fence or trellis, because it has no tendrils for gripping. Avoid planting where salt is a factor, for it has no tolerance for it. It should be noted that all parts of the plant are poisonous if eaten. Symptoms of poisoning include fever, swollen lips, thirst, nausea, and diarrhea. It is toxic only if large quantities are eaten. I can't imagine that this would be a problem for anyone, because I don't believe it would be very tasty. Skin irritation upon contact with the milky sap that oozes from any broken part may cause dermatitis in sensitive individuals.

Try the beautiful allamanda vine for a summer-long show. Decide for yourself whether to keep it over winter or buy a new one each year.

Begonia [Color 9]

Begonia spp.
Family: Begoniaceae (Begonia family)
Origin: South America
Type: Annual
Size: 8 inches–3 feet
Zones: All
Light: Part sun to shade
Water: Moderate
Varieties: Wax, Dragon Wing, Angel Wing, Rex Hybrids, others
Color: Red, pink, white, rose
Soil: Well-drained
Salt tolerance: Slight

We gardeners sometimes buy the same plants again and again every summer. Whether we need them or not. Because we always have. Because they do so well in certain circumstances, and we can find nothing else that does better. Because we like them.

Such is the case with wax begonias. They do so well in my bench containers that I have seldom tried anything else. My bench is constructed so that five terra cotta pots fit into holes cut out of the top. Viewed from the top, it appears that plants are growing in a shallow container because the bottoms of the pots are hidden by the bench. It is one of my favorite container arrangements, and wax begonias are the flowers of choice for them during the summer. Wax begonias (Begonia x semperflorens-cultorum) flower all summer. For my full-sun location, the ones with bronze-colored leaves work best. Green-leaved selections do better in partial shade. In full shade, however, they tend to stretch and flower poorly.

Wax begonias have flowers in shades of red, scarlet, pink, rose, or white. Most are weather-resistant, compact plants that are excellent when used for edgings, in window boxes, and in planters or containers. Because begonias bear hundreds of small flowers, the best show in a landscape is achieved if they are planted en masse.

Favorites include the Cocktail series, which has bronze foliage. 'Brandy', 'Gin', 'Rum', 'Vodka', and 'Whiskey' offer compact, six- to eight-inch plants with flowers of various colors. Other selections include the Victory, Challenger, Ambassador, and Prelude series.

Once in a while the begonias in my containers get too lanky and start flopping around a bit, so I know it's time to give them a trim. Then they're attractive for another few months. I don't throw away the trimmings, however. They root in a snap when placed in soil and kept damp.

Also among my favorites are the rex begonias (*Begonia x rex-cultorum*). These plants are grown mostly for their beautiful leaves in a multitude of shapes, colors, and patterns. They do exceedingly well in both my greenhouse and in a brightly-lit room in my home. Collecting all the different cultivars could keep a gardener busy for a lifetime. I only have to plant them in very well-drained, good quality potting soil and place them in bright light, fertilize them occasionally, and keep them from freezing. They reward me with year-round beauty.

These rex begonias are rhizomatous in habit, and most of their stems grow horizontally across the soil surface. I make sure that my plants dry out completely before watering; then I water thoroughly and discard drainage water. These begonias can be propagated by rhizome or leaf cuttings. For me they are strictly tender indoor plants. I do not attempt to grow them in outdoor conditions.

Most gardeners in the Deep South do best to leave growing the beautiful tuberous begonias (*Begonia x tuberhybrida*) to our friends farther north. I look at them and wish. I admire the two- to four-inch-wide flowers in white, yellow, orange, rose, red, and pink. However, experience has shown me that they are very short-lived in our heat and humidity. They prefer temperatures between 50°F and 65°F, and the leaves are very easily wind-damaged. The angel-wing or cane-type begonias are other members of the family worth knowing. Clusters of beautiful flowers bloom in summer and the plants last for years if protected from the cold. Leaves are diverse in color, size, and variegation, and may be solid green, red, or spotted with silver. The best known are the angel-wing begonias, which have large leaves that are silver-spotted on top and red underneath. Some from this group grow quite large. They are easily started from stem cuttings. Like the rest of the clan, soil should be well drained, for they are subject to crown rot in overly moist conditions.

Other kinds of begonias are available. Hardy begonia (*B. grandis*) is one of the superb Southern heirloom perennials that is passed from gardener to gardener. Since no generous gardener has been kind enough to pass one along to me, I will have to be content with the wax, rex, and angel-wings.

Blue Daze [Color 10]

Evolvulus glomeratus
Family: Convolvulaceae (Morning Glory family)
Origin: S. Dakota, Montana to Texas
Type: Grown as annual
Size: 9–12 inches
Zones: All
Light: Sun to part sun
Water: Moderate
Varieties: 'Blue Daze', 'Hawaiian Blue Eyes', others
Color: Blue
Soil: Well-drained, organic
Salt tolerance: Moderate

Hot! That's not the word for it! Try muggy, sweltering, and miserable! Such words describe a typical Southern summer day. What's a body to do? More to the point, what will our poor plants do? Humans can go inside. Plants, however, have no choice. They must endure the capriciousness of nature if they are to survive. Those that are marginal in our heat and humidity will probably succumb. Even such stalwarts as zinnias, marigolds, celosia, and other annuals that we plant for summer color will sometimes burn out during the worst of summer's heat. However, several tropical perennials will carry us through this difficult time in the garden. Although they are not winter-hardy in most of the South, they bloom for an extended time during the worst of summer's heat.

Let's consider one of the best of the lot. Blue daze grows about 9 to 12 inches tall. Throughout the summer, blue, three-quarter-inch flowers that resemble small morning glories bloom at the ends of each growing shoot. By noon the flowers close, but the soft, silver-green leaves are reason enough for its space in the garden. Ground-hugging stems make blue daze a good choice for a sunny ground-cover. A cascading tendency makes it effective in hanging baskets or tumbling over the edges of containers. For the flower border it's an ideal front-of-the-bed plant. Planting it in front of spiky plants such as African iris or ornamental grasses makes an interesting contrast in form. Next to large-leaved plants such as black-eyed Susan or purple cone flower, it offers differences in size and texture. Blue and yellow color combinations are always satisfying, so planting melampodium behind it and yellow or white purslane in front of it makes an unbeatable association. In fact, this artful mixer would be pleasing in almost any grouping. As is recommended for most landscape situations, plant in drifts instead of isolated specimens. A pleasing arrangement might be achieved by planting three to five blue dazes and as many or more of a contrasting plant.

Blue daze prefers good soil to which organic matter has been added. Flowering is best in full sun. Though fairly drought tolerant once established, poor flowering will result if it is drought stressed or if there is not enough light. Blue daze is readily available at garden centers during the spring and summer. Four-inch pots are perfect for spring planting. Quart- or gallon-sized containers can be planted anytime and expected to last until frost.

Though dependably hardy in frost-free areas, blue daze must be treated as a summer annual in the Deep South or overwintered in a greenhouse or other protected location. Propagation is easy from tip cuttings. If space allows, cuttings may be taken before frost and planted out the following spring. Fortunately blue daze is fairly salt tolerant, so gardeners living where salt is a factor might find it a suitable addition to their gardens.

Buttonflower [Color 11]

Centratherum intermedium
Family: Asteraceae (Daisy Family)
Origin: Brazil
Type: Tropical perennial, reseeding annual
Size: 6–18 inches
Zones: 9–11, elsewhere grow as annual
Light: Sun to part sun
Water: Low
Varieties: Sold generically
Color: Wisteria blue to lavender
Soil: Well-drained, organic
Salt tolerance: Unknown

A few years ago District I of the Florida Federation of Garden Clubs held a plant exchange. Each participant was invited to bring a plant and exchange it for one they didn't have. All of us were excited about the prospect of acquiring a new plant.

I don't remember what I took to the exchange, but I still have what I brought home. The plant I selected had simple, elliptic leaves about one and one-half inches wide and three inches long. Serrated leaf edges decorated the olive to light-green foliage. A crushed leaf imparted a fragrance almost like that of pineapple sage. Most important, I did not recognize it, and it was labeled simply "button-flower."

That was all the incentive I needed for selecting that particular plant. I brought the interesting little temptress home and found a likely spot for it in my garden. There it commenced to grow, and during the course of the summer it attained a height of about a foot and a spread of about three feet. From June until frost it was covered with pretty, one-inch, buttonlike lavender flowers. Its fine texture and massed, spreading form added a softness to my flowerbeds that effectively contrasted with the sharp forms and spikes of nearby plants.

I have since learned that the plant is named Brazilian button-flower. Native to Brazil, buttonflower is an herbaceous perennial in USDA Zones 9 to 11. In other areas of the Deep South, it is a tender perennial that is treated as an annual because it cannot withstand our winter temperatures.

Even so, it has been fruitful and multiplied, for it sets seeds prodigiously. Each spring, seedlings spring up as thick as hair on a dog's back and thinning is necessary for optimal growth. These cuttings can be potted up and shared with friends or offered at plant sales.

Buttonflower is effective as a ground cover, edging, or cascading down a wall or planter. I like it best massed at the front of a border where its softness and refined character may be best appreciated. It grows well in full sun to partial shade and prefers well-drained soil. Once established, it is very drought tolerant, and no pests or diseases are of major concern.

Combine this soft, fine-textured beauty with plants that have spiky foliage, such as grasses or African iris. In front of dramatic plants like purple-leafed cannas, they provide a soft transition from the ground to the high-flung giant canna's leaves. They combine beautifully with yellow lantanas and are stunning displayed against the oranges and golds of cigar plant, butterfly weed, and cosmos.

Buttonflower may be a bit difficult to find unless you have a friend who can share it with you. Keep your eyes open. You may get lucky.

Coleus [Color 12]

Solenostemon scutellarioides
Family: Lamiaceae (Mint)
Origin: Asia, Tropical Africa
Type: Annual
Size: 1–3 feet
Zones: All
Light: Sun to shade according to variety
Water: High
Varieties: Many, including varieties for sun and shade
Color: Grown for variegated foliage
Soil: Fertile, well-drained
Salt tolerance: Moderate/Slight

A few years ago coleus was primarily a plant for shady locations, along with caladium, hosta, and impatiens. Choices included several selections such as 'Carefree' with deeply lobed leaves, 'Fiji' with ruffled leaves, and 'Dragon' with gold-fringed leaves. The Wizard series was an improvement over the old Rainbow coleus because it had more compact growth and better branching. Other series include Saber, Brilliant, and Fairway. Many cultivars from these series are still available.

However, new varieties of coleus have become available recently that far outdo their shade-loving cousins. These coleuses flourish in the sun—right out in the bright, open, middle of it. Most of them form few if any flowers, and that is a significant improvement. I remember coleus grown in previous years that put on so many flowers that the colorful foliage was hidden. No matter how often I snapped them off, they finally won the battle because they were so determined to bloom.

According to Dr. Allan Armitage of the University of Georgia, about 60 species of coleus have been identified, but only *Coleus blumei* is used in the garden as a landscape plant. Taxonomists have even decided to change this name from *Coleus blumei* to *Solenostemon scutellarioides*.

Confusion exists in naming new cultivars, and I have seen as many as three different names assigned to the same cultivar. For example, is it 'Duckfoot' or 'India Frills' or 'Indian Frills'? Or is my favorite cultivar 'Alabama Sunset' or 'Coppertone'? With so many new cultivars being introduced, it may take a while for the names to become established.

Several varieties are found in garden centers, and all are excellent landscape plants. I have added several of them to my borders for the last couple of years. Their performance is remarkable. All summer long, in sun or part shade, these plants provide a colorful addition to the border.

The Sunlover series emerged in 1993, and includes such colorful varieties as 'Red Ruffles', 'Rustic Orange', 'Gay's Delight', and 'Thumbelina'. Each grows quickly and adds bright color to flowerbeds during our long, hot summers.

The Solar series was released in 1994 from Hatchett Creek Farms in Gainesville, Florida. Some favorites include 'Solar Morning Mist', 'Solar Sunrise', 'Solar Flare', 'Solar Red', and 'Solar Furnace'. Several of these grow in my garden and work hard all season long, adding color and interest to the border.

The Duckfoot series has foliage that reminds one of ducks' feet. 'India Frills' grows to about 13 inches tall and has dark green leaves with purple accents. The University of Florida teaching-research display in Milton, Florida, also contains green duckfoot and orange duckfoot coleus. Relatively small leaves make this group more drought tolerant than some of the larger-leaved groups.

From the Lake Brantley Plant Corporation in Longwood, Florida, comes the Florida series of coleus. Each cultivar is named for a Florida city. Among the best, according to the Florida Nurserymen and Growers Association, are 'Altoona', 'Bonifay', 'Immokalee', 'Micanopy', 'Yalaha', and 'Yulee'. New cultivars are added annually.

These sun coleus, as they are called, should thrive in gardens throughout the South. Give them moist, well-drained soil improved with organic matter, and fertilize them as you do other annuals. They will respond by putting on a dramatic show. Pinching back the growing tips encourages bushiness and provides an easy way to obtain additional plants.

Propagation is easy. Simply take tip cuttings from actively growing stems that are at least three inches long. Remove leaves from the bottom of each cutting and place it in a small pot filled with potting soil. Keep the newly struck cutting moist, and within ten days or so it will be well rooted. In a couple of weeks it can be transplanted into the garden.

Friends who visit my garden frequently leave with cuttings from my coleus plants. In a few weeks they, too, will have these beautiful plants growing in their gardens.

Fanflower

Scaevola aemula
Family: Goodeniaceae (Scaevola family)
Origin: Australia
Type: Tropical perennial
Size: 6–12 inches
Zones: All, Perennial 9–11
Light: Sun to part sun
Water: Moderate to Low
Varieties: 'New Wonder', 'Sapphire Blue', Outback series, others
Color: Blue, purple, pink, white
Soil: Fertile, well-drained
Salt tolerance: Excellent

A champion blooms in my garden, a performer of great merit. From mid-April until first frost I'm enchanted by the show.

Perform, you ask? Well, yes. In front of my perennial border, delightful lavender flowers bloom nonstop from early spring. Spreading slowly, a mass of small, purple, fan-shaped flowers sizzles at the edge of the border. They are equally suited to life in hanging baskets, where they cascade gracefully over the edge and bloom continuously. The higher the temperature rises, the more this little stout heart blooms!

What is the mystery plant? It's an Australian import that's becoming ever more popular in gardens across the country. *Scaevola aemula* is the Latin name, but most folks simply call it fanflower. The name comes from Latin *scaevus,* which refers to flowers that have petals on one side and are fan shaped. According to Norman Winter, Mississippi horticulturist, it is named for the Roman hero Mucius Scaevola, who showed unparalleled bravery (and questionable judgment) by burning off his own left hand. The blossoms do slightly resemble a human hand.

I know that I am not the only gardener to be smitten by this relative newcomer. It has won honors in Mississippi, Louisiana, and Georgia, where it has been named winner of such prestigious awards as the Mississippi Medallion, Louisiana Select, and Georgia Gold Medal. In trial gardens in Milton, Florida, it bloomed throughout the summer with thousands of blue-to-purple, nickel-sized fans.

Several cultivars are available. Gardeners can choose from 'New Wonder', 'Blue Wonder', 'Purple Fanfare', 'Outback Purple Fan', and others. All are good choices. This eye-catching annual's popularity stems from its prolific blossoms, low maintenance requirements, and ability to withstand extreme summer temperatures. It grows best in full sun but also does well in dappled shade.

Small, medium-green leaves take a back seat to the showy flowers that radiate in clusters from each node. A solid carpet of flowers is formed as the stems branch, overlap, and tumble over each other.

It combines well with other low-growers such as melampodium, threadleaf and Profusion zinnias, verbena, and lantana.

Fanflower can spread three to four feet by fall, so a spacing of at least 18 inches between plants is recommended. Trimming is rarely needed, but recovery is quick if cutting back becomes necessary. For best results, plant in well-drained, mulched, organic soil. Keep well watered if grown in containers. In the ground much less water is needed, and the plants are moderately drought tolerant.

Low rates of fertilizer are recommended. Complete balanced fertilizer, such as 10-10-10, should be broadcast at a rate of one pound per 100 square feet at planting time and again at eight-week intervals throughout the growing season. Use of slow-release fertilizer lessens the need for frequent application.

Try this exciting bedding plant in your garden. Put its versatility to use in a hanging basket, a planter, or in the landscape. You're sure to be as pleased with the performance as I have been.

Firespike [Color 13]

Odontonema strictum
Family: Acanthaceae (Acanthus family)
Origin: Central America
Plant Type: Shrub
Size: 4–6 feet
Zones: 7–11
Light: Shade to part sun
Water: Moderate
Varieties: Sold generically
Color: Bright red
Soil: Well-drained, organic
Salt tolerance: Moderate/Slight

Once back in my other life when I was a schoolteacher, I had a friend who had the most beautiful clothes imaginable. Every day she came to school looking like a model for a fashion magazine. I never quite understood how she always managed to look so perfect. She could breeze through the stores in the mall and immediately know if something new was on the racks, or she'd know if a particular item she had been wanting was on sale.

Now that I'm retired and living my next life, I understand just a little better. I don't think that I have become a clotheshorse, but I do realize that I behave much the same way in garden centers. It's all related to passions and things we value. My friend valued clothes. I value plants. I can walk through the nurseries and immediately know if they have something new. I quickly recognize a bargain, and I'm a sucker for a plant sale. When I find something new and interesting, I immediately grab it up and take it home to try in my yard.

One of my recent acquisitions is firespike (*Odontonema strictum*). Sometimes called cardinal spear, cardinal guard, scarlet flame, or scarlet butterfly lily, this showy shrub blooms in my yard in late summer and fall. It delights me with abundant 9- to 12-inch spikes of brilliant red, tubular flowers. The first freeze of winter kills it back to the ground, but it reemerges dependably each spring.

Hummingbirds and butterflies are just as enamored with the flowers as I am, for they swarm about for sips of nectar. Whitetail deer also love the plant, so that is a consideration for gardeners who must be concerned with such things. Pests have not visited my plants at all. Usually I cut the dead stalks back to the ground and add a bit of fertilizer when growth resumes in the spring.

Strikingly beautiful flowers and glossy leaves of firespike make it a handsome addition to the landscape. Individual flowers are small, but impact is great because the whole spike is often flattened or contorted like a cock's comb. The plant spreads by underground runners, but not nearly as rapidly as I'd like it to. I have a single plant that I've had for four or five years. Division has not been necessary, though I have managed to root some cuttings from stems cut early in the growing season.

Although we in the South must treat firespike like a perennial that gets killed to the ground in winter, it is a showy evergreen shrub in frost-free parts of the country. Hardiness is rated for USDA Zones 7 to 11, which makes it truly a plant for the South. It is native to open, semi-forested areas in Central America. Sturdy stems grow four to six feet or more, and though it is recommended for shade, it does well in considerable sun as long as adequate water is available.

Learning about plants and flowers can keep many of us occupied for a lifetime. Firespike was one of my most rewarding "discoveries." To my way of thinking, every garden should have this highly adaptable, carefree plant.

Forsythia Sage [Color 14]

Salvia madrensis
Family: Lamiaceae (Mint family)
Origin: Mexico
Type: Shrubby perennial
Size: 6–8 feet
Zones: 7b–10
Light: Sun to part sun
Water: Moderate
Varieties: Most often sold generically
Color: Yellow
Soil: Fertile, well-drained
Salt tolerance: Slight

One of the things that makes the fall garden particularly beautiful is forsythia sage. All spring and summer the stems shoot skyward. Finally, in late September when it has grown to about eight feet tall, many 12-inch spiky clusters of bright yellow flowers bloom on the ends of each branch. Individual flowers are a little over an inch long, and they bloom in succession from the bottom to the top of the spike.

The blossoms are held in sticky calyces (outer whorls of protective leaves) that many kinds of bees tend to avoid. The stickiness seems to pose no threat to butterflies and hummingbirds that zoom in to dine on the plentiful nectar. Cut blossoms last a long time in a bouquet, but it is sometimes difficult to clean all the little bits of debris from the sticky calyces.

Forsythia sage is native to Mexico. I remember the first time I ever saw it. A garden club friend entered a spray of it in a flower show a few years back. I thought it was one of the most beautiful things I'd ever seen.

Needless to say, I looked in every garden center, checked all my mail-order sources, and made an exhaustive search for the plant. Just when I was ready to give up, I found it at a local garden center. I snapped it up and brought the treasure home. Since then it has grown and multiplied. It is one of the things that marks a change of season; it ushers in the fall and blooms until the frost nips it back to the ground. In spring it emerges from the ground again and spends the whole spring and summer getting ready for another show.

In my garden, it grows up through a sturdy wire cage. Some means of support is necessary because of its eight-foot stature. Even though the one-inch-thick or more square stems look strong, they are very brittle. A forceful wind will send them hurtling to the ground, and the long wait for the glorious blooms will be for naught.

Forsythia sage spreads by underground rhizomes and makes broad thickets. I was able to dig up a few last spring and offer them at a plant sale. They went quickly. Unusual square stems and deeply textured, elongated heart-shaped leaves make these plants ornamental even out of flower.

The largest leaves are eight or more inches long and four or more inches wide. Held almost horizontally on five-inch stems, they are very prominent. It's tempting to reach out and touch the leaves each time I walk by. Velvety texture on the top surface and very prominent veins on the bottom side give the plant an interesting texture. Like most of the salvias, the leaves have a distinctive odor.

Light to filtered shade and organically rich, well-drained soil provide optimal conditions for this plant. Though it is drought tolerant, a bit of extra water may be needed during dry spells. High humidity does not bother it, and little or no fertilizer is required if it is well mulched with pine needles or other organic material. Forsythia sage is hardy throughout USDA Zone 8 and roots easily from cuttings.

Choose carefully the spot for this sage in the garden. Because of its height and bold character, it should be placed toward the back of the border. Remember that it will not reach its potential size until late summer and fall. It requires a great deal of space and could potentially overwhelm a small garden.

Keeping these thoughts in mind, place one in your garden if space allows. You'll be delighted next fall when it takes the spotlight in the garden.

Globe Amaranth [Color 15]

Gomphrena globosa
Family: Amaranthaceae (Amaranth family)
Origin: Panama, Guatemala
Type: Annual
Size: 9–24 inches
Zones: All
Light: Sun to part sun
Water: Low
Varieties: 'All Around', Gnome series, 'Buddy', 'Cissy', others
Color: Red, purple, pink, white, rose
Soil: Fertile, well-drained
Salt tolerance: Slight

With the arrival of hot weather comes the end of some of the flowers that carried our gardens through the spring season. Gone are the snapdragons and petunias, the ornamental cabbages and kales, and the beautiful daffodils and narcissi of early spring.

It is not the time to give up on all flowers, however. Some species thrive in hot weather and grow and bloom until frost. One such plant, and one of my favorite annuals, is globe amaranth. My mother and aunts back in Mississippi mistakenly called these plants "bachelor's buttons." Attractive cloverlike blossoms in colors ranging from rose, purple, lavender, light pink, orange, and white are borne on stiff stems throughout the summer.

These plants are readily available from nurseries and garden centers. They may be bought in handy cell packs ready to be planted in the garden, or they can easily be started from seed. Although they prefer fertile soil, they are drought tolerant.

Plant globe amaranth in the hottest, driest part of the landscape. Expect them to grow from nine inches to two feet tall, depending on which variety is chosen. Place them twelve to eighteen inches apart for a massed effect. Insects are not usually a problem, but mildew may occur if plants are stressed by extreme drought or if they are watered with an overhead sprinkler and not allowed to dry thoroughly between waterings.

In fall before the first frost, I always pull up the plants and pick off the individual blossoms. I use them in dried floral crafts, in floral designs, or for a colorful addition to potpourris. Sometimes I glue hundreds of the individual flower heads onto styrofoam balls. These balls are pretty decorations set about the house, or they can be put on dowels and made into stunning topiaries. With a pretty ribbon added, the balls are a beautiful Christmas tree ornament. One of my favorite "contrived" flowers for creative floral designs is made from one of these balls.

Sometimes I simply put the collected flowers in a pretty basket or bowl and set them in a strategic place where I can admire them all winter. The following spring, I shred a few of the dried flowers into a new planting bed. After they sprout and are about two or three inches tall, I transplant them to permanent locations in the garden.

The flower head is made up of many small inconspicuous individual flowers. The colorful bracts are what we see unless we examine them closely, but butterflies and insects have no trouble finding the tiny flowers. Dwarf selections 'Buddy' (purple) and 'Cissy' (white) top out at nine inches and are ideal edging plants. They can also be planted about six inches apart in a large container, where they will make a long-lasting living bouquet.

Globe amaranth is a pleasing addition to gardens. Grow them just for the beauty they provide in the flowerbed, or pull them up at the end of the season and play with them all winter. Either way, you and your garden will be all the richer.

Melampodium (also Butter Daisy) [Color 16]

Melampodium paludosum
Family: Asteraceae (Daisy family)
Origin: Central and South America
Type: Annual
Size: 10–36 inches
Zones: All
Light: Sun
Water: Low
Varieties: 'Derby', 'Million Gold', 'Lemon Delight', 'Showstar',
    'Medallion'
Color: Yellow, orange
Soil: Fertile, well-drained
Salt tolerance: Slight

One spring my class of sixth-graders got tired of looking at an empty planter that was just outside the classroom door. For several semesters it had been a handy place to toss chewing gum wrappers or unfinished bits of candy or other forbidden items before entering the classroom. Together we decided to do something about the mess. What we needed, we decided, was some brightly colored flowers. The planter was in full sun most of the day and was surrounded by brick and concrete. I cast about for some annuals that would tolerate these conditions.

A visit to the neighborhood nursery brought melampodium to my attention. Bright yellow daisylike flowers about the size of a nickel literally covered the plants in the tray. "Those," I thought to myself, "would look great in the brick planter." I bought the tray of plants and took them to school the next day.

The children and I cleaned out the planter, added some new soil, and sprinkled it with slow-release fertilizer. Then we planted the melampodiums in a gridlike pattern down the length of the planter and watered them in thoroughly. After snuggling some pine needle mulch around the tiny plants, we returned to the arduous task of learning about possessive nouns.

Obviously I made a good choice. All spring the plants grew until no space remained in the planter. They became a solid mass. Both the children and I were pleased with their performance. When summer vacation time rolled around, we left the flowers to fend for themselves. Quite truthfully, that is what they had been doing all along. Luckily the planter was equipped with an automatic watering system, which was turned on infrequently.

Though the sixth-graders had progressed to the seventh grade and had no reason to venture back into the sixth-grade territory, many of them came to check on the welfare of their flowers. They found them in great shape, still blooming to beat the band.

Winter, of course, killed them. However, when spring came the following year, we did not have to purchase any more plants. Hundreds of tiny seedlings sprang up in the planter. Many of them were pulled and sent home with the children to plant in flowerbeds at home.

Since that time, melampodium has been one of my most reliable summer annuals. Several varieties are available, such as the compact 'Million Gold', 'Lemon Delight', and 'Derby', which top out at about ten inches. 'Showstar' and 'Medallion' are taller varieties that reach 24 to 36 inches tall.

One of the perks of growing these tough little plants is that diseases and insects seem to have no interest in them. They are self-cleaning, so deadheading (removal of spent blossoms) is not needed. Since they are self-branching, they need no pinching to encourage bushiness. Furthermore, they take the South's heat and humidity in stride and miss nary a beat. They are truly low-maintenance plants.

Melampodium combines beautifully with many other plants in the garden. I particularly enjoy growing it in combination with some of the dark-leaved coleuses or with 'Blackie' ornamental potato or dark-leaved ornamental grasses. It is striking when combined with ornamental millet 'Purple Majesty'. Pairing it with blue and purple flowers such as annual ageratum (*Ageratum houstonianum*) or spiky blue salvia brings out the best in both colors. Try it with colorful ornamental peppers or with red zinnias.

Mexican Bush Sage [Color 17]

Salvia leucantha
Family: Lamiaceae (Mint family)
Origin: Central and South America
Type: Perennial
Size: 3–4 feet
Zones: 7b–10
Light: Sun to part sun
Water: Average
Varieties: 'Midnight', 'Kab', 'Purple Velvet'
Color: Lavender, dark purple, bicolored
Soil: Well-drained
Salt tolerance: Slight

In the fall Mexican bush sage becomes a showstopper with its white flowers that protrude from velvety purple or lavender-blue calyces. Individual flowers are about two inches long and are arranged in whorls up stems that are six to twelve inches long and held well above the foliage.

All summer the Mexican bush sage grows and fills in its place in the landscape. Eventually it grows about four feet tall and wide. Soft, grayish, lance-shaped leaves are one to five inches long and willow-like. They are distinctly velvety on top, and the whitish undersides flash in the slightest breeze. The soft outline of the shrub provides a pleasant companion to other plants that bloom in summer. In fall, however, the purple spikes demand their turn in the spotlight.

As its name implies, this late-summer and fall bloomer hails from Mexico. In its native habitat and in south Florida and other tropical areas, Mexican bush sage blooms all summer. Here it gets killed to the ground each winter, but it returns reliably from the roots and spends all summer growing to blooming size. Generally hardy to about 25°F, it may be grown as a low-maintenance annual in areas outside its hardiness zone. Protection from the worst of our winter is achieved by protecting the roots and crown with a layer of organic mulch such as pine needles or pine bark.

This drought-tolerant plant prefers sunny, well-drained sites and will usually survive with no supplemental irrigation. It can be used as a massed bedding plant, a container plant in large pots, as part of a mixed perennial border, as a landscape specimen, or in almost any landscape situation that suits its cultural needs.

Propagation is easily accomplished by root or stem cuttings, so if you have a friend or neighbor who grows Mexican bush sage, ask for a few cuttings. Both you and the grower will benefit. Pruning in early summer promotes a sturdier, more compact plant, as well as abundant late-summer and fall flowers.

Fuzzy calyces (outer flower coverings) are the main show. They persist after the flowers fall and are often used in everlasting arrangements since they retain their color after drying. I've been known to cut a bouquet when frost threatens and bind the stems together with a rubber band. After hanging in my airy laundry room for a few weeks, these stems are ready to be placed in arrangements that will last throughout the winter.

For gardeners who dislike bicolored plants—though I can't imagine such an instance—Mexican bush sage is available in solid colors. The cultivars 'Midnight' and 'Purple Velvet' have dark purple calyces and flowers, so they are all one color.

The best time to plant *Salvia leucantha* is in the early fall or early spring. If planted in fall, best results will be had if a container of one gallon or larger is selected. For spring planting, however, a smaller container will be fine. After transplanting, water regularly until the plant becomes established. Afterwards, it is drought tolerant. This plant is moderately fast growing, so specimens planted in fall should provide some enjoyment before the cold weather begins.

Hummingbirds and butterflies also love Mexican bush sage. Keep that in mind when you decide where to plant it. Put it in a prominent place so you can watch who comes to dinner.

Ornamental Pepper [Color 18]

Capsicum annuum
Family: Solanaceae (Nightshade Family)
Origin: Central and South America
Type: Tropical perennials grown as annuals
Size: 4–24 inches
Zones: All
Light: Sun to part sun
Water: Moderate
Varieties: Many cultivars
Color: Fruits red, yellow, purple, orange
Soil: Fertile, well-drained, moist
Salt tolerance: Slight/None

My saintly mother had little time for growing flowers and things to decorate the earth. She was too busy populating it with her children, and in the process she was much concerned about having enough food to feed them all. Consequently, her gardening time was spent in the vegetable patch caring for peas, corn, potatoes, and all the other wonderful crops that the family grew for food.

However, after we all grew up and Mother realized that we were not going to starve to death, she began to grow a few things just because they were beautiful. She particularly enjoyed growing ornamental peppers like the ones that Grandmother grew. Mother saved seeds from these pretty peppers each year, and they were planted in flowerbeds around the house.

Each spring they bloomed tiny, inconspicuous flowers, followed by peppers that were smaller in circumference than a dime. As they matured, they changed colors, starting out in shades of light green, and then changing to lavender, orange, and red. I thought they were beautiful then, and my admiration has not diminished over the years.

They are, needless to say, constants in my summer garden. These peppers reach a height of 10 to 20 inches and are grown as annuals. Actually, ornamental peppers are perennial but are killed by our winter temperatures. The colorful fruits are produced from May until frost.

They grow quite easily in full sun or partial shade, and they prefer moist soil amended with organic matter. I like them best planted in masses 12 to 18 inches apart where they make a solid mass of sturdy plants covered with colorful fruits.

If plants are left after frost, seeds will fall to the ground. If the soil is not heavily mulched, seedlings will appear the following spring. If someone has shared seeds with you, spread them thinly over a prepared bed and pat them to insure contact with the soil. Do not cover the seeds, however, for they require light to germinate.

Volunteers are easily transplanted to other garden areas or potted up and grown in containers. Actually, they are one of our best bedding plants for hot weather, and they work beautifully as a ground cover in mixed flower borders. Those in containers can be moved into the greenhouse during the winter. In spring they will grow new leaves and give an even greater performance.

Many cultivars of ornamental peppers are on today's market. As a matter of fact, most peppers might be termed ornamental. New lines, ranging from small Tabasco-types and miniature bells to large, orange, banana-shaped peppers may be found that are attractive for ornamental use, culinary use, or both. They can be grown in the traditional vegetable garden, incorporated into landscape plantings, or used as decorative container plants for porches and patios. All are very attractive and colorful, and they vary in their relative "hotness."

It should be noted that many of these ornamental peppers are quite hot and should not be planted where inquisitive children might pick a pod and pop it into their mouths. However, do not despair, for nonpungent varieties are available. The cultivar 'Medusa' is "child safe" and has multicolor fruit displays. An All America Selections Flower Award Winner is the cultivar 'Chilly Chili'. The "heat" was bred out of these peppers, so they are perfect for households with children.

Ornamental Sweet Potato [Color 19]

Ipomoea batatas
Family: Convolvulaceae (Morning Glory family)
Origin: Central and South America
Type: Vine
Size: 6–8 inches tall and spreading 8–15 feet
Zones: All
Light: Sun
Water: Moderate
Varieties: 'Blackie', 'Black Heart', 'Margarita', 'Sweet Caroline',
       'Pink Frost', others
Color: Grown for foliage: chartreuse, black, purple, variegated
Soil: Fertile, well-drained, moist
Salt Tolerance: Slight

As the weather heats up, many gardeners start pulling out such plants as snapdragons and pansies that provided color during the winter and early spring. Some of the plants still look good, but we have to harden our hearts and do the deed. New bedding plants must be installed before the heat sets in.

Ornamental potatoes will fill the bill quite nicely. They can be used for ground covers in combination with small shrubs, or in perennial or annual beds. Cascading over the sides of hanging baskets or containers, they are unequaled. They can also be trained to grow up trellises or other plant supports.

Most folks need only one of each cultivar of ornamental potato. They need to be planted at least three feet apart, and they root easily from cuttings. So, buy one, and start some cuttings if you want them in more than one place. Cuttings root in a matter of a few days. Plants prefer full sun to partial shade and moist, well-drained soil.

Ornamental potatoes enjoy hot weather. In fact, they don't really start growing until the soil warms up. When it does, however, stand back. They grow rapidly to cover an area as much as 30 square feet per plant.

These beauties are real potatoes, and like the familiar sweet potato that we enjoy with Thanksgiving and Christmas turkey, they are edible. One potato casserole made from them, however, will convince you to stick with the regular sweet potato, for the ornamental varieties are not very tasty. Three main cultivars were originally sold. 'Blackie' has dark purple/black, deeply cut foliage. 'Margarita' is easy to spot because of its chartreuse-colored, heart-shaped leaves. 'Tricolor' or 'Pink Frost' has multicolored leaves with green, pink, and white foliage. A newer cultivar is 'Black Beauty', which has rounded black leaves. Other cultivars with different leaf shapes and colors have been introduced.

Unfortunately, ornamental potatoes are host plants of the sweet potato weevil that causes so much trouble for sweet potato farmers. In many areas, ornamental potatoes are banned from commerce because they can cause the spread of the sweet potato weevil. If you decide to grow sweet potatoes in the vegetable garden, it might be best to leave the ornamental potatoes at the nursery.

The colored foliage of these plants makes them stars in the garden. Dark ornamental grasses are highlighted in the landscape when 'Margarita' is grown at their feet. As a matter of fact, when 'Blackie' and 'Margarita' are planted together, they make a dramatic statement.

'Blackie' provides a background against which yellow, peach, or orange flowers positively glow. Like the basic black dress that is a backbone of almost every woman's wardrobe, dark purple goes with everything in the garden. It is stunning with red salvias, lantana, pentas, dusty miller and—oh, I cannot think of a color that does not go with this dark, unassuming purple. It is a great mediator. The only mistake might be its overuse without other plants to lighten the mood.

Pentas (also Egyptian Star Flower) [Color 20]
   Pentas lanceolata
   Family: Rubiaceae (Madder family)
   Origin: East Africa to South Arabia
   Type: Tropical perennial
   Size: 8–48 inches
   Zones: All (as annual), Perennial 9–11
   Light: Sun
   Water: Moderate
   Varieties: Butterfly, New Look, and Profusion series, others
   Color: Red, pink, lavender, white, violet, cranberry
   Soil: Fertile, well-drained
   Salt Tolerance: Slight/None

Many gardeners want just a few plants to spruce up their summer gardens. They want something that will bloom throughout the season. Perhaps the gardeners want a few plants that will do well in a planter or container. They want them to last all summer, perhaps around the edge of a pool, or on a patio or deck that is used mainly during the summer months. Some plants seem tailor-made for such demands.

One that fulfills the order quite admirably is pentas, sometimes referred to as Egyptian star flower. From the day they are planted until frost cuts them down, they provide an unending parade of clustered, star-shaped flowers. Some varieties grow approximately four feet tall, while other, newer cultivars such as 'Butterfly Sparkles' are compact plants that grow only eight to ten inches tall. Available in pink, lavender, red, and white, a color can be found for every garden.

In most of the Deep South, pentas are best treated as annuals and replaced every year. In reality, however, they are herbaceous perennials in frost-free areas. Sometimes they will return each year, but not dependably. I have some on the south side of my house next to the foundation that return reliably, but those in more exposed locations are killed by freezing temperatures.

Butterflies and hummingbirds are frequent visitors to the nectar-laden pentas. Those on the south side of my house are beside a window where I sit each morning to enjoy my coffee. It is here that I see hummingbirds and butterflies within a few inches of my face. What a way to start the day!

Pentas thrive in full sun to very light shade. Salt tolerance is poor, so protection from salt spray is necessary. Pentas are a choice plant for the confined spaces of planters or containers. Impact is maximized when groups of similar colors are planted together. A solid background such as a fence or hedge helps them to sparkle and stand out in the landscape. Do not worry about scalding from the sun; the hotter it is, the better they like it.

One year, members of the garden club planted pentas and ornamental potatoes in a container at the Valparaiso Communicty Library. We chose white pentas and 'Blackie' potatoes. All summer long these containers of plants were showstoppers. Club members got hundreds of cuttings from the potatoes, and the plants just kept growing and tumbling over the edges of the containers. The pentas bloomed until frost cut them down. Many times we have replicated this combination of pentas of one color or another with one of the colorful ornamental potatoes. All have been striking, long season arrangements.

Perilla (also Shiso, Wild Basil, Beefsteak Plant)
   Perilla frutescens
   Family: Lamiaceae (Mint family)
   Origin: Southeast Asia
   Type: Reseeding annual (herb)
   Size: 1–3 feet
   Zones: All
   Light: Sun to part sun
   Water: Moderate to low
   Varieties: Generic variety and 'Perilla Magilla' with brightly
              colored variegated leaves
   Color: Grown for foliage; purple, green, and variegated
   Soil: Well-drained
   Salt Tolerance: Slight/None

Several trays of perilla were for sale at one of the garden club plant sales. Shoppers picked a pot up every now and then, but most passed them by because they knew nothing about the plants. Everyone noticed their attractive dark purple leaves, but buyers were wary. Still small, the plants were not yet as beautiful as they would be in a few weeks. It was not until I started pulling the leaves and invited shoppers to take a sniff that the perilla began to sell.

Until recently, I had given this ordinary denizen of the yard next door little notice. Aunt Lois evidently planted it years ago. Year after year it reseeded, and always a few plants volunteered in the bed in front of her house. Could something so common and so easily grown be a candidate for my flower garden?

I decided to give them a try. I pulled up half a dozen of the plants and planted them in a large container, which I placed in a corner of the herb garden. There it flourished all summer, growing about a foot tall and filling the pot with its characteristic dark purple foliage. In fall it bloomed inconspicuous pinkish flowers on spikes that grew from the tips of each stem. Obviously each flower was fertile, because in spring hundreds of plants came up in the vicinity of the container. I potted these up for the plant sale.

The dark purple foliage of perilla is its main attraction. It is at its best when contrasted with white flowers such as sweet alyssum or the silver of dusty miller. In the herb garden, it mixes pleasingly with the lavender flowers of *Stokesia* in May, and in June it is an attractive accompaniment to the pink flowers of bouncing Bet (*Saponaria officinalis*). Throughout the summer, blossoms of 'Cosmic Orange' *Cosmos* glow even brighter against the dark-hued leaves.

In the herb garden, perilla—also known as shiso, wild basil, and beefsteak plant—serves a variety of purposes. Japanese and Korean cooks use the leaves fresh or pickled to flavor rice, fish, soups, and vegetables. They also use them in stir-fries, tempura, and salads. The seeds are sometimes salted and served as a snack. Green *Perilla* (shiso) leaves are used by the Japanese in western dishes as a substitute for sweet basil. The red leaves can be used to make a pinkish vinegar, and rice turns a lovely pink color when a few chopped leaves are mixed in just before serving. Ground seeds add a sweet, pungent taste when added to herb mustards.

A variety of ailments such as indigestion, colds, malaria, coughs, and even cholera have been treated with perilla. In commerce, the seed oil is used as a paint and ink dryer, in the making of linoleum, and as a preservative in soy sauce. It has also been used in the manufacture of a sugar substitute.

Perilla is an easily grown annual for the South. In fact, it has run wild in some sections of the United States. It can be found growing wild in much of Missouri, Arkansas, and the Blue Ridge Mountains. It thrives in poor, dry soil and requires little attention. Almost any light exposure will do, for it grows well in shade or full sun. To prevent reseeding, simply remove the seeds before they fall to the ground. If more come up than desired, they are easily removed.

Recently some breeding work has been done with perilla, and it is now available in a cultivar called 'Perilla Magilla' that sports beautifully colored leaves. They do not reseed like the species. Their cultural requirements are much like coleus to which they are related. This will be an interesting plant to watch, as other new cultivars are sure to follow.

STARS OF THE FALL GARDEN

Just as surely as the earth turns, autumn brings relief from the sweltering heat of summer. Because of all the spinning and tilting of our planet, our autumnal equinox happens around September 23. At that time, Earth is in such a position in its orbit that the axis is tilted neither toward nor away from the sun, and the sun's rays are vertical at the equator. As the earth continues to tilt on its axis, the vertical rays of the sun fall on ever increasingly southern points until around December 21, the day of winter solstice. On that day the sun shines its vertical rays on the Tropic of Capricorn, after which the earth begins its tilt in the other direction.

This means, of course, that in autumn the sun shines on the United States from ever-decreasing angles, and its rays are tempered. Temperatures begin to cool in sync with Earth's tilt. We gardeners venture back outside because there is much to be seen. Many plants are enjoying the season and are stepping out in celebration. They've donned their finest attire and are ready for their turn in the spotlight. They know that winter is approaching, and this is their last big fling.

Salvia

Salvia spp. (according to species)
Family: Lamiaceae (Mint family)
Origin: Mexico, Southeastern USA
Type: Perennial and annual
Size: Varies with species
Zones: 7–10
Light: Sun to part sun
Water: Moderate
Varieties: Many, both perennial and annual
Color: Red, blue, yellow, red, pink, salmon, cream,
     lavender, purple
Soil: Well-drained
Salt Tolerance: Slight

A prima donna of the perennial border is forsythia sage [Color 14] (*Salvia madrensis*). Near the back of the border, its clear yellow flowers are held aloft to herald the season. Other salvias, too, are at their best in the fall. Mexican bush sage [Color 17] (*Salvia leucantha*) has been regaling gardeners with its spikes of purple and white bicolored flowers for about a month. Pineapple sage [Color 21] (*Salvia elegans*) beckons butterflies and hummers alike with its bright red flowers, and we humans often cannot resist plucking a leaf and enjoying its fruity fragrance. 'Indigo Spires' [Color 22](*Salvia farinacea x longispicata*) has returned for a grand finale after its midsummer pruning.

Firespike (*Odontonema strictum*) dresses up its corner of the border. Large avocado-like leaves have been fueling the plant all summer in order to produce a stem suitable for displaying such finery. Now it stands about four feet tall and is adorned with tubular, bright red flowers that almost smother the 12-inch spikes. Near the firespike is firebush (*Hamelia patens*). This Florida native has been putting out its clusters of reddish-orange, tubular blossoms all summer. Now its leaves are beginning to turn red, and it is getting ready to go out in a blaze of glory.

Turks' Cap [Color 23]

Malvaviscus arboreus
Family: Malvaceae (Mallow family)
Origin: Mexico, Brazil
Type: Shrub
Size: 5–7 feet
Zones: 8–11
Light: Sun to part sun
Water: Moderate to low
Varieties: *M. arboreus* var. *drummondii, M. arboreus* var. *Mexicana*
Color: Bright red, pink
Soil: Well-drained
Salt Tolerance: Moderate/Slight

Turks' Cap (*Malvaviscus arboreus*) has adorned itself with bright red, spiraled flowers that hang from its limbs in glorious profusion. Sharing a shrub border with our native beautyberry (*Callicarpa americana*), the two upstage their less-colorful compatriots.

Ginger

Multiple genera and species
Family: Zingiberaceae (Ginger family)
Origin: Varies with Genus
Type: Rhizomatous perennials
Size: 9 inches–10 feet
Zones: 8–11
Light: Part sun to sun
Water: Moderate
Varieties: Many species and cultivars
Color: Varies with species
Soil: Well-drained, moist
Salt Tolerance: Moderate/Slight

Gingers are in rare form in the late summer garden. Some of the blossoms have faded, but tropical foliage stands tall and reminds one of the spectacular blossoms that were held on the ends of head-high stems on the likes of butterfly and Kahili ginger. The banana-like leaves of the *Curcumas* often hide the colorful spikes. Spiral gingers add texture and color of their own, and the dancing girls (*Globba*) frolic with careless abandon at the feet of their taller cousins. Pine cone ginger (*Zingiber zerumbet*) pushed up sturdy "pine cones" earlier in the summer, and for fall they have turned bright red. While the variegated foliage of the beautiful shell gingers (Alpinia) brightens the border, I do not expect them to bloom.

Golden Dewdrop (also Sky-Flower, Pigeonberry) [Color 24]

Duranta repens
Family: Verbenaceae (Verbena family)
Origin: Tropical Americas
Type: Shrub
Size: to 18 feet
Zones: 9–11 (resprouts in Zone 8)
Light: Sun to part sun
Water: Moderate
Varieties: 'Alba', 'Grandiflora', 'Variegata'
Color: Light Blue, White
Soil: Well-drained
Salt Tolerance: Slight/None

Princess Flower [Color 25]

Tibouchina urvilleana
Family: Melastomataceae (Melastoma family)
Origin: South America
Type: Shrub
Size: to 10 feet
Zones: 9b–11 (resprouts in Zone 8)
Light: Sun to part sun
Water: Moderate
Varieties: *Tibouchina granulosa* is a larger species
Color: Royal purple
Soil: Fertile, well-drained
Salt Tolerance: None

Golden dewdrop (*Duranta repens*) sports its lavender flowers and golden berries to delight humans and critters alike. Princess flower (*Tibouchina urvilleana*) enchants us with flush after flush of royal purple blooms.

Cuphea

(also Bat-Faced Cuphea, Cigar Plant, Mexican Heather, others)
Cuphea spp.
Family: Lythraceae (Loosestrife family)
Origin: Mexico, Guatemala, W. Indies
Type: Perennials (Sometimes grown as annuals.)
Size: 6 inches–5 feet, depending on species
Zones: All as annual, perennial (8) 9–11
Light: Sun to part sun
Water: Moderate
Varieties: Several cultivars of each variety
Color: Varies with species
Soil: Well-drained
Salt Tolerance: Moderate/Slight

Most of the cupheas are in fine fettle. Cigar plants [Color 26] (*Cuphea ignea*) are loaded with yellow-tipped red-orange flowers. Bat-face cuphea [Color 27] (*Cuphea llavea*) is laden with tiny purple bats' faces that have big red ears. Fine-textured Mexican  heather (*Cuphea hyssopifolia*) and *Cuphea varia* add gracefulness and refinement with their presence. Even though these long-blooming cupheas look delicate, they are anything but weaklings. They've been through the thick and thin of it, all summer long, and are none the worse for wear.

Blue Butterfly Bush (also Blue Glory Bower) [Color 28]

Clerodendron myricoides 'Ugandense'
Family: Verbenaceae (Verbena family)
Origin: Uganda
Type: Shrub
Size: 8 feet
Zones: 9b–11 (returns in Zone 8)
Light: Sun
Water: Moderate
Varieties: Sold generically
Color: Light and dark blue
Soil: Well-drained
Salt Tolerance: Slight/None

Blue butterfly bush or blue glory bower (*Clerodendron myricoides* 'Ugandense') is one of the unusual plants in the border. The blue flowers resemble a group of blue butterflies congregating on the stems. Flowers have five petals—four light blue and one cobalt blue. Stamens project gracefully from the center of the pale blue petals which makes the flowers look like upside-down butterflies.

Lion's Ear [Color 29]

Leonotis leonurus
Family: Lamiaceae (Mint family)
Origin: South Africa
Type: Shrub
Size: 4–5 feet
Zones: 9–11 (may return in 8)
Light: Sun to part sun
Water: Moderate to low
Varieties: Sold generically
Color: Bright orange
Soil: Well-drained
Salt Tolerance: Excellent/Moderate

Leonotis leonurus, a striking orange-flowered shrub, goes by the common name of lion's ear or lion's mane. It grows four to five feet tall with an almost equal spread. Lion's ear blooms in the fall with a profusion of bright orange flowers that hug the stems in circles at intervals along the stems.

Ornamental grasses combine beautifully with fall-flowering perennials. Their flowers and seed heads, backlit by the autumn sunlight, make spectacular additions to the garden. Enjoy it now, for it will soon be gone. That's part of what makes it so special, you know. If it looked like this all year, we'd quickly tire of it. For everything there is a season, and now is the time for fall.

Stoke's Aster [Color 30]

Stokesia laevis
Family: Asteraceae (Daisy family)
Origin: Southern USA
Type: Perennial
Size: 18–24 inches to 4 feet
Zones: 5–9
Light: Sun to part sun
Water: Moderate
Varieties: Generic and cultivars
Color: Lavender blue, blue, purple, yellow
Soil: Well-drained
Salt Tolerance: Excellent/Moderate

Aunt Lois used to live next door. Although she wasn't really my aunt, everyone called her that. She had no children, and she had been widowed for many years. Her nephew lived down the street, and he and the neighborhood looked after her. She fancied herself a horticulturist and delighted in correcting my real or imagined botanical misconceptions or mispronunciations.

One day we were talking about the beautiful Stoke's aster that was blooming in her yard. I called it STOKES-i-a. She replied in a haughty voice, "I believe that's sto-KE-si-a. I used to belong to the garden club, you know."

I conceded for a time. Now I know that either pronunciation is correct. I have seen it both ways in reputable horticultural references. Some say that because it is named after Dr. Jonathan Stokes, it should be pronounced with the Stokes part accented.

Stoke's aster, sometimes called cornflower aster, is native from South Carolina to Florida, and west to Louisiana. It occurs naturally on moist, acidic pine barrens and even in bogs. In cultivation, however, it insists on perfect drainage.

Flowers of the aster are large—up to four inches across—and they bloom over many weeks. The many-petaled ray flowers are frilly-edged and look as though someone had taken a pair of pinking shears to them. Leaves are evergreen and persist throughout the winter in dark green, attractive rosettes.

The most frequently encountered color is an unusual wisteria-blue. There are, however, other cultivars such as 'Alba' and 'Silver Moon' which both have white flowers. 'Blue Danube' and 'Blue Moon' tend toward lavender blue, and 'Mary Gregory' has yellow flowers. 'Purple Parasols' has deep violet flowers, and 'Omega Skyrocket' has stems up to four feet tall.

This easily grown perennial is rewarding even to the most negligent gardener. I particularly enjoy cutting the flowers and using them in my spring bouquets, for they are long lasting as a cut flower. Butterflies relish the nectar of the early spring blossoms.

Stoke's aster will perform best if it is divided and reset every two years or so. The clumps multiply and become crowded, which causes flowering to diminish. Simply dig them up, pull the individual plants apart, and set them back out about nine inches apart in soil to which organic matter has been added. Pot up extras to share with friends or to donate to a plant sale.

Aunt Lois is no longer with us. She surely must be puttering around some beautiful garden up in Heaven. Amiable Spouse and I bought her little house, and now I get to tend her flowers. Her Stoke's aster is scattered around both my garden and hers. Thanks, Aunt Lois, up there somewhere—if you can hear me. The STOKES-i-a is doing just fine!

Zinnia

Zinnia spp.
Family: Asteraceae (Daisy family)
Origin: Mexico, Central America
Type: Flowering annual
Size: 12–48 inches
Zones: All
Light: Sun
Water: Average
Varieties: Many, including narrow-leaf zinnias, Z. elegans,
and many hybrids
Color: All shades and blends except blue; yellow, orange,
white, red, pink
Soil: Fertile, well-drained
Salt Tolerance: Slight

The National Garden Bureau recently celebrated the year of the zinnia. Small wonder. Great strides have been made in their breeding during the past few years. Now we can celebrate by planting these winners in our summer gardens.

At one time zinnias were not an annual of choice for gardens in the humid South. Because they were plagued with powdery mildew and alternaria blight, their show was often not worth their space in the summer border. New breeding breakthroughs have produced zinnias that are resistant to these fungal diseases. Today's home gardener has at his or her finger-tips results of tests performed in experimental gardens throughout North America and the world. One such series of tests is done by All-America Selections. Trial gardens across Canada and the United States grow selected flowers and rate their performance. Winners are named All-America Selections Winners (AASW). Fleuroselect Gold Medal Winners are chosen from similar trials across Europe and South Africa.

The results of these trials are in. We are the beneficiaries. We can purchase plants that have passed the tests, and we can grow them with the reasonable expectation that they will do well in our gardens. One outstanding winner of both the AASW and the Fleuroselect Gold Medal was the Profusion series of zinnia, which boasts three cultivars: 'Profusion Orange' [Color 31], 'Profusion Rose', and 'Profusion White'.

Zinnias are members of the daisy family. More than a dozen species exist, but only three are regularly grown. All are annuals that bloom from early summer until frost.

Zinnia elegans, or common zinnia, is the most familiar. It has been grown in gardens for decades. More recently the narrow-leaved zinnias, *Z. angustifolia* (also known as *Z. linearis*), have gained in popularity. The species has golden-orange flowers, but the variety 'Crystal White' (AASW in 1997) has pure white blooms with yellow centers. Narrow leaves, disease resistance, long-lasting flowers, and a spreading, compact growth habit make them a choice selection.

The recently introduced Profusion zinnias (*Zinnia interspecific*) are the result of crosses between *Z. angustifolia* and *Z. elegans.* They represent the best of both: heat and humidity tolerance, disease resistance, easy maintenance, pretty two- to three-inch single flowers, and compact growth. Topping out at 12 to 18 inches tall, they are particularly suited for the front of the border.

Most zinnias are easily started from seed that can be sowed directly in the place where they are to grow. If, however, you choose to buy cell packs from garden centers, look for plants with compact growth and good branching. Buying plants before they are actually in bloom is best, but flower buds should be present. If flowers are already in bloom, remove the blossoms when they are planted. This is difficult for a gardener to do, but the plants quickly send out additional stems and reward the gardener with many more flowers.

Choose a spot for your zinnias with at least six hours of direct sun daily. Dig in about two inches of organic soil amendments such as peat moss, cow manure, compost, well-rotted leaves, or other organic materials. Transplant into the garden on a cloudy day or in the late afternoon. Don't crowd zinnias because air circulation around the plants will help to keep them disease free. Tall *Z. elegans* should be placed 12 to18 inches apart, *Z. angustifolia* 6 to 10 inches apart, and the new Profusion zinnias 12 to18 inches apart.

Few garden flowers are as suited to the vase as zinnias. For best results, gather flowers in the early morning before the sun dries the dew. Select blooms that haven't fully opened. Cut and place them immediately in a bucket of water. Once indoors, recut the stems under water. Remove any leaves that would be under water and let the flowers "rest" for a few hours before arranging them.

Plant zinnias for yourself, because they bloom for months in the summer garden. Plant them for the butterflies, too, for they like the pretty blossoms as much as we humans do.

CONTAINER GARDENING [Color 32]

No place to garden? Don't despair. Everyone can garden, even if it's in a pot on a balcony or in a washtub under the shade tree. Nothing beats a pretty container of plants for adding quick and easy color right where you want it. It's a great way to dress up an entry or to deck out the patio for a special party or backyard barbeque.

Container gardening is the method of choice for people who have limited gardening space. Folks who want to garden but whose time is extremely limited may find much pleasure in planting and maintaining a simple container garden. For those with limited mobility, working in raised beds or containers makes gardening possible. Sometimes we choose to garden in a container because the soil in our garden for one reason or another is unsuitable for growing plants. Not to be forgotten are the facts that containers are moveable, and creating them is just plain fun.

Sometimes the creative artist that resides within the gardener needs a means of expression. A successful container garden encompasses all the principles and elements of art. Like a floral design, it should have pleasing rhythm, scale, proportion, balance, dominance, and contrast. Elements used in its construction are the same as other art forms: light, line, size, space, form, pattern, texture, and color. When we create a container garden, we seek to attain the attributes of beauty, harmony, distinction, and expression.

Choosing an appropriate container is a part of the process. Of course, a container can be anything that will hold soil and allow proper drainage. Some traditional containers include clay pots, hanging baskets, wire baskets lined with sphagnum moss or fibrous liners, concrete planters, planter boxes, whiskey barrels, buckets, tubs, and bushel baskets.

Don't limit yourself to traditional containers. Be creative. Choose a container that lends itself to the look you are trying to create. Consider tires, bags of potting soil, your favorite old boot, or a worn-out chair. An old wheelbarrow or wagon can be made into a portable garden, and whimsical items appropriate for containers can be found at thrift shops. Keep your eyes peeled at your neighbor's garbage. Unimaginative people cast out perfectly good containers that gardeners with vision often put to good use.

Planning and placing a container garden is much like choosing a picture to decorate your home. Choose one that looks good and meets your needs. It will add beauty to your surroundings and provide months of pleasure.

Be cautious, however, when selecting a container. It must have a hole for drainage, and it must be large enough to hold the amount of soil required for the plants you choose. Black containers heat up to dangerous temperatures in sun, and terra cotta and other porous containers may wick water away from plants.

Weight may become a factor if the container needs to be moved. Lightweight decorative containers are available that are made from molded resins, fiberglass, or plastic. Many of these containers capture the look of expensive containers and are easy to move around. Another way to lighten weight is to use Styrofoam peanuts or crushed aluminum cans.

Master Gardener Jim McCarthy uses aluminum cans in containers and feels that they offer several advantages over Styrofoam peanuts. "Just placing Styrofoam peanuts in the bottom of the container will lighten it," he says, "but this procedure effectively reduces the height of the potting soil and provides no oxygen reservoir for the roots to respire." McCarthy recommends using aluminum cans placed throughout the container (not on the bottom). He says that this procedure maintains the original height of the potting soil and also provides an oxygen reservoir throughout the container to overcome the problem of drowning the plants by overwatering.

McCarthy suggests that aluminum cans are most effective if they are punctured to provide the roots access to oxygen. He stabs the cans with a sharp instrument such as a penknife with a lock back blade and then rotates, making eight to ten punctures a can. "This goes very quickly," he says, "and the cans are reusable and indestructible."

Making an attractive container garden involves more than just choosing an appropriate container and plants. The proper potting mixture is also important. Choose one that drains well but that also holds enough moisture to keep the plants from drying out between waterings. The best mixture is one that is soilless. These mixtures are free of diseases, insects, and weed seeds. Also, if a good quality potting soil is chosen, it is lightweight and porous. Usually the more expensive potting soils are best. You get what you pay for, generally speaking.

Frances Crissman, Okaloosa County Master Gardener, sometimes mixes her own blend for use in her container gardens. Her recipe contains two parts sphagnum peat, one part processed cow manure, one part potting soil, two parts perlite, and granular fertilizer as directed on the package. She adjusts the perlite as needed to match the drainage requirements of the plants that she chooses. Crissman points out that the best soil will eventually break down and need to be replaced. For very large containers too heavy to repot, some of the existing soil should be removed and new soil added.

Most container gardens are created for a season, or even for part of a season. They are, by their very nature, somewhat temporary arrangements. By the time plants have grown together in a container for a few months, the container is filled with roots and the plants have outgrown their space. Maintenance becomes difficult and plants become less vigorous. It will be more rewarding at this point to start over. Pull out the old plants, renew the soil, and pop in some saucy new plants to carry the container through the remainder of the season.

Close attention must be given to maintaining container gardens. They often need fertilizing every week or so with soluble fertilizer such as Miracle Gro or Peters 20-20-20, particularly if fertilizer was not added to the original potting mix. Including a time-release pellet fertilizer at the time of planting simplifies container care because fertilizer is released with each watering.

Sometimes container gardens need to be watered every day, particularly if they are in full sun or if temperatures hover above 90°F as they frequently do in our neck of the woods. Be sure to water thoroughly, making sure that plants are adequately soaked. Water until it runs out the bottom of the container. Wait a minute and water again.

Be sure that the soil does not become hydrophobic so that water simply runs over the surface and down the sides of the soil. If such a condition occurs, let a slow trickling stream of water run into the container for thirty minutes or so. Alternatively, place the container in a tray of water and allow it to hydrate from the bottom.

Watering crystals are available and may be added to potting mixes to help maintain moisture. These particles swell into gelatin-like crystals, absorbing and retaining many times their weight in

1 Border Grass *Liriope* spp. (p. 9)
2 Holly Fern *Cyrtomium falcatum* (p. 14)
3. Japanese Sedge *Carex morrowii aurea* 'Variegata' (p. 16)
4. Dwarf Variegated Mondo Grass *Ophiopogon japonicus* (p. 20)
5 Muhly Grass *Muhlenbergia capillaris* (p. 21)
6 Portulaca *Portulaca grandiflora* (p. 25)

14 Forsythia Sage
   Salvia madrensis (p. 87)
15 Globe Amaranth *Gomphrena
   globosa* (p. 89)
16 Melampodium *Melampodium
   paludosum* (p. 91)
17 Mexican Bush Sage
   Salvia leucantha (p. 93)
18 Ornamental Pepper
   Capsicum annuum (p. 95)

19 Ornamental Sweet Potato
   Ipomoea batatas (p. 97)
20 Pentas *Pentas lanceolata* (p. 98)
21 Salvia *Salvia elegans* (p. 102)
22 Salvia 'Indigo Spires' (p. 102)
23 Turk's Cap
   Malvaviscus arboreus (p. 103)

24 Golden Dewdrop
   Duranta repens (p. 105)
25 Princess Flower
   Tibouchina urvilleana (p. 105)
26 Cigar plant *Cuphea ignea* (p. 106)
27 Bat-face cuphea *Cuphea llavea* (p. 106)
28 Blue butterfly bush
   Clerodendron myricoides 'Ugandense' (p. 107)

39 Snapdragon *Antirrhinum majus* (p. 129)
40 Sweet Alyssum *Lobularia maritima* (p. 131)
41 Mexican Petunia *Ruellia brittoniana* (p. 146)
42 Cashmere Bouquet
   Clerodendron bungei (p. 146)
43 Mock Orange *Philadelphus coronarius* (p. 147)

water. As plant roots draw moisture from the potting mix, the crystals slowly release water, helping to maintain a consistent moisture level longer than potting mixes without moisture crystals.

Use these crystals with caution, however. Tammy Winchenbach of Niceville Nursery in Niceville, Florida, says that they do maintain moisture, but in some of her containers they seemed to promote root rot by holding too much moisture around the roots of plants. She advises users to follow directions carefully. "A little goes a long way," she cautions.

Careful attention must be given to pruning and grooming plants for attractiveness. Many plants would quickly outgrow their space if allowed to grow unchecked. Prune as needed to promote dense plants and to keep them in scale with the container. Deadhead (remove spent blooms) regularly. Do not hesitate to remove a plant that is performing poorly, and treat for pests and diseases if necessary.

With a little effort and attention to details, anyone can have a pretty container garden. Since they don't last a lifetime, they are easily redone if the first effort is not pleasing. Just get a container, put some plants in it that you like, and go from there. You'll soon find a combination that is just right.

Listed below are some favorites that were treated more thoroughly in *Gardening in the Coastal South*. Consult that book for more information about these plants.

Perennials

Asclepias tuberosa	Butterfly Weed
Cuphea spp.	Cigar Plant, Bat Face Flower, Mexican Heather
Echinacea purpurea	Purple Coneflower
Gaura lindeheimeri	Gaura, Whirling Butterflies
Hamelia patens	Firebush
Phlox divaricata	Louisiana Phlox
Phlox paniculata	Summer Phlox
Plumbago auriculata	Blue Plumbago
Rudbeckia, spp.	Black-eyed Susan

Salvia spp.	Salvia
Sedum acre	Goldmoss, Stonecrop
Tibouchina urvilleana	Princess Flower
Verbena spp.	Verbena 'Homestead Purple'

Bulbs

Bletilla striata	Hardy Orchid, Chinese Ground Orchid
Caladium spp.	Caladium
Crinum spp.	Crinum Lily
Gloriosa rothschildiana	Glory Lily, Gloriosa Lily
Hippeastrum spp.	Amaryllis
Iris spp.	Iris
Lilium longiflorum	Easter Lily
Lilium	Oriental Lily
Lilium lancifolium	Tiger Lily
Tulbaghia violacea	Society Garlic
Zephyranthes spp.	Rain Lily, Fairy Lily
Zingiberaceae	Assorted Gingers

Vines

Basella alba	Malabar Spinach
Cardiospermum halicacabum	Love-in-a-Puff
Gelsemium sempervirens	Carolina Jessamine
Ipomoea alba	Moon Vine, Moon Flower
Lonicera sempervirens	Trumpet Honeysuckle
Mandevilla sanderi	Mandevilla
Passiflora incarnata	Passion Vine
Thunbergia alata	Black-eyed-Susan Vine
Trachelospermum jasminoides	Confederate Jasmine

4

HARDY PLANTS FOR
WINTER AND EARLY SPRING

Ornamental cabbages and kales, pansies and violas, and snapdragons and calendulas are standard bedding plants in winter gardens. These hardy annuals can withstand all but the very worst Southern winters. Purchased from nurseries in the fall and set out for color in the winter garden, these annuals far outperform their spring-planted kin.

Hardy annuals, generally speaking, are flowers that relish cool weather and whose seeds or seedlings can withstand winter's freezing temperatures. In the South most of them can be sown at any time during the fall. Many will sprout, grow, and even begin flowering in winter. Though many of them will not bloom until early spring, fall planting gives the seedlings time to grow into sturdy, vigorous plants that will bloom earlier than spring-planted seeds. For many of them, cool temperatures are required for germination. Many are self-seeding and are part of what makes gardening a year-long activity in the South. Gardeners who skip these fall-planted hardy annuals miss some of the most beautiful flowers of all.

Bachelor's Button (also Cornflower) [Color 33]

Centaurea cyanus
Family: Asteraceae (Daisy family)
Origin: Europe
Type: Hardy annual
Size: 1–3 feet
Zones: All
Light: Sun
Water: Low
Varieties: Dwarf Hyacinth Hybrids, Giant Double Hyacinth
      Hybrids, Thompson and Morgan Improved Hybrids,
      others
Color: Blue, lavender, pink, white
Soil: Well-drained
Salt Tolerance: Slight/None

Most years I save space in my garden for bachelor's buttons, or cornflowers. My favorites are the clear blue ones, but they are also available in shades of white, red, lavender, and pink. These annual flowers are native to Europe but have naturalized throughout North America.

One interesting story about cornflowers goes back to the time of Napoleon. When Napoleon forced Queen Louise of Prussia from Berlin, she hid her children in a cornfield. There she kept them entertained and quiet by weaving wreaths of cornflowers. Wilheim, one of her children, later became emperor of Germany. He made the cornflower a national emblem of unity in remembrance of his mother's bravery.

Bachelor's buttons are usually planted in November or December, though they may be planted as late as January or early February and expected to make a good showing in the spring garden. Seeds germinate better if they have been kept in the refrigerator for a few days before sowing. Sow them in place and cover with a thin layer of soil since darkness is required for germination.

Usually I wait for the first killing frost of winter to plant my bachelor's buttons. When the dead foliage of the summer annuals is removed, I clear a spot and sow the seeds. Tiny seedlings appear in a week or two, and I thin them to about a foot apart. The first blooms appear about 12 weeks after planting and last for about a month. If they are deadheaded regularly, they can last longer. Successive plantings can also extend the bloom period.

Though cornflowers do best in full sun, they are also suitable for planting in partial shade. They have no special soil requirements and are drought tolerant. They grow anywhere from one to three feet tall depending on the variety. If conditions are favorable, they will self-sow and come back from year to year.

My favorite planting of cornflowers ever was around the base of one of my birdbaths. They grew about as tall as the birdbath and their grayish-green foliage added a beauty and distinction of its own to the flower border. They were particularly pleasing for me because I cut them fresh for long-lasting bouquets, and I dried many of them for use in dried flower arrangements and floral crafts.

They are one of the flowers that blooms in early spring. In hot weather they do not fare well, so as soon as they begin to look bedraggled, pull them up and plant something that can withstand our summer heat.

Seeds can be had from friends who grow them or can be found in most mail order and on-line seed sources. You can usually find a package on seed racks at garden centers and other places where flower seeds are sold. I have seen this flower on a list of exotic invasives for some of the western states. If bachelor's buttons reseed to the extent that they disrupt native habitats in your area, do not plant them.

Candytuft [Color 34]
Iberis umbellata
Family: Brassicaceae (Mustard family)
Origin: Mediterranean Area
Type: Hardy annual
Size: 1 foot
Zones: All
Light: Sun
Water: Moderate
Varieties: 'Appleblossom', 'Dwarf Fairyland', 'Flash'
Color: Pink, purple, red, white
Soil: Well-drained
Salt Tolerance: Unknown

Some flowers require a considerable leap of faith. We plant seeds in the fall or winter, and then we wait three or four months before the plants grow large enough to bloom. Oh, they come up all right, but then they just seem to sit there. Later, when spring's warming breezes blow just right, they leap from the earth in a sudden frenzy to stretch their stems skyward, bloom, and then set seed before the heat of summer arrives.

These hardy annuals often do not receive the attention they deserve, because most of them take a bit of advance planning. One cannot rush out to the garden center in spring, purchase them, and set them out in the garden the way we do summer annuals. Gardeners must think of them in fall or early winter, prepare the bed, plant the seeds, and then wait for spring.

The diligent gardener who has thought things through and has not lazed through the fall of the year letting life pass by with nary a thought of tomorrow's garden, will be rewarded in due time. One of my favorite hardy annuals, globe candytuft (*Iberis umbellata*), requires such forethought.

One of the hardest things for gardeners to do is to thin their plants sufficiently. It seems a shame, say, to plant 500 seeds, have them all come up, and then pull up and throw away the vast majority of the small seedlings. That, however, is what one must do if candytuft is to grow and bloom to the greatest extent of its beauty. Crowded plants grow weakly, and since they do not transplant well, they do best when planted where they are to bloom. Since individual plants grow about one foot tall and wide, at least 12 inches of space must be allowed between each plant. Globe candytuft appreciates full sun and moderately rich to average, well-drained soil.

I have never seen plants of candytuft for sale at a nursery. Seeds are, however, available in various garden catalogs. Thompson and Morgan lists 'Appleblossom', 'Dwarf Fairyland Mixed', and 'Flash Mixed'. If the gardener has a friend who grows candytuft, perhaps a few can be begged. One blossom is made of many tiny flowers clustered closely together, each of which produces a seed. I simply cut off and save the whole blossom when the color has faded and only the green clusters of seeds remain. The following fall I shred them into a prepared bed, stir them around a bit, firm the soil, and sit back and wait for the considerable beauty that they add to my spring garden.

Nasturtium [Color 35]

Tropaeolum majus
Family: Tropaeolaceae (Nasturtium family)
Origin: South America
Type: Hardy annual
Size: Vining types 3–8 feet; bush, compact dwarf types
    8–12 inches
Zones: All
Light: Sun
Water: Moderate
Varieties: Dwarf, semitrailing, and climbing
Color: Creamy-white, yellow, orange, rose, crimson
Soil: Well-drained
Salt Tolerance: None

Every spring I enjoy eating stuffed nasturtium blossoms, and I relish the peppery leaves and flowers in salads and on sandwiches. Besides, the delicate fragrance and colorful flowers remind me of Grandmother's garden and the uncomplicated gardens of my childhood, so I simply must have them. I realize, though, that if they are going to be a part of the spring garden, I'd better get busy right after Valentine's Day.

Nasturtium seeds are best planted in February. Plants will tolerate light frosts, but a hard freeze will kill them. The watchful gardener will be prepared to protect them from a late freeze. Getting them growing this early is necessary so that they will have time to bloom and set seed before the heat of summer arrives. Native to the mountainous areas of Central and South America, they are grown as cool season annuals in the South.

Nasturtiums come in three types: dwarf, semitrailing, and climbing. Dwarf types are bushy and compact and include such cultivars as 'Alaska', 'Empress of India', 'Strawberries and Cream', and 'Whirlybird'. Semitrailing types reach a length of two to three feet, which makes them ideal for hanging baskets. The climbing types like 'Jewel of Africa' send out six- to eight-foot runners that are perfect for trellises, fences, and other structures. Flower color ranges from creamy white to yellow, orange, rose, and crimson. Leaves may be variegated or green.

Plant seeds where they are to grow, because they do not transplant well. Seeds should be soaked overnight and planted one-half to three-quarters of an inch deep and about six inches apart in a garden bed or container. The plants appreciate a sunny place and light, sandy soil. Rich, fertile soil and fertilizers are not necessary and will cause them to have lush foliage and few flowers. If they do not seem to be growing well, they can be lightly fertilized with a low-nitrogen fertilizer.

Second to the fun of growing nasturtiums is eating them. Pesticide-free flowers should be picked early in the morning and immediately placed in a cool, saltwater bath. The salt loosens any insects that may be lurking deep inside the blossoms and causes them to dislodge easily under a gentle stream of running water. After they are thoroughly clean, they are ready to eat.

The pretty blossoms are delightful stuffed with tuna and chicken salad or flavored cream cheese. After the cream cheese is softened, it can be piped into the blossom with a pastry tip. The flowers and leaves are a beautiful, tasty, and nutritious addition to a fresh spring salad. They contain ten times as much vitamin C as lettuce. My grandmother dried ripe seeds, ground them, and used them like black pepper. Today's cooks gather green nasturtium seeds, pickle them in vinegar, and use them as a substitute for capers. The blossoms are always an attractive garnish to dishes, and they look very pretty when frozen in ice cubes and used in iced teas or lemonades. If you choose not to eat the pretty flowers, pick them and place them in a vase for a colorful and fragrant bouquet.

Nasturtium seeds are readily available at most garden centers. Plant some for the hummingbirds who relish their nectar. Don't wait until spring and expect to run out to the nursery and pick up a few nasturtium plants. You most likely won't find them, and if you do they will never attain the vigor of the flowers you should have planted in February.

Nemesia [Color 36]

Nemesia fruticans
Family: Scrophulariaceae (Snapdragon family)
Origin: South Africa
Type: Short-lived perennial; grown as annual
Size: 8–10 inches
Zones: All
Light: Sun
Water: Moderate
Varieties: Several cultivars: 'Bluebird', 'Innocence', 'Banana', many others
Color: Red, pink, purple, lavender, white
Soil: Well-drained
Salt Tolerance: None

Here we go again. Little new flowers are on the market—or maybe they're not new and I have just become aware of them. Nemesia is the name of one of these latecomers. On my initial encounter with the plant, I bought only one. The plant had beautiful blue flowers and was a cultivar called 'Bluebird'.

Buying only one of a plant is not really like me. Usually I buy at least three, but since I was unfamiliar with this plant, I purchased only one. I expected it to wither and die with the first frost. Surprisingly it flowered all winter and well into the spring, and I wished that I had bought at least a dozen of them. I planted the tiny plant in my sunniest area in a bed I had amended with organic matter. It was watered regularly by the sprinkler system. I was delighted by its compact habit and freely blooming nature.

Since then I have added more nemesias to my garden. 'Blueberry', 'Innocence', and others give the same performance as the pretty 'Blue Bird' of past seasons. The diminutive plants grow eight to ten inches tall and have a similar width. Cultivars include 'Banana', 'Blue Lagoon', 'Candy Girl', 'Compact Innocence', and many others. Flowers are vanilla scented and resemble miniature snapdragons on tiny light green leaves.

I also noticed that seed can be purchased from some of my favorite seed companies. This would surely be a better way to go if large numbers of plants are desired. They should be planted in early fall. Since light is not required for germination, the seeds should be covered lightly. Seeds will germinate in about seven days.

Nemesia is a short-lived perennial. While it can take some frost, a hard freeze will kill the top and the plant will grow back with the return of milder days. Unfortunately, the plants are not tolerant of our summer heat, so we must grow them as winter annuals.

Diascia (also Twinspur)

Diascia barberae
Family: Scrophulariaceae (Snapdragon family)
Origin: South Africa
Plant Type: Hardy Annual
Size: 12 inches
Zones: All
Light: Sun to part sun
Water: Moderate
Varieties: 'Ruby Field', 'Coral Belle', 'Emma', others
Color: Mostly pink to mauve, salmon, shades of red
Soil: Well-drained
Salt Tolerance: Unknown

Another little newcomer that must be tried is diascia, or twinspur. This member of the snapdragon family is hardy to about 20°F or lower. Trailing stems take root and rebranch to form broad mats. Blooming stems are held a few inches above the foliage. As the flowers start to fade, the plants can be cut back with scissors to about three inches above soil level and they will reflower. As a matter of fact, an employee at The Garden Gate in Gulf Breeze, Florida, told me that if they were frozen to the ground, they could be cut off at soil level and expected to come back. Several colors are available, such as salmon, lavender, pink, and deep rose.

Both nemesia and diascia are versatile plants with many uses. Try them on the patio or balcony in combination planters, hanging baskets, or in landscape beds. Wherever you put them, they will delight you with flowers throughout the winter. They just might be a refreshing change from pansies and snapdragons.

Ornamental Cabbage and Kale [Color 37]

Brassica oleracea
Family: Brassicaceae (Mustard family)
Origin: Europe
Type: Hardy annual (actually biennial, but grown as an annual)
Size: 1–5 feet (in flower)
Zones: All
Light: Sun
Water: Moderate
Varieties: Many cultivars chosen for various colors
Color: Flowers yellow; foliage white, green, lavender, purple,
    pink, red, variegated
Soil: Fertile, well-drained
Salt Tolerance: Slight/None

Ornamental cabbages and kales are some of the South's most dependable winter bedding plants. Long after the zinnias and marigolds of summer have faded to a memory, the colors of ornamental cabbages and kales glow brightly in beds and containers. Indeed, as the winter grows colder and a few frosts visit the countryside, the hues of the cabbages and kales get ever more colorful.

These ornamental plants are cousins to many vegetables, including cabbage, broccoli, cauliflower, mustard, and turnip. All belong to the Brassicaceae family. Both ornamental kale and ornamental cabbage are biennials that are grown as annuals. Though very similar, they can be distinguished from each other by differences in the leaves. Kale has curly, frilly leaves. Cabbages, on the other hand, have broad, flat leaves. Both have bright green, lavender, purple, red, pink, and white foliage.

Ornamental cabbages and kales can be started from seed, but they grow unthriftily in the heat of our summers. Most of us opt to buy them from nurseries which bought them from northern growers. They are readily available at garden centers during the early winter, and they make a quick showing in the landscape.

I often have to chuckle to myself when a reference states that certain plants require full sun and rich, damp soil. Well, yes, they do if they can get it. Do not give up, however, if you have less than full sun and your soil is devoid of nutrients. Put them in the most sun you can manage, add organic matter and slow-release fertilizer to the planting bed, and enjoy the less than perfect but still quite acceptable results. We do what we have to.

Ornamental cabbages and kales, like their cousins, are host plants for such butterflies as great southern whites and cabbage whites. The butterflies fly daintily among the cabbages and lay their eggs as nature intended. Soon little green caterpillars can be seen chomping on the leaves. This is not good unless you planted them in the butterfly garden for just this purpose. Damage from these insects is usually minimal because the plants grow in winter when the insects are inactive. If caterpillars do infest your ornamental plantings, they can be controlled with insecticidal soap or *Bacillus thuringiensis* (Bt), which is a bacteria that infects the caterpillars but is not considered harmful to people or animals.

Though edible, the ornamental cabbages and kales are grown more for their colorful foliage. However, individual leaves are very attractive when used to decorate a tray of fresh vegetables or to line a salad bowl or a turkey platter. Individual leaves can be washed in cold water, dried, wrapped in paper towels, and placed in a plastic bag in the refrigerator, where they will last for a about a week.

Floral designers always try to have a few of these beautiful plants on hand. One head makes a focal area or center of interest in a mixed design. Or a head can simply be set in a bowl or needlepoint holder for an attractive centerpiece or decoration for the coffee table or sideboard.

When spring arrives and the weather warms, cabbages and kales "bolt," or grow taller and begin to flower. Unfortunately the yellow flower clusters are not very attractive. Furthermore, the plants begin to smell like rotten eggs, so most gardeners pull them up and replace them with summer annuals.

Oh, well. Like many beautiful things, they're here today and gone tomorrow. We cannot keep it all forever. We must notice and enjoy beauty when it is in season and close at hand.

Petunia [Color 38]

Petunia spp.
Family: Solanaceae (Nightshade family)
Origin: Argentina, Tropical South America, Australia
Type: Hardy annual
Size: 6–30 inches
Zones: All
Light: Sun
Water: Moderate
Varieties: Over 300
Color: All shades and blends
Soil: Fertile, well-drained
Salt Tolerance: Moderate

I remember the old-fashioned petunias that grew in my garden when I was a child. Never did I have to plant these old, open pollinated strains. They came up with exuberance in every nook and cranny where seeds had fallen from the previous season's crop. Flowers bloomed in magnificent profusion on vining plants in hues of purple, white, and pink. They perfumed the whole garden with their powerful fragrance. These wild petunias (*Petunia integrifolia*) were chosen as Texas Superstars (plants that are highly recommended by the Texas A&M Agriculture program) because of their cold and heat tolerance and resistance to diseases.

Today over 300 different varieties of petunias are available, so it is hard to know where to begin. The buyer is greeted with such terms as grandiflora, multiflora, floribunda, miliflora, and even hedgiflora. Trailers, doubles, minitunias, and supertunias further confuse the issue. Generally, the floribunda hybrids have medium-sized flowers with heavy blossom production. Varieties include the Celebrity, Primetime, and Madness series. (Series refers to a cultivar that comes in a range of colors.) The grandifloras include the Avalanche series. They tend to bloom early and have large flowers. Multifloras include the Wave petunias.

The Wave petunias offer several choices that boast greater heat and cold tolerance than many of the others. The original Wave series was introduced in 1995 when 'Purple Wave' was designated an All-America Selection winner. Following closely on its heels were 'Pink Wave', 'Rose Wave', 'Misty Lilac Wave', 'Blue Wave', and another

AAS winner, 'Lavender Wave'. Next came the Easy Wave series, which are more mounding, and then the Tidal Wave group, which can grow up to three feet tall if planted close together.

From Australia come the supertunias (*P. axillaris*), which are ever-blooming, long-lived, and available in a wide range of colors and growth habits. 'Trailblazer' and 'Surfinia' offer still more choices. Look also for the 'Kahuna', 'Supertunia', and Suncatcher series. To further cloud the issue, the *Calibrachoa* hybrids such as 'Million Bells' and 'Lirica Shower' are sometimes called minitunias but are in fact bellflowers. One of the most gorgeous hanging baskets I have ever seen was filled with hundreds of terra cotta–colored bellflowers. They are also available in dark blue, white, dark red, and yellow, and are reportedly hardy to 15°F.

Petunias are usually cool-weather plants for most of the South. In my garden, I find that they grow well in late fall and early winter and again in spring before the hot weather arrives. Most of us in the South can keep them growing vigorously all winter if they are in containers that can be moved to protected places in freezing weather. In my experience, they burn out during the heat of summer.

Many of the new hybrids, however, exhibit increased cold and heat tolerance and less susceptibility to diseases and pests. Petunias are heavy feeders and should be planted in rich, organic soil and fertilized regularly throughout the growing season. Pinching or cutting back the stems will generate growth and more blooms. A good layer of mulch will keep soil temperatures more constant and prevent rapid moisture loss.

If you have not grown petunias in a while, now may be a good time to give them another try. Some of them may surprise you with their vigor and floriferousness.

Snapdragon [Color 39]

Antirrhinum majus
Family: Scrophulariaceae (Snapdragon family)
Origin: Southwest Europe
Type: Hardy annual
Size: 6 inches–4 feet
Zones: All
Light: Sun to part sun
Water: Moderate
Varieties: Several series, including Floral Carpet, Floral Showers,
          Royal Carpet, Tahiti, Liberty, Sonnet, others
Color: Lavender, orange, pink, red, yellow, white
Soil: Fertile, well-drained
Salt Tolerance: Excellent

Snapdragons are frequently seen in full bloom during our cool season. They bloom best in fall and spring day length. Winter days are too short for blooms to initiate, so plants spend the winter growing and becoming established. In spring they put on a show that cannot be equaled with spring-planted snaps.

Unfortunately, a disease lethal to snaps sometimes establishes itself in the soil. Planting snapdragons in the same place year after year is not a good idea because new plants may become infected and die. If the disease is present in your garden, try growing snaps in containers.

Cut off any flowers that are present when planting snapdragons. No matter how hard you have to grit your teeth, do it anyway. Stocky plants with many more blossoms will be your reward. Regular deadheading also extends the bloom season, because snapdragons, like most annual plants, are single-minded in their efforts to produce seed. Once the seeds are produced, the flowers die. Deadheading keeps flowers blooming for a much longer time because the seed-producing process is interrupted.

My garden club had a very interesting experience with snapdragons. One particular work day we were all there, weeding and planting new annuals in the butterfly garden. During the preceding month, we had planted several trays of snapdragons. Some of the members were working among them, weeding, fertilizing, deadheading, and generally doing what gardeners do in snapdragon beds.

We were chatting among ourselves about one thing and another when one of the ladies said, "Hey, you all. Come look at this." We all moved near to see what she had found. Munching on the snapdragons were numerous caterpillars. Such a state of affairs would send less hale and hardy gardeners squealing and running for the poison. To the environmentally aware ladies in the garden club, however, it was a cause for excitement and jubilation.

We all gathered near to admire the black and white caterpillars. We took one into the library to study closely. Orange markings ran down the sides, and a row of branched spines ran down the length of its body. A pair of very short spines stuck out from the top of its head. Some of the members searched for a book that would identify this caterpillar. We finally found it to be the larval form of the beautiful common buckeye butterfly. We should have known without looking, however, for these were the critters we invited when we planted the snapdragons.

Besides being larval plant food for buckeye butterflies, snapdragons are one of our most colorful winter annuals. Modern varieties provide faintly fragrant, blossom-laden flower heads in a wide assortment of colors. They are available in three heights: small (from six to nine inches); intermediate (eighteen to twenty-four inches); and large (three or four feet). Although they are perennials, they are usually treated as annuals.

Snapdragons may be started from seed, but they are very tiny, and controlled growing conditions are almost a necessity. Since seeds need light for germination, they should not be covered with soil. In the South they should be started in a sheltered seedbed in summer and planted out in the fall for winter and spring flowering. However, seedlings bought from a garden center will flower earlier than plants started at home from seeds. Our summer heat is detrimental to snapdragons, so buying plants from northern growers seems a better way to go.

Snapdragons are particularly fun in the butterfly garden where children are frequently present. When individual blossoms are pinched from the side, they make the "dragon mouth" open and close. They are equally useful in the home garden, because the tall varieties make excellent cut flowers. However, they require staking. The intermediates need no staking, and they have stems long enough for use as cut flowers. Choose from among the dwarf series for a colorful carpet of flowers at the front of the border.

Cultivars include the dwarf Floral Carpet, Floral Showers, Royal Carpet, and Tahiti series. If intermediates are desired, check out the Liberty or the Sonnet series. The Rocket series is recommended if tall plants are desired. Select the desired size of plants and set them out in a sunny bed that has been amended with organic matter.

We garden club members are prepared to plant additional snaps if the buckeye caterpillars completely decimate the crop. We expect, however, that cold weather will send the larvae scurrying to protected places, or that they will overwinter as chrysalides. Payback for club members will come in spring when we see the adult buckeyes nectaring on the bountiful snapdragon blossoms. This, folks, is gardening at its best!

Sweet Alyssum [Color 40]

Lobularia maritima
Family: Brassicaceae (Mustard family)
Origin: Mediterranean Area
Plant Type: Hardy annual
Size: 6–10 inches
Zones: All
Light: Sun to part sun
Water: Moderate
Varieties: 'Easterbasket', 'Wonderland', 'Snow Crystals',
          'Carpet of Snow'
Color: Wine-red, salmon pink, orange, lemon, and silver white
Soil: Well-drained
Salt Tolerance: Slight

Sweet alyssum is a tiny plant that I like to call a little giant, because no matter how small it is, it makes a giant contribution to my flowerbeds each year.

Though it is best suited to the fall, winter, and early spring garden, I usually have some of it growing year round. My favorite places to grow it are at the edges of sunny beds and around the edges of my herb garden. It is equally suited for hanging baskets and other types of containers. For gardeners who want fragrance in their gardens, it is a must, for the honeylike scent is most pleasant.

I learned the hard way that the seeds require light for germination. I bought a packet of seeds and planted them, covering them lightly as I usually do. No plants came up. It was not until I bought a new packet and read the directions that I discovered what I had done wrong. It plainly stated on the packet that light was required for germination. I prepared my bed as usual, sprinkled the tiny seeds on the surface of the soil, and patted lightly to be sure they had good contact with the soil. Lo and behold, I think every one of them came up. The tiny white flowers bloomed all spring and well into the summer. The following fall more plants came up where the old flowers dropped seeds.

Seeds germinate in 8 to 15 days at temperatures between 65°F and 75°F. Light frosts seem to have no effect on sweet alyssum, but research indicates that a hard freeze might kill it. In my Valparaiso garden, however, I have never lost it to cold weather. Colors range from wine red, salmon pink, lavender, purple, to silver white. Cultivars include such popular choices as 'Easter Basket', 'Wonderland', 'Snow Crystals', and 'Carpet of Snow'.

Amiable Spouse and I frequently comment about the insects that buzz around the sweet alyssum. Some bees are always flying around, and I have seen butterflies and hundreds of tiny wasps gathering pollen or sipping nectar from the minuscule blossoms.

Sweet alyssum grows best in full sun, but it also blooms in partial shade. Six to ten inches tall is its usual height, but plants are smaller on sunny sites with poor soil. I plant it in beds that have been amended with organic matter, and though it is moderately drought tolerant, it prefers to be kept moist.

White is my favorite color since it seems to be more visible in the landscape than some of the other colors, especially when it is planted in masses. Many tiny four-petaled flowers about a quarter of an inch in diameter bloom in clusters at the ends of each stem. Each cluster measures about three-quarters to one inch in diameter, and each plant has many of these tiny clusters.

Sweet alyssum is readily available in flats at most garden centers in the spring and fall. Pick up a tray or so of these tiny giants to add a bit of sparkle to your landscape.

OTHER CHOICES

Besides the obvious and frequently seen snapdragons, pansies, dianthus, and ornamental kale and cabbage, many other plants may be used to add variety to the winter or early spring garden.

Love-in-a-mist (also Nigella)

Nigella damascena
Family: Ranunculaceae (Buttercup family)
Origin: Mediterranean Area
Type: Hardy annual
Size: 1–2 feet
Zones: All
Light: Sun to part sun
Water: Moderate
Varieties: 'Miss Jekyll', 'Persian Jewels', 'Persian Rose', others
Color: Blue, pink, white
Soil: Well-drained
Salt Tolerance: Slight/None

Not to be left out is the delicate and beautiful love-in-a-mist (*Nigella damascena*). It has bloomed in my garden for several springs. Though I had never seen it "in person," I had seen and admired it in garden catalogs and magazines. "Oh, well," I thought to myself. "That's just another of those things like peonies and lilacs that won't do well in the South."

Much to my delight, I was mistaken. My friend Shari brought me a bouquet of the delicate blue flowers from her garden one spring. That's all it took. She saved some seeds for me. I scattered them around the garden that fall, and since then they have enhanced my garden each spring with their unusual, frilly flowers and seed pods.

Nigella grows about two feet tall. Leaves are finely cut and almost threadlike. In spring, blue, white, or pink flowers about an inch wide adorn the ends of each stem. Following the blooms, attractive seed heads are formed which are useful in everlasting arrangements or in floral crafts such as wreaths and contrived flowers that many of us enjoy making.

Larkspur

Consolida ambigua
Family: Ranunculaceae (Buttercup family)
Origin: Southern Europe
Type: Hardy annual
Size: 1–7 feet
Zones: All
Light: Sun to part sun
Water: Moderate
Varieties: Thompson and Morgan's Improved Hybrids, others
Color: Lavender, pink, white, purple, blue
Soil: Well-drained
Salt Tolerance: Slight/None

Larkspur (*Consolida ambigua*) is another of those beautiful flowers that must be planted in late fall or early winter. I must confess that I cannot be absolutely positive about the correct botanical name of this flower. Research reveals the following names for annual larkspur: *Delphinium ajacis*, *Consolida orientalis*, *Consolida ajacis*, and *Consolida ambigua*. I will follow Mississippi horticulturist Norman Winter's example and go with *Consolida ambigua*.

Regardless of its exact name, I remember the tall, stately spikes of larkspur in Grandmother's garden in Mississippi. They were one of the first flowers that bloomed in the garden in early spring. She cut many beautiful bouquets, and still the garden was full of them. They were a rainbow of colors ranging from light and dark pink, blue, rose, lavender, and white. In her cottage garden they grew about three or four feet tall in bold drifts where they were allowed to reseed every year.

Larkspur is a member of the Delphinium family. Many varieties are in the trade, and they range in height from one to seven feet. Most garden centers have larkspur on their seed rack, and they can easily be ordered by mail. I particularly enjoy Thompson and Morgan's Improved Hybrids.

Plant larkspur seeds on top of loosened, well-drained soil and tamp lightly to insure contact with the soil. Thin to about 12 inches apart and fertilize lightly. Enjoy early spring spikes of blooms, and be sure to let some of them mature in order to make seeds for next year's garden. Simply shred the mature seed heads in place or allow them to fall naturally. Their tiny, internal clocks tell them when it is time to germinate and grow in the garden.

Stock (also Gillyflower)

Matthiola incana
Family: Brassicaceae (Mustard family)
Origin: Mediterranean Area
Type: Hardy annual
Size: 8–30 inches
Zones: All
Light: Sun to part sun
Water: Moderate
Varieties: Harmony series, others
Color: Red, rose, purple, white, yellow
Soil: Well-drained
Salt Tolerance: Moderate/Slight

Another of my favorites in the winter and early spring garden is stock (*Matthiola incana*). In addition to great fragrance, this hardy annual offers dense spikes of both pastel and rich-colored flowers in shades of red, rose, purple, white, and yellow. Stock is equally at home in cottage gardens, formal beds, or mixed borders. Narrow, gray-green leaves and sturdy stems make it an excellent choice for long-lasting cut flowers. As with most annuals, stock offers greatest impact if planted in masses.

Grow stock in fertile soil in either full sun or partial shade, and thin so that some air space remains between plants. Depending on which cultivar is chosen, expect stock to grow from 8 to 30 inches tall. Moderate salt tolerance makes it well suited to coastal gardens.

Pot marigold

Calendula officinalis
Family: Asteraceae (Daisy family)
Origin: Egypt, Southern Europe
Type: Cool-season annual
Size: 12–24 inches
Zones: All
Light: Sun to part sun
Water: Moderate
Varieties: 'Orange Porcupine', 'Citrus Smoothies', 'Touch of Red', others
Color: Orange, yellow, apricot, cream
Soil: Fertile, well-drained
Salt Tolerance: Moderate/Slight

Pot marigold (*Calendula officinalis*) may also be grown in beds or containers during our cool season. Flowers resemble gerberas and come in colors ranging from orange, apricot, and bright yellow, to lemon, cream, and nearly white. Dwarf cultivars are available that grow to about 12 inches tall, but standard cultivars grow twice that tall.

Though I grow pot marigold for the color it adds to the winter garden and to my bouquets, it has medicinal properties that are of interest to those who enjoy growing herbs. A variety of compounds are contained in the flowers which are known to stimulate the healing of wounds. It is anti-inflammatory and constricts blood vessels to stop bleeding. During the Civil War it was used to treat infection, and the Romans used it to treat scorpion bites.

With so many hardy annuals available, gardeners needn't limit their winter gardens to the more obvious choices. Search for these flowers and grow something different. All are easily started from seed, and nurseries often carry cell packs in the late fall.

HERBS FOR THE WINTER GARDEN

A friend e-mailed me a few weeks ago asking for a list of herbs to plant in her new herb garden. This friend is a Master Gardener (see sidebar), so of course, she knows how to amend her soil and prepare her planting bed. I'm sure that she has already selected a sunny spot, dug the area thoroughly, removed weeds and competing roots, added compost or organic matter, and readied it for planting. No doubt she has had her soil analyzed at the extension office and has made corrections if needed for pH and nutrient deficiencies. She has a general idea, too, of herbs that will work in her garden, but she wanted to be sure that she was not overlooking anything.

Several favorites come to mind immediately. Every year I make sure to sow seeds of cool-weather crops that grow easily from seed. These include mustard, kale, spinach, collards, turnips, carrots, chard, cabbage, broccoli, and cauliflower. Most people think when I mention these plants that I am talking about the vegetable garden. True, these are vegetables that can be cooked by the potful and served hot with cornbread and onions, but that is not how some people prefer to grow and use them. Just a few plants of each will enliven a salad or serve as an interesting garnish. They can also be a colorful addition to the garden if red mustards or vibrant 'Bright Lights' Swiss chard is planted. A few Oriental greens are also available and beckon from seed racks. One might try some of the Chinese cabbages, pac choi, or Japanese or Chinese greens with tantalizing names like mibuna and mizuna. Any of these plants will do well in my friend's herb garden.

Other annual winter herbs that will spice up salads and dishes include dill, fennel, and coriander. Green leafy vegetables like lettuce, mesclun mix, radishes, chervil, and arugula or roquette will add an interesting mixture of tastes and textures. Loose-leaf lettuces are particularly rewarding and are available in a wide range of leaf forms, flavors, and colors. Tasty green onion sets are available at most garden centers ready to plant in the fall herb garden.

In my garden, sorrel rebounds from summer doldrums and throws up fresh tasty leaves. Horseradish that has sulked all summer sends up new leaves up to two feet tall. Chives and garlic flourish in the cooler weather. Now is a good time to add these perennials to the herb garden.

Sage, rosemary, oregano, and thyme are absolute must-haves in the herb garden. These perennial herbs are probably most easily started from plants purchased from the nursery. Selecting them can be confusing for beginning gardeners. It helps if you go to the nursery knowing that there are several different varieties of these herbs. Sage (*Salvia officinalis*) can be purple-leaved, variegated with gold, white, and green, or solid green. All are equally effective in recipes. Rosemary can be upright or prostrate and trailing, and so can thyme. The most popular oregano used for seasoning is Spanish oregano

(*Origanum vulgare*), but also frequently chosen by discerning cooks is Greek oregano (*O. v.* var. *prismaticum*). Other oreganos are popular garden subjects, but not all are suitable for spaghetti sauce and pizza.

Save plenty of room for parsley. Readily available from most garden centers, it is essential for the herb garden. However, if several plants are wanted, it is easily started from seed. I even fill spots in the flower borders with the emerald green, curly-leaved variety of parsley. Some cooks prefer the smooth-leaved kind and claim that it offers better flavor in recipes. I know that my friend will want to plant enough (and also dill and fennel) to share with the Eastern black swallowtail butterfly caterpillars that will surely come next spring.

Flowers are not forgotten in the winter herb garden. Pansies, violas, and calendulas offer edible flowers. Nasturtiums supply an ample harvest of edible, peppery leaves as well as beautiful flowers that can be stuffed and eaten. Seeds of nigella and chamomile may be planted for early spring flowers.

My friend is starting her herb garden at an ideal time. She will enjoy it all winter. Next summer a new group of herbs can be grown, for growing herbs in the South is a year-round pleasurable activity.

What is a Master Gardener?

In 1972, an Extension Service Agent in the State of Washington reasoned that well-trained volunteers could respond to many everyday homeowner questions and free him and his colleagues for more technical and difficult problems. The Extension Agent selected, trained, and certified volunteers as Master Gardeners. They soon succeeded in meeting his desired objectives—in fact they exceeded his expectations. And so the Master Gardener Program began.

Since that time, the Master Gardener Program has grown and is now active in 45 states. Florida's program began in 1979. The program has been a tremendous success and is now active in over half of Florida's counties. The Florida Master Gardener Program is sponsored by the University of Florida's Institute of Food and Agricultural Sciences (IFAS) of which the Cooperative Extension Service is a part.

II
The Environmentally Sensitive Landscape, Some Considerations

THE EVOLUTION OF ENVIRONMENTAL CONSCIOUSNESS

Sometimes I think back to the days of my childhood in Mississippi and the gardens that I knew then. They were mostly vegetable gardens because a large and growing family depended on them for food. The ground was bare except for the plants we cultivated, and Daddy had plows and tools that kept the middles of his rows free of weeds. The weeds that remained were removed with a hoe. These gardens were enclosed with fences to keep out the cattle and deer. Dogs kept raccoons, 'possums, rabbits, and armadillos out of the yard and garden, just as the cats kept the mice under control in the barn.

Flowers that I grew were at the head of the vegetable garden in a special row that Daddy plowed for me. It was in this very special row that I spent many happy hours tending the flowers that I managed to collect from generous aunts, neighbors, and grandparents. Tending the flowers was fun, but I didn't mulch, and I knew nothing about insecticides or poisons. Fertilizer came from the cows, and it was the real stuff.

When a garden plot became unproductive, Daddy cleared a section of new ground. Trees and all other vegetation were removed, and the new plot was fenced in. Pete and Pat, the mules, were harnessed and put to work removing stumps and pulling the sod buster. For a few years we could count on vegetables that grew with renewed vigor and freedom from diseases that had built up in the old garden's soil. I guess Daddy was not much of a soil scientist. Fortunately, though, he had a few hundred acres from which to choose a new garden plot.

Also, in the country gardens of my childhood, there was not much ornamental horticulture. I suppose the people in town had shrubs attractively arranged around their houses, but we country children often bathed under the eaves during the summer showers that came with regularity. Our favorite jumping-off place was the front porch. Foundation shrubs would have been a nuisance.

Mother had a few bushes scattered around, but they were not in any seeming order. They were not arranged with an eye for how they would combine with other plants. Often they stood in isolation somewhere out in the yard—or in the far corner of it. They survived if they were strong enough. Others died as children and dogs ran along the edges of the fences with total disregard for the welfare of the plants.

We also used the sides of the house as protection from the sun during summer days. Early mornings were often spent picking peas or butterbeans. The rest of the day was spent shelling them and preparing them for the canning jars or for the freezer. We propped our chairs up on the shady side of the house until the sun changed sides. Then we moved to the other side so that we could continue our work in the shade. Pea hulls and corn shucks were fed to the cows. Tomato and potato peelings went to the pigs. We knew nothing about composting.

We burned everything that would burn, and we had a gully down the hill a good piece from the house. Glass bottles, tin cans, and items that could not be burned or consumed were tossed into the ravine. My brothers used the bottles and cans for target practice when they got new BB guns. I suppose over a period of years most of the items in the gully were reduced to rubble and leaves and other debris covered the refuse. That was our landfill.

Back then it was our way of life, and it was all we knew. Times change, though. The world today is different. We've learned a few things about taking care of the earth. Because of more people. Because of more garbage. Because of lots of reasons. Because we've had to.

Environmental consciousness has evolved.

POLLINATORS

Pollen in the air at certain times of year is troublesome for those of us who suffer seasonal allergies. What are these millions of tiny particles that cause such discomfort?

Pollen grains contain genetic information necessary for viable seed development, which is part of the reproductive cycle of flowering and cone-bearing plants. Genetic diversity, so important to healthy plant communities, is boosted when pollen is carried from one plant to another.

Of course, plants themselves cannot transport pollen from one to the other, so they must depend on another means of pollen transferal. Some depend upon the wind to blow the tiny grains from flower to flower. Others depend on wildlife to perform this essential function.

Exactly who are the wildlife participants that provide such a necessary service to life as we know it? According to the National Wildlife Federation, somewhere around 200,000 animals and insects serve as pollinators. They accept flowers' invitations to dine and drink the nutritious nectar offered. When they sip nectar, they gather pollen grains and transport them to the next flower, thereby accomplishing the critical task of fertilization.

The most common and perhaps most effective pollinators are bees. Hairy bodies and outstanding flying ability help them to perform this task. Generally, flowers pollinated by bees are those upon which they can land and in which they can crawl around to get nectar. More than 4,000 species of bees are native to North America.

Beetles of many kinds are attracted to plants that produce heavy pollen. Generally these beetles eat flower parts and pollen. With their clumsy flight, beetles need a flower that provides a handy landing platform. Often they are attracted to spicy or fruity odors.

Flower and bee flies pollinate many flowers. Some of these flies are attracted to foul-smelling flowers that smell like rotting meat or dung. Some flowers, such as our native buckeye, depend upon hummingbirds for pollination.

Butterflies are also important to the welfare of many plant species. They must have a place to land but are able to get nectar from deep within a flower with their long tongues. Night-blooming flowers are often visited by moths, which serve as their pollinators.

If we stayed up at night, we would likely see nectar-eating bats around pale or white night-blooming flowers. They seek flowers like those of the agave plant and many species of tall cacti. Usually these plants contain much nectar and have a strong musky or fruity odor.

Providing habitat for all of our pollinators is an important task. As a group, they are on the decline worldwide. Habitat destruction, use of chemical pesticides, spread of invasive exotic plants and animals that displace native species, and ignorance are some causes of this decline.

Our yards can be part of the solution. We can include a wide variety of flowers to attract each group of pollinators to our landscapes. By doing so, we not only increase the likelihood that they will survive; we increase our own chances, as well.

DIMINISHING WILDLIFE

Two causes for concern recently made their way to my mailbox. A United States Commission on Ocean Policy reported that about 40,000 acres of coastal wetlands are disappearing each year. They are being drained or filled in and paved over as houses, condominiums, and resorts spring up in their places. These disappearing wetlands provide essential spawning, feeding, and nursery areas for most of the nation's commercial fish catches. Coupled with continued harvesting and overfishing, 40 percent of our fish stocks have been depleted. The commission determined that the once seemingly boundless ocean resources have limits. Furthermore, ballast water from ships is spreading invasive alien species to new locales around the world.

The commission has concluded that our oceans, coasts, and

marine resources are in trouble. It reports that ocean pollution is caused largely from farmland and urban runoff. To compound the problem, human populations are increasing so much near shorelines that coastal management organizations are overwhelmed and unable to adequately process applications for new construction. Are we surprised? Is this news?

Another warning came from Bob Sargent of the Hummer/Bird Study Group in Clay, Alabama. The population of birds in general is decreasing, but Sargent specifically cited the case of neotropical migrants. These birds, of which there are at least 361 species ranging from herons and raptors to swallows and warblers, winter in Central and South America and then move northward each spring into the United States and Canada to nest and raise their young. Often they find their breeding grounds altered or destroyed. This means, sometimes, that there will be no baby birds in these disturbed areas. It happens season after season, and the results are catastrophic.

Sargent suggests several things that we can do. We can preserve the trees we have in our own yards. We can resist the temptation to turn our yards into wastelands of grass to be mowed, sprayed, and fertilized. Existing shrubbery and naturally occurring native plants can be left in place, and we can continue to add more. At the polls we can elect officials who are environmentally sensitive to the plight of wildlife and its rapidly disappearing habitat. Support of groups like The Nature Conservancy will help to secure lands that can be set aside for wildlife.

Sargent reminds us that the land we have now is all that there will ever be. The most insidious killer of wildlife and loss of their habitat is a "let-the-other-fellow-do-it" attitude. It's an attitude that we master gardeners and educators cannot afford to have. We must take corrective measures in our own yards and neighborhoods, and we must spread the word. The birds and fish can't talk, but we can. We're the only voice they have.

MAKE WISE PLANT CHOICES

Gardeners try hard to select plants that can live in harmony with each other, be healthy, and contribute to the beauty of our gardens. We continue to work for a balanced system in which all the plants and critters live together amicably. We make our choices, and then we live with the results—or spend much time and effort trying to overcome and correct our mistakes. We learn quickly that the plant choices that we make contribute to or detract from a balanced system.

Selecting a wide variety of plants is one key to a healthy garden. Planting a large number of the same species in an area gives insects and diseases a good chance to find all they need to survive for a long time. Consider lawn grasses, for example. Here thousands of grass plants are grown. If a disease or insect attacks, it finds all it needs for itself and for all of the offspring it can produce. So that is what it does—at the speed of light or faster, unless some action breaks the cycle or until all the grass is consumed.

A similar thing has happened with red-tip photinia. Introduced to the trade in the 1950s, this fast-growing evergreen shrub with red-tipped foliage quickly became popular. Everyone and his neighbor had to have at least one hedge made of this attractive shrub. Overplanting led to the quick spread of a leaf-spot fungus that caused the plants to decline or even die. Today this shrub is no longer a dependable landscape shrub for the South.

Often we plant exotic or nonnative plants in our yards. Some of these imports (though thank goodness, not all) find no natural enemies to keep them in check, and they proliferate exponentially. Consider the beautiful Mexican petunia [Color 41] (*Ruellia brittoniana*). Until a few years ago, I touted this perennial as one suited to our area—and I shared it with friends and wrote about it in newspapers and magazines. I thought it was a native plant.

Imagine my surprise when this plant was listed as an exotic invasive species for Florida. *Ruellia carolinensis* is native to the eastern U.S., but *Ruellia brittoniana* hails from Mexico and has naturalized in many parts of the South. This in itself does not make it bad. We learn of its wickedness when we notice that it is out-competing some of our native species and displacing them. In my own yard, I have been working hard to get rid of Mexican petunia. I had it in a bed with some beautiful native Stoke's aster. Before I became aware of it, the Stoke's aster was in trouble, and the Mexican petunia was headed for the herb garden and the rose bed.

A similar story could be told about the beautiful cashmere bouquet [Color 42] (*Clerodendron bungei*). I admired it in a friend's garden where delightful clusters of rosy red flowers bloomed with abandon. Of course, I wanted it for my garden. Ever since I planted it, though, I have been pulling it up—out of the lawn, out of the neighbor's garden, and wherever else it has managed to spread its suckering roots. Pulling it up has no effect. Three or four grow from the roots to take its place. Now I wish I had never seen this flower!

It's amazing just how gullible we gardeners are. Several years ago, our neighbor Aunt Lois had some pretty lavender-colored flowers that bloomed in late summer. They bloomed on spikes about a foot tall. I noticed that she never seemed to do anything to encourage them. As a matter of fact, they struggled for existence amid the briars and weeds that grew around them. "That," I thought, "is a plant for me!" I took a few of them and planted them in my enriched garden bed. Ever since, I've had a constant struggle to keep these plants in their place. I've done my best to get rid of them, including digging and practically sifting through the soil for pieces of root that were left in the ground. In spite of my best efforts, obedient plant (*Physostegia virginiana*) continues to be a pest in my garden. I realize that it is a native plant and is desirable in certain places where it can grow unimpeded in natural areas or in unimproved soils.

The same thing might be said of mock orange [Color 43] (*Philadelphus coronarius*). Somewhere I read that the flowers of this shrub were fragrant, and that it was even more beautiful than our native dogwood in the spring when it was completely covered with blossoms. To be perfectly honest, the shrub was beautiful in the spring. It attracted the orchard orioles that flitted from flower to flower in pursuit of nectar. However, it had not even a whiff of fragrance, and it was nondescript during the rest of the year. Several years after I planted it, I noticed little ones coming up all around it. They extended out into the lawn and under the fence into the neighbor's yard. I could plant nothing near it because its root system was so extensive.

Finally I tired of battling the hundreds of plants that came up in ever-increasing distances from the shrub. It became leggy and straggly and lost its favor with me. I had a hankering for a loquat, and I could find no other place to plant it than the exact spot occupied by the mock orange. The task of removing the ill-fated mock orange fell to Amiable Spouse. We could not believe the mass of roots that grew underneath the shrub. I understand that some cultivars of mock orange may have greater landscape value than the species. I will, however, think long and hard before I plant another one in my landscape.

ROOM FOR ALL

Thank God, I'm not a butterfly. The praying mantises, big-eyed bugs, and many of the other creatures that inhabit my garden eat butterflies—all stages of butterflies, from eggs to caterpillars to adults. The wasps that fly around the house search for handy chrysalides in which to deposit their eggs. The wasps' eggs hatch out and use butterfly chrysalides for food. Birds swoop down and claim the biggest, juiciest caterpillars for themselves

I thought I was doing something good when I bought the praying mantis egg cases at the garden center. I brought them home, hung them in a shrub, crossed my fingers, and hoped for the best.

I cheered each time I saw a big-eyed bug or an assassin bug. "These critters," I thought to myself, "will help me win the war against insect pests in my yard." I welcome lizards and toads of all kinds, and view many wasps as beneficial. Birds are also welcome in my wildlife-friendly yard. I have not always thought about the butterflies.

I've been trying to make my yard attractive to all these creatures. I know that others who are serious about butterflies rescue them in the egg stage and place them in rearing boxes. This protects them until they become adults and increases their chances for survival. Butterfly enthusiasts actively hunt down and kill some of the creatures I've worked hard to attract.

Lately, though, I've come to some realizations. I believe that in a balanced ecosystem there is a place for all these creatures. There must be enough bugs for the bugs that eat other insects, as well as for the frogs, wasps, and birds. It's the nature of things. If I just do my part to keep the poisons and other pollutants out of the ground and air, I will help them all to survive.

Part of being a good environmental steward is recognizing which bugs and critters are beneficial and which are not. Learning to control the bad ones and have minimal negative impact on the environment is another step in the right direction. No one wants the farmers' corn crops to be ruined by corn ear worms. If I plant a few tomato plants, I do not expect to share them with tomato horn worms. All the critters are not friendly, and some control measures are necessary.

CONTROLLING PESTS

Cultural Practices

Eek! It's a bug—and it's on my flower! Oh, horrors! What shall I do?

Every gardener at some time needs to control garden pests. Grabbing a sprayer full of poisons is tempting, but it is usually not the best course of action. Before reaching for the poisons, we should try every other means at our disposal to gain control over the diseases and insects that harm our gardens. It should be remembered that over 99 percent of all insects are either beneficial or harmless, and almost all spiders are beneficial.

Sometimes certain cultural practices are all we need to control insects and diseases. I don't know how many times I've heard Horticulture Extension Agent Larry Williams exclaim, "You've got to put the right plant in the right place!" He knows that no amount of care will make an impatiens perform well in the sun and that a blueberry or azalea must have acid soil. Zinnias must have sun to do their best. Gardeners near the beach have little success unless they choose salt-tolerant plants. Greatest success will be experienced if plants are matched to the conditions they need for optimal growth.

Another practice over which gardeners have control is when and how irrigation water is applied to the landscape. Many people believe that watering late in the day allows the soil to absorb more of the water and that less is lost to evaporation. Like I often told sixth-graders, folks must put on their thinking caps. Consider such diseases as molds, mildews, and fungi. One condition that encourages their growth is dampness over a long period of time. Watering late in the day keeps plants wet for the longest possible time and gives diseases a good foothold.

Furthermore, frequency of irrigation is important. Plants should be watered only when a need is evidenced, and not every day come heck or high water. Infrequent but deep watering encourages deep root systems and vigorous plants that can withstand droughts and other adverse conditions. Some plants that are overwatered are simply not allowed to develop into the strong plants that they are capable of becoming.

The gardener should therefore figure out the watering schedule that will allow the plants to be wet for the shortest amount of time. Best results seem to be achieved when plants are watered early in the morning while the dew is still on the ground. When the sun comes up, the drying process begins, and in our humid climate plants need all of the drying hours that can be managed.

When we do see a disease or insect problem, we might try some nonpolluting options. Sometimes it makes sense simply to remove and destroy infected plants or plant parts. After a few seasons of putting this action into practice, you will have gardens filled with plants that are resistant to diseases and insects. With so many plants from which to choose, why choose one that requires constant care to keep it healthy? Get rid of insect and disease-ridden plants that cause worry and extra care!

Sometimes all we need is a bit of tolerance. Felder Rushing, horticulturalist from Mississippi, advises gardeners to step back three large paces, remove their glasses, and then look to see if an insect is causing great damage. If damage is not evident during the performance of this test, the problem requires no action. Of course, a watchful eye must be kept on the offending insect to be sure that the population comes under control through some appropriate action, such as releasing beneficial insects, hand picking, or spraying with a strong jet of water.

A healthy plant is perhaps our best line of defense against insects and diseases. Often the best course of action is to build the soil and give plants a fighting chance. Soil and soil-dwelling creatures that promote plant growth appreciate lots of organic matter. Do not shortchange your garden by failing to provide this important component. Organic mulch will enrich the soil as it decomposes, as well as retain moisture and retard weed growth.

Overfertilizing is another harmful practice. When more fertilizer is applied than a plant can use, the extra is simply washed through the soil and on to China, or into our water system, whichever comes first. Excessive growth caused by overfertilization makes caring for the garden more labor intensive since more pruning and mowing may be required. Fertilize just enough to promote adequate growth and leaf color.

Other cultural practices, such as crop rotation, yield beneficial results. Do not give diseases and insect pests an advantage by planting the same plants in the same place year after year.

Companion planting may also help. Did you know, for instance, that onions repel cabbage butterflies and help all members of the cabbage family? Did you know that chives are good companions for fruit trees and tomatoes, and that roses love garlic? And did you know that growing peas and beans fixes nitrogen in the soil and makes the earth more productive?

Before reaching for the sprayer full of poison to keep insects and diseases under control, think on these things. Let's put some of these cultural practices to work. How much better it will be for us and for the earth if we can leave the poisons out of our gardens!

Physical Controls

Many times pest plants or insects can be controlled simply by using physical methods to remove a pest from an area or to block its entry into an area. Often a little more work is involved, but the results are great. No insecticides are necessary, the environment suffers no ill effects, and the pest is dealt with effectively.

Sometimes all that is needed is a fly swatter. Bugs can be knocked to the ground and stomped on, or they can be picked by hand and dropped into a pail of soapy water. They can be vacuumed, or they can be prevented entry by various means. Entry points around doors and walls can be caulked. Floating row covers (netting designed to spread over plants) prevent insects' access to vegetable plants. Barriers can be made by removing both ends of a can or plastic cup and placing them around plants to form a collar against cutworms or certain vine borers.

Weed control offers several options. Weeds can, of course, be pulled by hand before they set seed. Large areas of infestation can be covered with black or clear plastic and left for four to six weeks. A good layer of mulch often inhibits weed growth. Corn gluten meal sprinkled on turf grass will inhibit root formation during germination of annual weeds such as dandelions and crabgrass.

Traps provide another physical means of controlling insects. Yellow jackets can be lured into narrow-necked bottles or jars containing fruit juice. I remember a time at Ruckel Middle School in Niceville, Florida, when the pesky critters entered the classroom every time the door was opened. One of the science teachers saved the day (many days, actually) when she had her students make simple traps out of plastic soda bottles with a bit of sugar water in them for an attractant. They were hung in trees and bushes around the school. Our problems with the critters diminished dramatically.

Nocturnal insects like to hide in rolled-up pieces of moistened newspaper or paper towel rolls. Simply lay them out in the evening. The next morning pick them up, tie them in a plastic bag, and toss them into the garbage.

Sticky fly strips are effective when hung in small enclosed areas. Flies like to light on narrow yellow strips, where they get stuck and cannot fly away. Similar sticky traps catch aphids and whiteflies attracted by the bright yellow color. These sticky traps can be bought ready for action, or they can be made with plastic strips coated with Tanglefoot or other sticky substances.

Many physical means may be employed to control slugs. Stale bread attracts them in droves. Sprinkle it around your plants and pick it up the following day—loaded with the slimy critters. Circle plants with crushed eggshells to stop them in their scummy tracks. Diatomaceous earth, a mined material composed of the fossilized remains of ancient sea-dwelling diatoms (plantlike creatures), cuts their nasty bodies into shreds. Lay down some wooden planks along the garden path and look under them the following morning. You'll have to scrape the slugs off with a stick or piece of wood. Sprinkle coffee grounds around slug-infested plants. They dislike the taste, I suppose. They don't return for seconds, and they avoid the area. Of course, we've all learned that beer attracts the pesky mollusks. Simply pour some beer in a shallow container such as a cat food can and sink it in the ground level with the soil. Slugs will come to the party and will drown in the brew.

According to one gardener, birds go after his tomatoes and straw-berries only if the birdbaths have no water in them. As long as he kept water available for the birds, they left his vegetables alone. That, of course, did nothing to solve his problem with squirrels, but we often face such dilemmas and have to figure out a solution. Persistence pays.

Next time you're in the garden and observe plant damage caused by pest weeds, insects, or other critters, try some of these physical controls. You may find that both you and the environment will be healthier.

Beneficial Insects

So we struggle along in our efforts to have a beautiful garden. We have paid attention to certain cultural practices that help our gardens stay healthy. We've chosen noninvasive plants and put them in the right places. Correct watering practices have encouraged strong root systems, and mold and mildew are minimal. Plants that were decimated by diseases or insects have been removed and replaced with plants that tolerate the conditions we're able to provide. We've become tolerant of a few chewed leaves, and we have improved the soil to get plants off to a good start. Crop rotation, companion planting, and correct fertilization have helped our gardens thrive.

We've made conscious choices about how we tend our gardens, and in the process we have tried to do our part to care for our planet. Our decisions have been based partly on our determination to cause no damage to the environment. The ideal is not to interfere at all with the natural system but to aim for a condition in which the good bugs police the bad ones.

Often when pests are repeatedly treated with the same insecticide, they become immune to it so that repeated spraying has little effect. At other times, gardeners may use a broad spectrum insecticide that kills all insects—beneficial as well as destructive. When all the beneficials are killed, no natural controls are left in the garden. When pests return, they multiply rapidly and a phenomenon called pest flareback occurs. Then we gardeners must face a larger-than-ever population of the pests we were trying to control.

Beneficial insects in our gardens go a long way toward helping us win the battle against pest insects. Ladybugs and green lacewing larvae, for instance, prey on aphids, mites, and other soft-bodied insects. Certain small wasps lay eggs on the eggs, larvae, or chrysalides of other insects. When the wasps hatch out, they feed on the host, which kills it. Other useful insects include spined soldier bugs, ground beetles, minute pirate bugs, praying mantises, syrphid flies, and predatory stink bugs.

Where are these beneficial creatures to be found? Often we can grow plants that are particularly useful in attracting them. Plants like caraway, coriander, blazing star, coreopsis, cosmos, and goldenrod entice a large number of beneficial insects. Sunflowers, yarrow, sweet alyssum, candytuft, and many of the salvias are also excellent. A natural area complete with wildflowers and "weeds" provides a safe haven for these insect friends to live and breed.

Also, many companies sell beneficial insects in containers. Lacewings, praying mantises, and lady beetles come nicely packaged and ready for release. Be sure to purchase a nectar food spray to encourage the young larvae to stay in your garden and work for you.

Following a few easy rules will encourage predators and parasites of plant pests to stay in your garden. Provide a diversity of nectar- and pollen-producing flowers that bloom throughout the growing season. Water in a birdbath or pond is helpful in attracting many beneficials.

One of the most important things for the gardener to do, of course, is learn to recognize the beneficials. Little is gained if the gardener can't tell the heroes from the villains. Pictures of beneficial insects can be found in various books, publications, and websites.

Keep in mind that beneficial insects must have a food supply, so if all the bad guys leave, the beneficials will, too. We would all do well to remember that in the best of circumstances, it's a bug-eat-bug world out there. Our efforts to augment this process will benefit us all.

Biological Controls

Adding to the effectiveness of good cultural practices is another method of control that will give gardeners additional weapons in their battle against insect pests. Environmentally conscious gardeners have learned about certain biological controls that may be enlisted in the fight.

Biological controls—commonly called biologicals—include insects, mites, nematodes, and microbial organisms as well as other organisms like birds and bats. When a gardener decides to use biologicals, he simply uses organisms that feed upon or infect plant pests as a method of keeping them under control. Natural enemies exist for most of the major pests of vegetable and ornamental crops. Some of these natural enemies are biologicals that can be purchased and introduced into the garden, and others are usually present or easily attracted.

Beneficial insects are important biological controls. Some of the insects are predators, and others are parasitoids. Predatory beneficials kill by chewing or stabbing with tubelike mouthparts.

Particularly useful predators are lady beetles, assassin bugs, and praying mantises. Parasitoids include certain flies and wasps which lay their eggs in or on other insects. Then the parasitoid eggs hatch and the larvae become predators of their host insect.

Certain mites and spiders are predaceous. Predaceous mites feed on plant-eating spider mites. Many spiders catch prey in webs, and others hide among foliage and flowers and snatch a meal at opportune times.

Beneficial nematodes are helpful in controlling many lawn and soil pests. The very word "nematode" strikes fear in the heart of the gardener. We're all too familiar with the dreaded root knot nematodes (tiny soil-dwelling worms that damage plants by feeding on roots). Some nematodes, however, are beneficial. They are microscopic parasites that attack and kill such pests as cutworms, squash borers, Japanese beetle grubs, mole crickets, and more. They bore into their victims, feed on them and reproduce without attacking plants in any way.

Beneficial nematodes are sold in packages of 5, 10, or 25 million. They may be packaged on a wet sponge or in some other medium. Those that I purchased were packaged in a box of vermiculite, and to activate them, I simply mixed the vermiculite with about five gallons of water and then sloshed it out all over my lawn area. I have my fingers crossed, because they are supposed to control mole crickets and other lawn pests.

Certain bacteria are used to fight specific pests. For instance Bt (*Bacillus thuringiensis*) is a naturally occurring bacterium that affects larvae of various insects, including mosquitoes and black flies, as well as a wide array of the butterfly and moth larvae. Different strains produce toxins that affect different insects. To be effective, it must be eaten. After ingestion, it destroys the gut lining which results in death.

The primary benefit of Bt is that it is highly selective in its action. Most Bt products kill only the caterpillars that eat it. Therefore it has no effect on most beneficial insects. It is considered safe to humans and can be used right up to harvest. It should be remembered, however, that Bt kills not only the larvae of pests, but also the larvae of butterflies. It is absolutely essential to target specific insects and keep it away from plants where butterfly larvae feed.

Milky spore is a bacterium used to control Japanese beetle grubs. Grasshoppers can be controlled with grasshopper pathogen (*Nosema locustae*).

It is important to remember when using a biological control that results will not be immediate. Sometimes multiple applications or regular releases are necessary. Also, do not expect all pests to vanish. Natural enemies rely on pests for food, so if they completely eliminate their food supply, they will starve.

Use of these biological controls will enable us to minimize the use of insecticides. Even so, they should be used knowledgeably and with awareness of the effect they have on the environment and other critters. We still won't rush out and spread biological controls willy-nilly throughout the landscape. We will, however, store them in our memory banks and pull them out when conditions warrant.

Insecticides

Once a pest population becomes unmanageable, a decision must be made. The gardener can decide to uproot and discard the plant, to simply live with the damage, or hope it will correct itself. Sometimes the decision may be made to try to control the pest by spraying or treating with something that will kill the offending critter.

This is a difficult decision, and one that must be approached with knowledge and awareness of the consequences the action will have on the environment. Such a decision should be made, of course, only after cultural practices, physical and biological controls, and beneficial insects have not achieved acceptable results.

It stands to reason, then, that if a decision is made to spray, the gardener will use the least toxic control and the one that will decompose most rapidly. It also stands to reason that the gardener will mix just enough of the killing spray to do the job, and then will confine the spraying to the smallest possible area.

We know, of course, that the least toxic spray is water. Many times, a strong jet of water is all that is needed to dislodge and displace insects. Studies show that high-pressure sprays knock off aphids, spider mites, thrips, caterpillars, and other wingless pests. Once knocked to the ground, they often either drown or are eaten by birds and other predators.

Insecticidal soap is a frequently used insect control that has little toxicity to the environment. Soap penetrates the insect's outer coat and appears to cause suffocation and/or membrane disruption. Effects are rapid and usually result in the death of susceptible insects within a few minutes after exposure. The insect must come in contact with the wet spray. Once it is dry, the insect will not be affected by walking over or ingesting plant material that has been treated with soap. Consequently, soaps should be applied at times when the plant can remain wet for the longest possible time, and foliage should be sprayed thoroughly on upper and lower leaf surfaces, on stems, and all parts of the plant. Insecticidal soap does not leave a residue, and crops can be harvested the same day. It is said to be no more toxic to humans and other mammals than dishwashing or bath soap. However, like other soaps, it may cause some eye irritation.

Insecticidal soaps may be toxic to some plants. If symptoms such as yellow or brown spotting on the leaves, burned tips, or leaf scorch occur, discontinue use. Some plants, such as Japanese maple, jade plant, lantana, gardenia, bleeding heart, and crown of thorns, are known to be sensitive. Certain cultivars of azalea, poinsettia, begonia, impatiens, ferns, palms, and succulents may also be sensitive. It makes sense to spot treat part of the plant and wait at least 24 hours to see if symptoms develop. Young, tender growth, drought-stressed plants, or young transplants are also more likely to be harmed.

While effective against most soft-bodied insects, insecticidal soap generally does not affect adult beetles, bees, and wasps because of the hardness of their body cuticle. Adding horticultural oil to the soap mixture may increase the effectiveness for harder-to-kill insects.

Horticultural oils are sometimes used to control aphids, mites, leafhoppers, mealybugs, scales, plant lice, and mosquito larvae. While most of these oils are made from refined petroleum, some vegetable oil-based sprays are now available. Horticultural oils are divided into two categories—summer oil and dormant oil. Summer oil is light and can be applied during the summer months to green foliage. Dormant oil is thicker and should be applied to deciduous trees and shrubs while they are dormant in late winter or early spring.

Horticultural oil suffocates soft-bodied insects and mites by blocking the air holes (spiracles) through which they breathe. Like soaps, oils act strictly through contact. Be sure when using oil to spray under the leaves, in branch crotches, and around the trunks. Insects can hide in tiny crevices.

Horticultural oils are designed to be mixed with water, so it is important to read directions thoroughly. Damage can occur if oil sprays are applied at temperatures below 40°F or above 90°F. Damage can also occur on plants suffering from drought. Certain plants such as maples, walnut, and cedar cannot tolerate oil sprays, so caution is advised.

Sometimes insecticidal soap and oil are mixed together. Then pests have a double whammy. Many homemade recipes exist for both insecticidal soap and horticultural oil and mixtures of both, but commercially prepared mixtures are less likely to cause harm to foliage. The effects of homemade mixtures on plants and insects have not been tested and are more likely to cause damage. If you try homemade mixtures, use pure, mild soaps such as Dove, Ivory, or Castile. The soap should have no perfumes or detergents that could cause harm to plants. It should not be extrastrength, grease-cutting, or antibacterial soap.

As with other insecticides, oil and soap sprays cannot distinguish between beneficial and pest insects, so care must be taken to apply them to pest infestations only. Never, ever, should an insecticidal spray be applied in hopes that it will prevent a pest outbreak.

"Why, then," you may ask, "should I use insecticidal soaps or horticultural oils instead of more traditional insecticides?" The answer is that many traditional insecticides cause a great deal of damage to humans and other mammals, not to mention the environment. Generally, soaps and oils pose little or no threat us, and they degrade rapidly in the environment. They are, therefore, a more environmentally friendly approach to pest control.

Botanical Controls

Botanical insecticides are naturally occurring plant extracts and compounds that have insecticidal properties. Many people believe them to be safer or less dangerous than synthetic insecticides. In fact, botanical insecticides (botanicals) include some of the fastest-acting, most deadly toxins known. They vary greatly in their toxicity to humans as well as to nontarget organisms. All pesticides, whether natural or synthetic, are regulated as pesticides by the Environmental Protection Agency.

The main advantage of botanicals over synthetic insecticides is that they decompose quickly in the environment since they are broken down by oxygen and sunlight. This means that their residues are less likely to endanger our soil, water supply, pets, people, or wildlife.

Botanical sprays or dusts may be another weapon in the pest control arsenal, but they should be used with all precautions recommended when using synthetic pesticides. Resort to them only after less drastic measures have been tried, like insect predators and parasites, traps, and barriers. Be sure that saving the crop is worth the risk, and by all means, know exactly what the risk is.

Rotenone is a botanical derived from the roots of several leguminous plants. It is a broad-spectrum contact and stomach poison, affecting nerve and muscle cells. It causes insects to stop feeding and die within a few hours or days. It is extremely toxic to fish and aquatic life, and is moderately toxic to humans and other mammals. Inhaling large amounts of Rotenone can be dangerous.

Sabadilla dust comes from the ground seeds of a tropical lily. The alkaloids in the product affect the nerve cells of insects and cause paralysis and eventual death. The dust is considered the least toxic of all registered botanical insecticides. In its pure, extracted form, however, it is as toxic as the strongest synthetic insecticide. A person can become sick if it is ingested or absorbed through the skin and mucous membranes. It is a broad-spectrum contact and stomach poison. Use it to control such pests as stink bugs, blister beetles, and other adult insects which are hard to control by other means. Be aware that Sabadilla also kills honeybees and other beneficial insects.

Ryania comes from the stems of *Ryania speciosa*, a South American shrub. It is a stomach poison which causes insects to stop feeding soon after they eat it. Ryania is considered relatively nontoxic to mammals, but it breaks down more slowly in the environment than other botanicals. It is sold primarily as a control for codling moths that frequently harm apple crops.

Nicotine is one of the most toxic substances sold for use in the garden. Extremely fast-acting, it causes severe disruption and failure of the nervous system. It must be a weapon of last resort. It should be noted that no insect has ever developed immunity to this poison.

Pyrethrum is another broad-spectrum insecticidal powder which is made from the dried flowers of the pyrethrum daisy, *Chrysanthemum cinerariifolium*. It is fast acting and disrupts the nervous system and causes paralysis. Many insects, however, have the ability to metabolize Pyrethrum, and they can recover. It is not particularly toxic to humans and other mammals, or to birds and other wildlife. Also, it degrades rapidly when exposed to light, air, or moisture.

Neem is derived from the seeds of the neem tree, *Azadirachta indica*. It is used as a general cleaning chemical and is found in many toothpastes, cosmetics, pharmaceuticals, and other products. It seems to act as a systemic with repellent and growth regulator effects on insects and mites. It affects the hormones many insects need to develop, so they are killed as they attempt to molt or emerge from eggs. Many leaf-chewing beetles and caterpillars can be controlled with neem insecticides. Aphids and most other sucking insects seem to be less susceptible. Because of its lack of toxicity to humans, it was recently exempted by the EPA from food-crop restrictions. It is marketed for use on any edible or ornamental plant.

Other botanical insecticides exist, but these are the most commonly available ones. As with all insecticides, use them cautiously and with full knowledge of their effects on the environment and you.

Sometimes we gardeners are so concerned about pest insects and diseases that we forget that plants can be pests, too. Often we are rudely awakened when we see such pests as Japanese honeysuckle and kudzu running at breakneck speed across the countryside. Sometimes these invasives grow in our own backyards.

EXOTIC INVASIVES

What are They, and What's the Big Deal, Anyway?

They're everywhere, and they're running amok across the country. Exotic space-grabbing, tree-smothering, stream-choking invaders are here. Infesting acres of land and threatening plants and animals throughout the region, they are cause for great concern. They are a group of plants that we call exotic invasives.

The term "exotic plant" is not in itself bad. In the U.S. the term refers to a plant with a natural range that did not include particular places at the time of European contact (1500 CE). And really, they're not from outer space, but they have been brought here from other countries. Some of our most popular landscape plants—camellias and some azaleas, for example—are exotics.

A native plant is a species whose natural range included any given area at the time of European contact. A naturalized exotic is an exotic that sustains itself outside cultivation. An invasive exotic, however, is an exotic gone wild that has naturalized and is expanding on its own in plant communities. These are the ones about which we are most concerned.

The Florida Exotic Pest Plant Council separates exotic invasives into two groups: Category I and Category II. Category I invasive exotics are altering native plant communities by displacing native species, by changing community structures or ecological functions, or by hybridizing with natives. This definition relies on documented ecological damage caused.

Category II invasive exotics are those that have increased in abundance or frequency but have not yet altered Florida plant communities to the extent shown by Category I species. They may be ranked Category I in the future; therefore, they bear close scrutiny.

Examination of lists of invasive plants from other Southern states reveals that many of Florida's invasive plants are of concern throughout the South. The Southeast Exotic Pest Plant Council and exotic pest plant councils from other Southern states are all concerned about such pests as kudzu, Chinese tallow, Chinese privet, and mimosa.

Several characteristics allow the exotic invasives to do their dirty deeds. Many are heavy seed producers. Their seeds can be spread by wind, water, yard trimmings, or by birds and other wildlife that eat the fruit. Many spread by well-protected, below-ground rhizomes. Invasive exotics are able to spread partly because natural predators that controlled the plants in the country of origin were not imported with them. Native predators in our country are too few or even nonexistent.

Often we don't know immediately if an imported plant is invasive. Sometimes there is a "lag phase" of decades to centuries before a plant spreads exponentially. In the case of kudzu, there was an apparent lag phase of 10 to 20 years before any problems were noticed.

Many are shade tolerant, so they become established under developed forest canopies. Before the problem is noticed, they are well established and in the process of taking over the forest. Others quickly invade riparian (relating to or situated on the banks of a river; lake, pond, bay, or other body of water) habitats and quickly exclude native understory plants. Regeneration of native trees and plants is prevented.

The initial spread of exotics along highway and utility rights-of-way, disturbed habitats, and riparian systems, enables them to migrate easily into adjoining forest areas. Because many disturbed habitats occur in cities, exotics present severe problems for urban forestry programs. Natural succession and reforestation are often prevented or retarded by invasive exotic plants. Often they grow in groups, and efforts to retard one of them may allow another one to spread exponentially.

Biodiversity is decreased in natural reserves and parks and detracts from the parks' primary mission of preserving native species. The reduction in biodiversity can also adversely impact wildlife and alter natural processes such as fire and water flow.

According to the U.S. Fish and Wildlife Service, invasive plants out-compete agricultural crops for soil and water resources, reduce crop quality, interfere with harvesting, and reduce land values. On rangelands, invasive plants crowd out more desirable and nutritious forage, cause soil erosion, and poison some wildlife and livestock species. Alarmingly, three million acres are lost to invasive plants each year.

There are many culprits. Living and spreading profusely in Northwest Florida include what University of Florida Extension Agent Sheila Dunning calls "the dirty dozen." Plants included in this group are chinaberry, Chinese privet, popcorn tree, cogon grass, hydrilla, Japanese climbing fern, Japanese honeysuckle, kudzu, mimosa, torpedo grass, tropical soda apple, and water hyacinth. Although these may be some of the worst invaders, this list is far from complete. According to an article published by the Nature Conservancy, ecologists rank invaders second only to habitat loss as threats to biodiversity. Among imperiled species in the United States, 49 percent are threatened by invasive alien species. Exotics cost the nation an estimated $138 billion a year, according to scientists at Cornell University. On one section of Sanibel Island in Florida,

Brazilian peppers and Australian pines are the only plants that exist in an area that once had 70 species of native plants. The U. S. government estimates that alien species of plants invade approximately 4,600 acres of land daily.

SOME WIDE-SPREAD EXOTIC INVASIVES
Are They Growing in Your Yard?

Air Potato *(Dioscorea bulbifera)*
A few weeks ago while I was visiting a friend, she asked me to identify a vine that had recently appeared in her garden. I recognized it at once. It was that infernal air potato.

"You'd better pull that thing up immediately!" I cautioned her. "If you allow it to grow, it will overtake everything in your yard!"

I spoke from experience. A few years back I admired the vine growing in a friend's yard and asked for a start, which she willingly gave. The first year I enjoyed its presence in my garden. The second year wasn't so bad, so I planted some on my back fence. The fourth and fifth years saw its spread to the vacant lot behind mine, and I have begun to fight a seemingly losing battle against the exponential spread of this aggressive pest. Other people, too, fight constant battles. Each year in Gainesville, Florida, groups of people get together to remove the vines from natural areas. They vow to "take back their natural areas, one potato at a time."

I am not proud to say this, but my next-door neighbor admired the vine. She pulled some potatoes from the vines that I am struggling to remove from the fence that separates our properties. She planted them in her yard, and the neighbor across the street admired hers. Now they are climbing the beautiful live oaks across the street. Very recently I have seen potatoes for sale at some individual plant sales. They sell like hot cakes to unsuspecting and inexperienced gardeners.

On each of my trips to Winter Park, Florida, I am amazed at the air potatoes that I see invading our state garden clubs' headquarters and Meade Gardens next door. Air potato, like kudzu and other exotic invasives, is a monster on the loose that is intent on establishing a monoculture where nothing except itself will grow.

Air potato has spread throughout much of Florida, as well as parts of Louisiana, Mississippi, and Texas. Research documented this statement, and I cannot help but believe it is equally as aggressive in Alabama, Georgia, South Carolina, and other southern states. It is a relative of the yam, and it is highly decorative as it climbs up various supports. Any gardener who sees it would want a start—until they learn of its malicious intent. It can reach well into the canopy of trees 60 or more feet tall.

Ridding an area of air potatoes can be an endless, frustrating task. The vines grow as fast as eight inches a day, and tubers of various sizes and shapes form in the axils of the leaves. In late summer and fall as many as 200 of these tubers may drop to the ground from each vine. If not collected, each one will sprout the following spring. Oaks, palms, and other trees are devastated by the vicious vines.

The vine is native to tropical Asia and Africa. It disrupts native plant communities by forming impenetrable thickets on native trees and shading out understory vegetation. It therefore negatively impacts wildlife that is dependent on native plants for forage, nesting, and cover. Also, it interferes with ecosystem integrity by threatening biodiversity and ecosystem stability in natural areas.

If the warning is a little late and your property is well on its way to being an air potato jungle, you may wish to consider some control options. The vines can, of course, be pulled by hand, and they can be disconnected from the stems to prevent aerial "potato" production. Underground tubers can be dug and placed in a black plastic bag until they have degraded, or they can be burned. Diligence is required. Continue to hand-pull all sprouting vines.

Once we know about the invasive potential of this vine, of course we do not plant it in our landscapes under any circumstances. We never share with our neighbors, even if they ask, and we discourage offers at plant sales and other sources where uninformed people dispense them willingly.

If each of us works to inform all our friends and neighbors of the potential of this vine, maybe we can make some difference to the health of our environment. We must, if we are to continue to enjoy natural areas with diverse plants that sustain wildlife and ultimately even ourselves.

Chinaberry Tree (*Melia azedarach*)

All around the South, chinaberry trees bloom in spring. Fragrant clusters of lavender flowers appear from March to May on plants just a few years old. In the early evening, walking by a blooming Chinaberry tree is a pleasant experience. It is an eye-catcher in woods and landscapes where it is easily spotted while in bloom.

Chinaberry is native to southeastern Asia and northern Australia and is a member of the mahogany family of plants. It is a fast-growing, short-lived tree that has a rounded crown and can grow up to 50 feet tall with a 20-foot spread. For more than 200 years it has been a popular landscape tree in the United States because it has attractive flowers and large compound leaves, and it provides quick shade.

Flowers mature to greenish-yellow and then to tan. Fruits about a half inch in diameter persist after the leaves fall. They made excellent bullets to use in battles against my brothers and boy cousins half a century ago. The shiny, hard seeds have been used as beads for rosaries. The Chinese use extracts from the bark and fruit to kill parasitic roundworms. Research shows it to have insecticidal, antiviral, and possibly anticancer properties. The wood has been used as fuel wood, as well as for flooring.

Unfortunately, this tree has escaped cultivation and become naturalized in Florida and in 11 other states, including Hawaii and Texas. In Florida it is listed as a Category I exotic invasive species. Like other invasives, its seeds are readily dispersed by birds. A single tree in a yard can cause a thicket of chinaberry trees in a short time. It thrives in a variety of soils and is hardy from Zones 7 to 10.

All parts are toxic. In humans, ingestion of the berries can slow heart rate and can cause diarrhea, vomiting, depression, weakness, seizures, and shock. Reportedly, eating just six berries can result in death. Although birds seem to love the berries, some have been known to become paralyzed after eating them. Bark, leaves, and seeds are poisonous to farm and domestic animals.

Chinese Privet (*Ligustrum sinense*)

Finally Amiable Spouse responded to my request and cut down the variegated Chinese privet, also called Chinese ligustrum. It had been in the yard for years and had been pruned back countless times. Usually it was quite attractive in its place in the side yard, and the birds liked it. I think that maybe Amiable Spouse liked it, too, but he understood the situation after I showed him problems it was causing around the neighborhood.

I felt that it was our responsibility to remove the variegated shrub. Foliage on some of the branches kept reverting to solid green, seed-bearing branches. Also, the variegated cultivar is capable of producing seeds. When these seeds germinate, it is the solid green form of the plant that comes up.

I have also noticed a number of these shrubs in neighbors' yards. In some instances, as much as half the shrub has reverted to solid green. The homeowners evidently don't know the havoc that these fruiting branches will cause to delicate ecosystems nearby. The shrub is capable of forming dense, impenetrable thickets. It can dominate the shrub layer of an invaded habitat. Like other invasives, it alters the ecosystem by choking out native plants.

A drive through any of the southeastern states reveals miles and miles of Chinese ligustrum. It comes up along fence rows and then spreads out into the woods. Mississippi State University lists it as one of Mississippi's ten worst invasive weeds. The Georgia Exotic Pest Plant Council also has it on its top ten, and the Florida Exotic Pest Plant Council lists it as a Category I invasive plant. Tennessee and Kentucky list it as a severe threat, and it is on Virginia's list of highly invasive plants.

This invasive plant is a member of the olive family which was introduced into the South as an ornamental in 1852. By 1933 it had naturalized, and a few years later it was recognized as a noxious weed. It grows to about 12 feet tall and wide and is hardy to Zone 6.

Ligustrum sinense thrives in sun or heavy shade and in flood plains or low wet places. It frequently invades disturbed sites, but it also finds its way into less disturbed upland hammocks and pinelands. So adaptable is this hardy shrub that it can even thrive in the crack of a sidewalk.

Chinese privet is distinguished from other privets by the presence of fine hairs on the twigs and undersides of leaves. Clusters of small, four-petaled white flowers bloom in spring and give way to fleshy blue fruits less than a quarter-inch in diameter. Birds like the fruits and scatter them widely. Michael Dirr confirms that this privet can be found in the South anyplace that birds fly.

The Virginia Department of Conservation and Recreation recommends controlling plants by hand if the stem is less than one inch in diameter. The entire root must be removed. Any root not removed will sprout, so plowing or mechanical methods that cut the roots into pieces will result in many new plants. To kill the plant effectively, apply a foliar application of glyphosate or apply it to the stump immediately after the plant is cut down.

Many people continue to plant these invasives in their landscapes. They are fooled by the pretty variegated form of this ecosystem-destroying monster. It is hoped that more and more people will learn to recognize it and refuse to give it a chance.

Elephant Ears (*Colocasia esculenta*)

Other plants that cause great concern are the large elephant ears that grow in streams or damp places in many parts of the South. Sometimes called taro, wild taro, dasheen, or cocoyam, these perennial herbs look beautiful lining the streams. The arrowhead-shaped leaves grow to be about 24 inches long and 20 inches wide, and an exotic flower blooms near the ground. The upper leaf surface is dark green and velvety. Plants grow about four to six feet tall and make a bold statement in the landscape.

Elephant ears grow from a large corm (enlarged underground stem) that produces offsets from which new plants grow. Slender stolons, or prostrate stems, grow at the surface of the ground and produce new plants. They can grow in a wide range of dry to wet sites in either sun or shade and are primarily spread by movement of vegetative fragments. Only a small piece of corm is needed to produce a new plant. With such easy means of propagation, they spread at lightning speed under favorable circumstances.

In areas outside the coastal and tropical South, elephant ears may not be as invasive. The tops get killed to the ground at 30°F. In areas where the ground freezes, corms may be lifted and stored during the winter and set back out the following spring. Caution is advised, however, for these plants can escape cultivation, and they are difficult to confine near bodies of water or in wet areas.

Taro was brought from Africa to the Americas as a food crop for slaves. It was introduced into Florida and other southern states in 1910. The Department of Agriculture recommended it as a substitute crop for potatoes. By 1974 it had been labeled an aggressive weed. Until the 1980s, however, it was promoted as a food, feed, and fuel crop for Florida. It is now naturalized in Florida and other areas of the South along streams, marshy shores, canals, and ditches. In 1990 it was reported as naturalized in 183 of Florida's public water bodies. By 1994 it had spread to 235 public water bodies. Today it continues to march across the tropics and much of the subtropics. It has been reported in natural areas in southern Georgia, Alabama, Louisiana, Mississippi, and Texas.

So what makes it an exotic invasive? Of course, one main thing is its ease of propagation. Another is its allelopathic characteristics. It produces a toxin that suppresses growth of nearby plants. It is therefore able to out-compete native plants. Wildlife that depended on the natives that once grew on the site now has nothing to support it. The area becomes a monoculture that sustains nothing but itself.

What can we do about the taro growing in nearby waterways? We can encourage the city crews to remove it from the streams. We can eliminate any plants that grow on our own property. Mechanical harvesting or mowing does not control taro. Repeated treatments with herbicides like 2,4-D or 2,4-D and glyphosate provide acceptable temporary results. However, physical removal of the corms is required for eradication from aquatic sites.

Mimosa (*Albizia julibrissin*)

Once in my other life, before I met Amiable Spouse and when I lived on Bayshore in Niceville, Florida, I had a beautiful mimosa tree. Underneath it was a comfortable bench and group of chairs where friends and I sometimes sat and visited while we enjoyed the ambiance of the garden. In spring, pink, pleasantly fragrant pompom flowers bloomed, and hummingbirds buzzed by for their share of the plentiful nectar. It was a sight to behold, and I considered myself lucky to have such a beauty in close proximity.

To my absolute dismay, the beautiful tree died. I learned that it was susceptible to a vascular wilt which is often fatal. I did notice even back then that little mimosas came up everywhere and that I had to pull them out often unless I wanted a mimosa forest in my back yard.

And now, many years later, I'm living my next life in Valparaiso with Amiable Spouse. Mimosa trees are everywhere in Valparaiso— on the vacant lot behind me, down the street in several yards, in Lincoln Park, and almost everywhere you look. In one house that was vacant for a few months, the front yard quickly became a small mimosa jungle. I frequently pull small seedlings from my yard. Not surprisingly, the tree is now on the hit list. It has been declared a Category I invasive exotic species by the Florida Exotic Pest Plant Council.

It is not hard to see why this tree pops up everywhere. Following the flower, elongated pealike pods develop. This large seed crop almost guarantees that hundreds of trees will come up in close proximity. Cutting a tree down does no good, because it simply resprouts. It is a strong competitor to native trees and shrubs in open areas or forest edges. Dense stands of mimosa effectively reduce the amount of sunlight and nutrients available for other plants.

Mimosa is native in a part of the world that stretches from Iran to Japan. It was introduced to this country in 1745 and is now natural- ized across the southern United States and to all of the states adjoin- ing the Pacific. It takes advantage of disturbed areas and is often seen along roadsides and in open vacant lots in urban/suburban areas. Along riparian areas where its seeds are easily transported in water, it is particularly troublesome.

Even though I miss the mimosa of my other life, I am not willing to let one grow on Amiable Spouse's and my property. Now I know of its aggressive nature. I will substitute a fringe tree (*Chionanthus virginicus*) or a redbud (*Cercis canadensis*) when I want a tree simi- lar in size to the mimosa. Then I can be sure that seedlings will not take over the world.

Popcorn Tree (*Sapium sebiferum*)

Some time back a work party was organized for the purpose of removing exotic invasives from the beautiful natural areas around

Turkey Creek in Niceville, Florida. Several people showed up, and the day was spent cutting down popcorn trees and other invasive species. City workers were present with their large truck and shredder chipper. Groups of volunteers cut down the trees, while others dragged them to the trucks to be shredded. Some of the professionals in the group applied a solution to the stumps to prevent the pest trees from resprouting.

This certainly was a worthy effort, and many exotic invasives were removed on subsequent work days. More effort is needed, of course, for the popcorn trees continue their march into this and other natural areas throughout the South. A drive through almost any neighborhood will reveal several of them growing right along with other landscape ornamentals.

No one disputes that popcorn trees are beautiful in the fall when their leaves turn brilliant shades of red, yellow, and burgundy. Over time people sought them out and planted them in landscapes because of their color. Even today popcorn trees are sold in some nurseries, and the unsuspecting public may find them labeled "Florida aspen" or some such moniker that hides their true identity. Sometimes they are called by names that are more revealing, such as "Terrible Tallow" and the "Melaleuca of northern Florida."

The popcorn tree (sometimes called Chinese tallow tree) is native to China. It is a small- to medium-sized tree, topping out at about 40 feet tall, though usually it is a bit shorter. It is deciduous, and leaves are broadly round at the base and taper to a slender point. In spring yellow-green, drooping catkins (spikes of flowers) are produced. Yellow-green, three-lobed fruits follow the flowers. In fall the fruits turn brown and split to reveal three whitish seeds that somewhat resemble popcorn and give the tree its common name. The seeds germinate easily and are spread by birds and water, for they can float great distances.

The trees grow rapidly and can produce seeds when only three years old. They are capable of invading wild land areas and quickly replacing natural communities. The surrounding ecosystem is degraded because tannins produced by the trees kill any competing plants. In a short time, a monoculture is formed.

In another common occurrence, leaves drop into water and increase the rate of eutrophication. I didn't understand that term when I first saw it, but I had heard that the popcorn tree was capable of killing fish and other aquatic creatures. Evidently, the leaves are rich in nutrients, and when they drop into the water they cause excessive growth of aquatic plants, especially algae. The resulting bacteria consume nearly all the oxygen, especially during warm weather, and fish and other aquatic creatures are suffocated.

As with many of our invasive species, Chinese tallow was purposely introduced into the United States as early as the 1700s. Although it was cultivated in China as a seed-oil crop, here it has been used primarily as an ornamental. Not surprisingly it has spread to every coastal state from North Carolina to Texas and inland to Arkansas. It has been detected in California and had become naturalized in 57 percent of Florida counties by 1996.

Control of the noxious tree is difficult. Sheep and goats have been known to eat the leaves. I didn't see any sheep or goats around Turkey Creek, and they are not free- ranging in most areas. Don't laugh, however. These days, ranchers, government agencies, and others are leasing goat herds to clear places where weeds have invaded. Goats can help control thistle, kudzu, purple loosestrife, and even poison hemlock. In Tallahassee, Florida, sheep are used to help control kudzu. The flock numbers 1,200 and can eat up to 200 acres of kudzu annually. Stationed all over the city and county in flocks of 60 to 300, they are guarded by electric fences and sometimes dogs.

Biocontrols for popcorn trees are not available. There seems to be no creature that eats it nor any disease that affects it enough to impede its growth. Some success has been reported by burning during the dormant season followed by burning or mowing during the growing season. Burning, however, is not an option in all localities. Cutting the trees down is not effective since they quickly resprout. Cutting and painting the stump with Triclopyr products is effective. This action should be done in spring to minimize seed spread.

Understandably the popcorn tree is one of the Nature Conservancy's "Dirty Dozen" of unwanted alien species. The other eleven include plants and critters. Plant offenders are purple loosestrife, hydrilla, tamarisk, miconia, and leafy spurge. Offending creatures are flathead catfish, green crab, brown tree snake, rosy wolf-snail, balsam woolly adelgid, and zebra mussel. All of them spell trouble for our native species and ecosystems.

Homeowners and residents can help by eliminating popcorn trees from their landscapes and by joining volunteer efforts to remove them from natural areas. We all need to pitch in if our valuable natural areas are to be preserved.

The List Goes On

Usually it is the uninformed who choose to plant invasive species in their yards. Aunt Lois, my sweet neighbor long passed, is a prime example. She admired a Japanese honeysuckle that she saw growing in the woods. Smitten by the glorious scent of its yellow and white flowers, she brought it home and planted it in her yard. For a year or two it was fine, but then, before its evil nature became evident, it had not only consumed the tree but was rampaging through the azaleas and sending up tendrils in search of its next victim. I have spent countless hours trying to rid my property of this tenacious vine.

Japanese honeysuckle may be a dependable ornamental in northern states where cold weather keeps its evil character in check. In the South, it is a good example of an exotic gone wild, and it is recognized by the Exotic Pest Council as a serious problem in 24 states. In the woods in Mississippi where I grew up, there are places where one can hardly walk because the honeysuckle is so thick. Its rampaging vines swallow everything in its track and shade the sun from more desirable native plants. Disturbingly, it is still promoted as forage for deer in many southern states.

Aunt Lois was also fond of common lantana (*Lantana camara*). Butterflies were frequent visitors to the nectar-laden blossoms. Birds visited during fall and winter and made off with the plentiful berries. Unfortunately, they spread them around the neighborhood, and many residents now have common lantana whether they want it or not. It grows in parks and other natural areas where it is hard to control. She also insisted on having a camphor tree (*Cinnamomum camphora*) in her yard. She used it medicinally. Unfortunately, those of us who do not desire it in our landscapes find that we must pull up stray seedlings on a regular basis.

I am another good example of a gullible gardener. Several years ago I saw the beautiful Mexican petunia (*Ruellia brittoniana*) blooming in a friend's yard. I asked for a start, which she gladly shared. It was a popular selection at plant sales and nurseries. Unwittingly, I planted it in my perennial border, and it was later added to the garden club's butterfly garden. Well, time told the tale. The Mexican petunia spread by rhizomes to places in the landscape where it was not welcome. I started digging it out several years ago, and I'm still at it. Even the smallest piece of root left in the ground can generate a new plant. Now it, too, is a Category I invasive plant in Florida.

Several years back I admired the striking red berries of coral ardisia (*Ardisia crenata*) in a friend's landscape. She willingly shared her plants with me, so now, I have that, too, with which to contend.

Heavenly bamboo (*Nandina domestica*) is on the hit list. This shrub has long been a favorite Southern landscape plant because of its attractive form and beautiful red fruits. Native to China and Japan and west to India, it is now naturalized in North Carolina, Florida, Georgia, Alabama, and other southern states. Yet it continues to be sold. Some cultivars are available that reputedly do not produce seed.

Homeowners continue to plant Chinese wisteria (*Wisteria sinensis*) and Japanese wisteria (*Wisteria floribunda*) in their landscapes. The object of admiration is, of course, long clusters of drooping flowers that bloom in spring and perfume the whole area. One has only to look in natural areas in almost any Southern state to find examples of these exotics gone wild. A much better choice would be our native wisteria (*Wisteria frutescens*).

Sword fern (*Nephrolepis cordifolia*) is coming up in many places in my landscape where I placed containers of ferns during the summer months. I had not thought them to be hardy in my area, but obviously I was wrong. They may get killed to the ground in winter, but they rebound with vigor in spring.

I remember when my brothers planted autumn olive (*Elaeagnus umbellata*) on their property in Mississippi because it was attractive to deer and other wildlife. Mistake! Sawtooth oak has been planted for the same reason. The plants will, of course, out-compete native species.

Water plants such as water hyacinth (*Eichhornia crassipes*), hydrilla (*Hydrilla verticillata*), green hygro (*Hygrophila polysperma*), and water lettuce (*Pistia stratiotes*) create havoc in many of the South's waterways.

With their climbing ability vines can be particularly troublesome. Infesting many acres are such pests as cat's claw vine (*Macfadyena unguis-cati*), Japanese climbing fern (*Lygodium japonicum*), and skunk vine (*Paederia foetida*). Grasses such as cogongrass (*Imperata cylindrica*), Japanese grass (*Microstegium vimineum*), Johnsongrass (*Sorghum halepense*), and torpedo grass (*Panicum repens*) rapidly invade natural habitats throughout the South.

Control of Exotic Invasives

As homeowners, we can do much to help. We can learn which plants are the exotic invasives and remove them from our property. Many attractive native species are commercially available that serve almost any landscape purpose. Furthermore, we can join organized eradication efforts when they are sponsored by concerned groups. We can contact local, state, and federal government representatives to let them know how concerned we are about the impact of these biological pollutants.

For the homeowner, many of the invasive plants can be cut as close to the ground as possible. If they are cut enough times and their food supply is consistently removed, they may eventually die. Sometimes plants can be dug, especially if they are small. Care must be taken to remove all of the roots. Small plants can be pulled up by hand. All plant parts should be bagged and disposed of to prevent reestablishment.

Control of exotic invasives outside the bounds of the home landscape is expensive, lengthy, and risky, because the culprit must be completely eradicated to prevent its return. Effective procedures require several treatments, continued monitoring, and extensive follow-up. Adjoining properties must be treated, and sometimes that is not possible. Infestations commonly occur along highway, railroad, and utility rights-of-way, and they are seldom treated. Many federal and state agencies have laws that prevent the use of some herbicides that might effectively control a specific exotic species. Costs are prohibitive, and funding has not been forthcoming.

In the best of all worlds, chemical treatment of pests would not be necessary. We, however, do not live in such a world. Our world is riddled with imperfections, and sometimes strong actions are needed. Exotic invasives can sometimes be controlled with certain chemicals. Usually the vine or trunk is cut and brushed with a product containing a herbicide such as Triclopyr found in products such as Brush-B-Gon®. Green leaves can sometimes be killed by the application of Round-up® or other glyphosate products. Use caution and do not allow these products to get on desirable plants. Retreatment with glyphosate may be necessary for any sprouts.

Triclopyr products, such as Brush-B-Gon®, and glyphosate contained in Roundup® and Rodeo® (labeled for aquatic areas), are available at retail outlets. Always use herbicides according to the label. The label is the law, and when herbicides are applied in a manner that does not conform to the label, the law is being broken. Of course, the law exists for the protection of the consumer and the environment.

Perhaps the future will see coordinated efforts of weed scientists and extension specialists who can research and develop environmentally sound, integrated control approaches. We can hope that all levels of government will adopt legal strategies to prevent future importation and spread of the offenders. Extension specialists and educators will surely continue to educate the public and help them learn to recognize the exotic invasives all around us. They will share the importance of halting the spread of the weeds as well as methods and procedures to achieve effective control.

It's Time for Mistletoe and Holly

Holly, yes. Mistletoe, maybe—if we know about it and use it responsibly. From early times, mistletoe has been one of the most magical, mysterious, and sacred plants of European folklore. Historically it has been used in the treatment of epilepsy, nervous disorders, apoplexy, and giddiness. Some people have used it as a heart tonic, as an aid to digestion, and to stimulate contractions during childbirth. It was believed that mistletoe hung in the home symbolized purity and strength and promoted happiness. Enemies meeting beneath the mistletoe threw down their weapons and kissed and embraced. In Germany and Austria, drugs made from extract of *Viscum album* (European mistletoe) have potential use as a treatment for cancer.

With all these reputed benefits, it's a wonder that people do not run right out and eat a few of the berries. Do not be tempted, however, for the side effects can be extremely dangerous and even fatal. They can slow the heart rate dangerously, cause hallucinations and convulsions, increase blood pressure, cause heart attacks or cardio-vascular collapse, and lead to death.

Florida Federation of Garden Clubs Wildflower Chairman Dara Dobson enjoys tying bunches of mistletoe with pretty red bows and giving them away during the Christmas season. They are a popular attraction at her wildflower programs. When asked how she managed to get the mistletoe out of the trees, she replied, "Oh, no problem. Lloyd shoots it out with his gun." That's better, I suppose, than the Celtic priests who cut it from a sacred oak with a golden sickle and caught it on a white cloth to keep it from touching the ground. They offered it along with two white bulls as a sacrifice to their pagan gods.

Although mistletoe is popular during the holidays, it is not good luck for the tree on which it grows. It is a parasite which eventually weakens and possibly kills its host. Once established, a mistletoe plant lives about ten years. After that time the weight of it causes it to fall from its weakened host or it is shaded out.

Birds assist in the spread of this parasitic plant. They eat the berries and carry them away to other trees. There they clean their bills or deposit their droppings. The sticky berries adhere to the bark, and after a few days tiny roots emerge. Flattened tips enable them to work their way through the bark and into the tree. Eventually the roots become firmly embedded in the branch and mistletoe begins to take nutrients from its host.

Control is very difficult. Removal of the plant will have no effect, since it will simply regrow. Removal of the entire limb is an effective means of control. Dr. Bob Black, horticulturist from the University of Florida, says that a plant growth regulator (Ethephon) has recently been found to be an environmentally safe control for mistletoe. When sprayed on the mistletoe, it causes it to decline and reduces the chances of its continued growth.

Mistletoe remains a popular plant for Christmas decorations and merriment. The dark green, oval foliage and white berries symbolize peace and love. Use it in that spirit, but with caution. Remember that it is extremely poisonous, so do not put it within the reach of small children who may be tempted to eat the pretty berries. Place it well overhead in a strategic position. Then use it as an excuse to kiss someone you love.

THE INDOOR ENVIRONMENT

Clean the Air with Houseplants

Grow fresh air, you ask? You bet your boots! In much the same way that the tropical jungles and temperate zone forests clean and purify earth's air, plants in the home can add much to the comfort and health of family members.

This is not a new idea. The following quotation is attributed to the nineteenth-century Ladies' Floral Cabinet:

> The highest mission of plants is not merely to please our eyes with color, our mouths with delicious fruits. Not only do they do this and more, but they are ever silently but surely eating up what is impure and injurious to ourselves in the atmosphere and in the earth all around our homes; and any dwelling in which plants are well and healthily grown will be more likely to be a clean and healthy house than if plants were not there.

A growing body of research suggests that the ladies were right on target. Cultivating plants may be the best medicine available for improving mental and physical health and wellbeing. Plants beautify a room and make it a friendly, attractive place to live or work. Businesses install interior landscaping to increase worker productivity and reduce absenteeism. Restaurants, hotels, and other businesses include plants in their decor to help attract customers.

The space program did much to increase our knowledge about the benefits of plants in indoor spaces. In 1980 the John C. Stennis Space Center in southwest Mississippi discovered that houseplants could remove volatile organic chemicals from the air. Formaldehyde, benzene, trichloroethylene, ammonia, and bioeffluents (chemicals released during human respiration) are a few such offenders that are effectively removed from the air by plants. This is not guesswork, but the results of experiments done by NASA under carefully controlled conditions.

Not only do plants successfully remove these and other chemicals from the air, they do so with no harm to themselves. They improve their ability to remove chemicals with increased exposure; that is, they "learn" the process. Airborne toxins are absorbed through tiny openings in the leaves called stomata. From there they are delivered to microbes living around their roots, which can then break down the toxins and use them as a source of food for themselves and the plant.

Through their biological processes, plants not only clean the air but make it more healthy and comfortable for us in other ways. Water vapor is released that makes our noses and throats less susceptible to assaults by airborne chemicals, viruses, mold spores, dust, and allergens. Phytochemicals are given off that suppress mold spores and bacteria found in surrounding air. Research shows that plant-filled rooms contain 50 to 60 percent fewer airborne molds and bacteria than rooms without plants. Houseplants are more than simple luxuries and decorative elements. Because they are nature's living air purifiers, they are important to our health.

Many houseplants are suitable candidates. Based on testing, some houseplants have been rated according to ease of growth and maintenance, resistance to pests, efficiency at removing chemical vapors, and transpiration rates. Some high scorers were areca palm, lady palm, rubber plant, dracaena, English ivy, ficus, Boston fern, peace lily, corn plant, pothos, philodendron, arrowhead vine, dumb cane, schefflera, snake plant, Norfolk Island pine, prayer plant, spider plant, Chinese evergreen, and calathea.

That sounds for all the world like a list of the most easily grown plants. Do yourself and your family a favor. Decorate your home and clean your air with beneficial houseplants.

III
Ruminations on Southern Gardening

A Few Lessons

Gardening in the South has its own particular set of challenges. We battle intense heat and humidity, nutrient- and water-deficient soil, hurricanes, and all kinds of diseases and insects that these conditions favor. Every advantage that we can wrest contributes to greater success in our gardening efforts. With a better understanding of our unique climate and environmental challenges, gardening in Dixie can be pleasurable and rewarding. Years of experience have taught me a few tricks of the trade.

One of the first strategies I learned was to keep every pine needle and leaf that fell in my yard. Previously I raked them up and deposited them at the curb for trash pickup. In their place, I sprigged grass into the sand. Then I began a vicious cycle of watering, fertilizing, poisoning, and mowing. I did achieve an acceptable lawn, but at a cost, both to my pocketbook and to the environment.

Now I know a better way. I let the pine needles and leaves fall where they may. I rake around the edges a bit to neaten things up, but mostly Mother Nature defines the edges of my mulched areas and I follow her lead.

181

Now don't misunderstand. I still have a lawn—just not as much of it. In open, sunny areas where leaves and needles do not fall, grass grows unhampered by competing tree roots and shade. Mowing is easily accomplished because lines are gently curving. Insecticides are infrequently applied in areas where problems occur. Fertilizer application has been reduced because my mulching lawn mower set at a high level deposits some natural fertilizer every time I mow. Grass grows taller and more vigorously, and its deeper roots require less frequent water. Too, I've learned that greener is not always better, and my idea of what is acceptable includes a few weeds interspersed among the blades of grass.

Most of us find that our soil is not perfectly suited for growing healthy annuals, perennials, and vegetables. Organic matter is the magic ingredient that makes a big difference. It doesn't matter whether the soil has too much sand or too much clay—the fix is the same. Copious amounts of peat moss, cow manure, compost, or other organic matter improve the soil tremendously. In addition, the use of slow-release fertilizers and a liberal application of mulch greatly improve the health of the soil and the growth of plants.

Perhaps one of my most satisfying lessons came from my early attempts at pest control. I didn't know one bug from another, and I looked upon all of them as plant-devouring enemies. Many met their demise at the end of my sprayer. Now I know that there are many more good guys out there than bad guys. I've learned to recognize assassin bugs, soldier beetles, lady bugs, spiders, green lacewings, and other helpers in the battle. Toad abodes dot my flowerbeds. Helpful snakes and lizards assist me in my efforts.

Now I spot spray only after I've identified the enemy, and then only if the level of infestation is critical and I don't see the natural pest patrol on the job. My plantings are diversified, so the bugs are kept quite wonderfully confused and therefore never quite gain the upper hand. I'm finding more and more of the beneficials and fewer and fewer of the pests. My yard has become a sanctuary for birds, butterflies, and such. Now that's rewarding!

DEALING WITH DROUGHT IN THE LANDSCAPE

We in the South are often required to cope with drought. Grass along the highways turns brown, and plants everywhere show signs of stress. Water use is restricted, and our yards get drier and drier.

Broiling temperatures and drying winds add to the problem. What can a homeowner do to help his or her landscape get through these drying times?

Providing shade is one energy- and water-saving technique. Plants that are in sheltered places out of glaring sun and strong winds need less water than those in unprotected places. Deciduous trees on the southeast and southwest sides of the house provide cooling shade for the house and its inhabitants. Shade-loving shrubs, small trees, and flowers are also protected when planted beneath such trees.

Using water wisely is a must these days. However, having a landscape that makes optimal use of water does not necessarily rule out all water-loving plants. We simply need to divide the landscape into moderate, low, and very low water-use zones. Then place the plants with the highest water demands in spots that receive runoff water or are naturally protected from sun and wind. Adjust irrigation to meet the needs of these plants. In very low water-use zones, select plants that are naturally drought tolerant and that can survive on existing rainfall.

Lawn grasses require more water and maintenance than most other landscape plants. While some grass may be good, limiting or reducing the amount of turf that is maintained around homes is an increasingly popular and sensible trend. Decks and patios provide places for relaxing and do not require mowing or watering. Drought-tolerant shrubs or groundcovers can replace much of the lawn area and add visual interest to the home landscape.

Improving soil with organic matter tends to lessen demand for water. Many plants struggle and need more water in poor soil. Nutrients and water are held in place directly in proportion to the amount of organic matter in the soil. Remember, though, that if organic matter is added, it should be incorporated into the entire planting area and not just dropped into a planting hole here and there. This practice tends to restrict plant roots to small, enriched areas and does not encourage them to spread out into the native soil.

Mulching is a beneficial practice that reduces evaporation of water from the soil surface and keeps both soil and plants cooler. An organic mulch breaks down over a period of years and enriches the soil. A mulch of three to four inches suppresses weed growth and reduces soil compaction. Areas that are well mulched need much less water to maintain healthy growth than areas with no mulch.

In a nutshell, we can refine landscape design so that plants are grouped according to water needs. We can limit turf areas and select plants that thrive on very little water. Effective irrigation, use of mulch, and addition of organic matter to the soil all contribute to more efficient use of water.

We must incorporate these water-saving practices into our daily lives, because periodic droughts have been the norm for the past several years. Gardeners and farmers talk about drought and cast their eyes heavenward searching for some sign of much-needed rain. They know that the absence of rainfall has depleted soil moisture and injured their plants. According to Dr. Gary Knox, turf researcher from the University of Florida, drought stress can reduce plant growth more than all other environmental stresses combined.

Effects of drought on trees and shrubs can be short term or long term. Short-term damage can be caused by just one dry spell, and may include wilting, leaf scorch, and some loss of leaves. Long-term damage happens over a period of years. Woody plants exhibit stunted growth. Some stems and branches may die back, and in the worst-case scenario the plant dies. It is the long-range damage that homeowners often notice.

One symptom that raises considerable concern is stem dieback. This malady is caused by a loss of fine feeder roots. As soils become dry, more feeder roots grow in an effort to take up all available water. However, these roots die if the soil remains dry. There may be more foliage on the plant than the roots can support. When the rain finally does come, the plant probably cannot take it up because of the loss of its feeder roots. As the roots and canopy try to achieve balance, part of the canopy begins to die back. If the drought persists through the following year or before the plant can recover, it may die. At this time, the concerned homeowner calls the extension office, seeking a cure for his sick plant. We know, of course, that it's a little too late to do the right thing.

Of course, during a drought, plants are in a weakened condition. Such pests as wood borers, aphids, spider mites, and other insects home in on the weakened plants. While vigorous, healthy plants can withstand much damage from insects and diseases, weak plants may succumb under the additional stress.

The best way to fight against drought, of course, is to select plants that are drought tolerant. Some drought-tolerant trees for home landscapes are redbud, persimmon, loquat, American holly, yaupon, Southern magnolia, pine, Chinese pistache, several species of oak, chaste tree, hackberry, green ash, cypress, eucalyptus, fig, wax myrtle, Southern red cedar, Eastern red cedar, and Japanese black pine. Choose drought-tolerant shrubs such as glossy abelia, Japanese aucuba, beautyberry, cassia, quince, fatsia, Burford and Carissa holly, juniper, Turk's cap, oleander, Indian hawthorn, and dwarf palmetto.

A more extensive listing of drought-tolerant plants can be downloaded from the web site at http://edis.ifas.ufl.edu. Download Circular 807, "Drought Tolerant Plants for North and Central Florida." Alternatively, call the extension office in your area. It has literature that will help you choose drought-tolerant plants for your landscape. It behooves all of us to seek out these drought-tolerant plants as our water supplies become more and more depleted.

ADDING ZING, ZAP, AND ZEST TO THE GARDEN

"I've spent months designing and installing this backyard," muttered Marcia. "I've planted the right plants in the right places. I've studied, visited nurseries, asked questions, and done my homework. The plants are growing according to plan. They're all healthy and well tended, and yet something is missing. There is no 'zest'. Why?"

"This backyard is making me mad!" muttered Mazie. "I have a healthy lawn and an exquisite evergreen shrub border bounded by a wooden fence. I don't want to spend a fortune, and indeed, I don't think I'll live here forever. What can I do meanwhile to add some 'zap'?"

"My entry is a sad sight," sighed Suzie. "The grass and shrubs that the landscaper installed are doing well. The door is freshly painted, and everything is neat and trim. Why doesn't it 'zing'?"

Marcia, Mazie, and Suzie all have a common problem. There is no focal point, no center of interest, no garden ornamentation. There's nothing that is attention arresting. It's a problem that is frequently found in home landscapes. How do you capture and hold a viewer's attention and create areas that cause one to pause and savor a scene? How do you add zest, zap, and zing to your landscape?

There are, of course, the ever-popular bench, the birdbath, the sundial, and the arbor. All of these garden features will add pizzazz to a place if they reflect the style of the structure and the personality of the gardener.

My own favorite focal areas came about quite accidentally. When I first moved into my present home, I had the luxury of beginning almost at the beginning. Already in place were some mature Florida longleaf pines, a scraggly lawn, and a few mature shrubs. Mostly, though, I had the luxury of a blank canvas. I raked the pine needles around a bit, generally letting them remain where they fell. I simply sharpened the edges and made them neat. Then I began adding shrubs into these naturally mulched areas. Things began to take shape. Lawns began to emerge in areas where few pine needles fell. Mother Nature defined my areas and I capitalized on and polished her lead. Lines were curving and graceful. Mowing was quickly accomplished because there were no awkward nooks to navigate.

Everything was peaceful. Calmness and tranquility reigned. Soon I began to be—well, bored. For some time I had been collecting bromeliads. My husband's hunting club tackled the taming of a new swimming hole in Turkey Creek, a popular local recreation area. They had to remove several cypress knees. Knowing of my penchant for such things, they brought them to me. I set the cypress knees up near my entry and displayed my bromeliads on them. Dy-na-mite!! People stop to stare. "Simply stunning!" some say.

In the back yard after the pine needles were swept into place, I separated the mulched area from the lawn with variegated liriope. Into the mulched area went shrubs and perennials, and it was all very pretty. Harmony and repetition had been achieved. BORING!

Providentially, my neighbor had some large pilings that he no longer needed. Did I want them? You bet! I cut them into various lengths and set three good-sized posts down just behind the *Liriope* in center-back of the yard. Over the pilings, I draped a large, green fishnet. A concrete pelican was placed on the shortest piling. Above him, on a taller piling was placed a draping pencil cactus in a container. Old Mr. Pelican peeked out from among its trailing branches. A vine was planted to clamber up the net. I circled the area with a brick edging and planted an ornamental sedge, a daylily, and some various complementary plants. "Wow!" folks say. "What a wonder!"

Another of my favorite areas is sited along my

woodland path. Since I have limited financial resources, a single residential lot of this prime real estate in the heart of the Vale of Paradise is all my schoolteacher husband and I could afford. Therefore, the length of my woodland pathway is not as long as I would like it to be. Something was needed to slow the progress of guests as they strolled along it so that it would seem longer. So, I created areas of interest along the curves and bends to encourage visitors to stop and look. A planting of aspidistra beneath an oak tree and some giant liriope were installed along the pathway, but that did not stop traffic. The needed "zing" came about when I placed a large potted caladium, a potted hosta, and a Saint Fiacre statue that was a gift from a friend in front of all the greenery. "Wow!" folks say. "Who'd 'a thought it?"

Several other focal areas have been added to my garden. Wherever they exist, they are placed in a line of sight straight out from a sitting area to create a vista, along a pathway to add interest, or at a major stopping place, such as beside my entry. Added as an exclamation point along a straight line of similar plants, they keep the landscape from being humdrum. An unpleasant scene over which you have no control can be disguised by skillful placement of a garden ornament or artfully arranged focal area. The eye naturally stops on striking compositions or unusual ornaments, and the offending structure or scene fades from consciousness.

Focal areas and garden ornaments can be added to your yard for similar reasons. Trellises, weather vanes, statuary, elegant pots filled with plants, great urns, gods, angels, striking and unusual plants or plant combinations, and anything else that can be found, made, or purchased can serve as a garden ornament. A garden swing or bench with an arbor over it makes an unbeatable place to add details. A vine growing over it, a hanging basket or two suspended from it, and a couple of containers or plants on the side make a pleasant composition. When choosing items to embellish your garden, choose things that you truly like. Anything goes. Restraint is in order, though, because a garden that is overly ornamented can become more like a junkyard than a tastefully furnished outdoor space.

Creating a garden and ornamenting it is a primary means of creative self-expression for many people. Maybe we can't draw, and we can't dance, but by golly we can create a garden that expresses who we are and what we're all about. Isn't that, after all, the real purpose for gardening?

LANDSCAPE DESIGN TRICKS

The landscape leading to the front door of my house is totally to my liking. Something of interest is there year-round, but it is never overpowering. Careful planning and a few simple design techniques enabled me to have the look I wanted.

First, visitors walk through the arbor that Amiable Spouse built over the walk. Beside it on both sides, old roses bloom and perfume the air. Scrambling up it on both sides are allamandas with soft yellow flowers that bloom all summer.

After walking through the arbor, plants of different kinds provide year-long interest. Plants are massed in groups: orchids in one spot, daylilies in another, and Oriental lilies in another. Shrubs are grouped together in masses of the same variety, and here and there a specimen plant demands special attention from the viewer.

In very early spring, the ground orchids (*Bletilla striata*) bloom. I have a bed of them with thirty or so planted together in a mass. When they bloom, the show is significant. For about a month I enjoy their lavender blooms. For the remainder of the summer their pleated foliage stands out in contrast to the azaleas and other nearby plants.

A few weeks later, lavender azaleas bloom at the foot of a pine tree. Initially I planted four azaleas in this spot— all the same kind. When they bloom, they are the only spot of color along the walkway.

Then the amaryllises steal the show. They border the entire right side of the walk. Mostly red, they are a much-anticipated event each year. When they are finished blooming, their strappy green foliage remains to add interest and variety.

Following the amaryllises, Confederate jasmine blooms and perfumes the whole area. It scrambles up a tall pine near the entry to my house. When it is not in bloom, its evergreen foliage remains to add structure and permanence.

After the jasmine, the daylilies bloom. The only ones I have near the walk are the fragrant 'Hyperion' given to me by a friend. Their pale yellow blossoms are a perfectly beautiful pocket of color surrounded by the green of the amaryllis and orchid foliage. Their delicate scent offers a superb extra dimension of enjoyment.

In summer, 'Casa Blanca' Oriental lilies unfurl for perhaps the most glorious show of all. In a bed about two-thirds up the walkway, the clump of white lilies with long anthers tipped with auburn pollen command attention. Their whiteness is striking in the surrounding green masses of plants whose foliage remains after their earlier bloom. The scent of the Oriental lilies is unforgettable. The display lasts about two or three weeks, but it is enough. So beautiful is the show that their place in the garden is secure even if they last for just a day.

Lending permanence to the succession of flowers are a few plants that add structure and mass to the perennials. A grancy gray beard (*Chionanthus virginicus*) planted a few years ago is just getting big enough to become interesting. Florida longleaf pine trees soar skyward and provide mulch and dappled shade that these plants enjoy. A specimen *Philodendron bipinnatifidum* (formerly *selloum*) stretches its massive leaves out and gives a tropical look to the scene. More evergreen azaleas round out the planting at the head of the walk and provide a mass of color in spring. Adding contrast in form, texture, and color is a tall evergreen juniper that rises above and behind the massed azaleas.

What landscape tricks did I use to make this area interesting? To begin with, the whole bed is mulched with pine needles, and plants are restricted to the bed. The mulch inside the bed and a wide sweep of lawn on the other side unify and bring order to the varied plants. Masses of single kinds of plants keep it from seeming jumbled, and spaces between different groups of plants offer relief from too much variety. Usually only one kind of plant blooms at a time, so interesting pockets of color appear in succession all summer. Some evergreen plants are present year-round. Interspersed among them are perennials whose color comes and goes in interesting succession, and whose foliage dies down in winter.

Amiable Spouse enjoys strolling down the walk each morning to get the paper. Always there is something beautiful to see. I love it all—the landscape, the morning, and the spouse. What more could one ask?

THE NEWLY SPRUNG SPRING

Just as we know it will, spring comes without fail each year. It's nature's revival—a new beginning and a reaffirmation of life. It was in spring many years ago that we Bullock children begged Mother to let us go outside without shoes on our feet. Long before the ground had warmed enough, we started a familiar refrain. "Please, Mother, let us go barefoot," we pleaded. Finally, when she figured it was time, she relented and we dashed outdoors, eager to feel cool, damp earth and the newly sprung soft grasses and tiny flowers beneath our feet.

Gardeners know the feeling. We've learned to keep the shoes on our feet most of the time, but we still love the feel of the soft grass and the promises held deep within the soil. We're happiest digging in the cool, moist earth, and claiming for ourselves riches that the land can deliver. It's not the actual digging, nor is it the hard work—though that may be a part of it. We love the smell of freshly dug earth, and we feel unbelievably relaxed and happy after a day of hard work in the garden.

Mostly, however, it's being outside, participating, seeing, hearing, feeling, sensing. It's a primordial response—our reaction to the age-old music of the universe. And it's more than just the soil; it's the sun that shines more directly with each passing day and banishes the darkness of winter and unleashes the lightness of spring. Our spirits soar with the ever-increasing brightness of the sun's rays, and we rise early every day to snare every precious moment of it. The birds and creatures who share our earthspace know, and their presence and activity add to our concept of rightness.

Think everyone sees it, feels it, hears it? Not on your life! Most folks have no concept—no basis of experience. They're rational folks who never allow themselves to drift beyond the bounds of conscious thought and enter into a purely sensory realm. Furthermore, most of my friends think that I have lost it about now. Gardeners, however, nod their heads in agreement. They know. Makes perfect sense. Been there.

Amiable Spouse knows. Not because he's a gardener, but because he's out and about in the woods and on the river—regularly, to charge his battery, to adjust his attitude, to keep himself amiable. And then, when I ask him to help me with some of the gardening tasks, he's agreeable.

Lately I've been asking him to help prepare my planting beds. We both know that if we skimp on this initial preparation, the results of our efforts will be disappointing. If we can come down from our dream state long enough to get the work done, the flowers will fulfill their mission with their greatest beauty.

We must dig organic matter into our sandy soil. It's a lesson that disappointment taught me. Disappointment because my sturdy seedlings grew into mere shadows of what they should have been. Disappointment because the sand that was between my toes did not grow plants like the Mississippi mud I'd left behind.

So, the organic matter is necessary—peat moss, compost, animal manures, rotted oak leaves, or whatever else we can find. How much? As much as we can afford or manage, or until the soil turns just a bit dark. A good shovelful per square foot or so. Then we supplement that with a sprinkle of slow-release fertilizer on top of the ground at planting time, and then again a few weeks hence.

After the ground is well prepared, we further improve our chances of a good show by covering the soil with mulch. I much prefer organic mulches that will eventually rot and enhance the fertility of my soil, and those that occur naturally in my yard are just fine. Fallen leaves. Pine needles. Chipped-up trimmings from pruned shrubs. Grass clippings (not treated with weed products). Sometimes I must supplement with pine chips or other materials that I can buy in a bag. I avoid cypress mulch because I know that cypress trees are cut from native stands and shredded to satisfy this market.

After Amiable Spouse has prepared the planting beds, I'm ready to plant the sturdy seedlings that I purchased from the nursery—or the perennials or other plants. Having provided my beds with adequate water, proper exposure to sun, and minimal care, I can now sit back and expect a long season of bloom from the plants that I have chosen.

First things first. Prepare the soil. Get the plants. Plant. Sit back. Enjoy. Or go to the next piece of ground and experience another bit of joy. Birds singing. Butterflies fluttering. Bees buzzing. Nature being. Gardening.

GARDENING MISTAKES

In a lecture that I attended recently, Okaloosa County Master Gardener Lyn Fabian made an interesting comment that really set me thinking. She suggested that gardeners should discuss their failures more often, for it is from our mistakes that many valuable lessons are learned.

I had not thought about it in just that way, but after considering the idea, I believe that she was right on track. We often talk about plants and techniques that are successful, and we tout this plant or that one because it grew so well in our garden. We become familiar with certain products and methods, and it is these we share.

We become successful gardeners because, as we experience failures, we discard the process, product, or plant that led to disappointment. We do it another way, or we try another plant. It grows well, so we tell others about the one that lived and performed admirably in our landscape. We forget about the one that died.

One might think that avid gardeners do not make some of the common mistakes that "ordinary" gardeners make. Actually, quite the opposite is true, probably because we engage in the activity far more often than casual gardeners. We're out and about in the garden almost every day. Our mistakes are numerous, and, as we make them, we store in the far reaches of our minds little bits of knowledge that keep us from making these mistakes again—usually.

Once I was asked to give a program about mistakes that I had made in the garden, and I had no trouble finding material for my presentation. As a matter of fact, I ran over the time allotted and didn't nearly cover the multitude of examples that came to mind when I searched my memory.

For instance, I remember the time I found many huge, striped worms on my parsley. I hastily set about killing them. I didn't realize that they were black swallowtail larvae. The same thing happened  to my tulip poplar tree. Funny green worms with large eyespots were eating the leaves. Of course, I rescued the young tulip poplar. It was much later that I learned that I had killed the larval stage of tiger swallowtail butterflies. Ignorance was fatal to the butterflies. The mistake was mine.

Lack of knowledge can cause us to make costly and time-consuming mistakes in the landscape. Usually we gardeners do the best we can when selecting plants that will enhance our landscapes. Nobody spends good money and hours planning for failure. Even so, some of our best efforts occasionally go awry.

A few poor choices stand out as obvious to many of us who have purchased certain plants and watched them grow and tried to care for them. I remember an early experience. My husband and I had a brand new business, and I wanted to landscape it attractively. We had a strip about 60 feet wide and three or four feet deep that ran along the side of a building. I decided that we could achieve color and textural contrasts with a couple of different shrubs. At the garden center was a group of beautiful Chinese juniper (*Juniperus chinensis* 'Hetzii') in cute little gallon-sized containers. I chose about seven of them and planted them four or five feet apart down the length of the bed. Between each I planted Japanese euonymus (*Euonymus japonicus* 'Aureus'). It sported leaves with bright yellow centers bordered with green. I alternated the two shrubs all the way down the side of the building. It was attractive, I thought, when it was finished.

Now those of you who know these shrubs are already snickering. The 'Hetzii' juniper is an appropriate selection for certain parklike situations, for its mature size is 15 feet tall and at least that wide or wider. It grew huge! The whole side of the building was obliterated in a few years. The euonymus very quickly became victim to several ailments; among them were mildew, leaf spot, aphids, and euonymus scale. After I spent considerable time spraying for one malady after another, I finally dug them up. A few years later the juniper had to be removed. Customers couldn't walk down the side of the building.

Other mistakes abound. I decided at that same residence to plant a hedge of red tip (*Photinia fraseri*) between my yard and the one next door. I wanted a well-mannered hedge that didn't need too much pruning. If only I'd had Michael Dirr's *Manual of Woody Landscape Plants* at that time! He stated it quite well when he said that this plant is so overused that the term nauseous is not sufficient. While the new red leaves are attractive, the plant grows to 20 feet high and about one-half as wide. Overuse contributed to a troublesome and often devastating leaf spot (*Entomosporium maculatum*) that killed many shrubs and made those that managed to survive unsightly. I could never keep it pruned to an acceptable height. I sold that house and let the next owners worry about the red tip hedge. I do not believe that this plant is sold in our area anymore.

I hesitate to mention the silver maple that I planted near a septic tank. Nor do I like to remember the Japanese pittosporum (*Pittosporum tobira*) that I planted as a foundation shrub under the windows of one house. I don't even like to think about a holly that I planted in front of my present house with the expectation that it would be a low-growing, mounded foundation plant. Now it is about as tall as the second story.

Amiable Spouse has spent considerable time removing plants that hugged the foundation of the house too closely. When it was time to paint, he couldn't get the ladder set up because the plants were in the way. On one side of the house he actually had to replace some of the siding because the shrubs and sprinkler system had caused the wood to rot.

Again, I have to confess. The mistake was mine. When I set about installing the landscape, I did not find out enough about the plants. I didn't know that the Foster's holly grew to be a tree, or that the tiny 'Blue Ice' juniper that I planted would one day be taller than the house. There were many things that I didn't know during those days. As a matter of fact, lack of knowledge remains a condition that will surely afflict me as long as I draw breath.

When so many plants are available, it is hard to make informed choices. It pays to do some homework before shopping. Do not rely, as I often did, on finding a pretty little plant at the nursery and buying it for its looks. Determine the mature size of plants and place them appropriately in the landscape. Ask reliable nursery personnel or call the extension service. Any master gardener can quickly consult a reference book and help you make informed decisions. They can look up pests and diseases, proper placement, cultural requirements, and any number of facts that will help you choose appropriately. With all the facts in hand, your new plants should add years of beauty to your landscape.

The longer I garden, the more I learn, both from my own experiences and from sharing with other gardeners and reading accounts of their gardening experiences. Maybe by the time I'm no longer able to garden I will have learned enough that I could garden successfully had I the strength.

Please notice, though, that these mistakes did not keep me from gardening. I stumbled on in my attempts, and at the very least, I learned a few lessons. Many butterflies have flourished in my garden since that first tragic encounter, and the next shrubs that I plant near the foundation will be far enough from the house that they will never touch—or this time Amiable Spouse might not be as amiable.

So in keeping with Lyn's suggestion, I will remember from time to time to share my failures as well as successes. Maybe we can all learn a bit more and garden just a little better.

PROPAGATING PLANTS

"Marie," friends want to know, "How do you get so many plants to sell at plant sales?" It's a simple question, but the answer is more complicated. First, people know that I contribute to several plant sales during the year, all of which support worthy causes. The garden club has one or two sales each year to support their projects. I contribute heavily to these. Then the master gardeners have a gigantic plant sale, and the butterfly association finances some of its projects by selling plants for butterfly gardens. I contribute to all of these groups because I believe in what they're doing.

Knowing this, people call and invite club members or master gardeners to dig plants from their yards. These specimens are potted up for our sales. One friend gave me a crowded Christmas cactus that needed dividing. I divided it and grew it in my greenhouse all summer. Now I have about a dozen Christmas cacti ready for the next plant sale. Another friend brought Louisiana irises and canna lilies freshly dug from her yard. I potted them up. Local garden centers give me cuttings when they prune their stock. Or they may donate root-bound perennials that can be rejuvenated by dividing and repotting. Actually, I have been known to buy root-bound plants with just that purpose in mind. Folks around here know that I start many plants each year, so they are eager to recycle their used plant containers by bringing them to me.

These donated plants are not the only source, however. I have become skilled at propagating plants from my own yard. Lately I am absolutely hindered when I work in the yard because I have to pot up every sprig that I prune or dig. Extra plants from perennial divisions are potted up and set aside. Prunings from assorted shrubs and perennials are stuck into pots or the ground where they will root. Before a killing frost I frantically take cuttings of everything that will be killed back to the ground. I put them in water until I can get them potted up. Seeds are collected and planted immediately or set aside until a better time. It's a continuous process.

I've learned several tricks that have made my propagation efforts more successful. First, regular potting soil is not always the best medium in which to start cuttings. Some of mine rotted because the medium stayed too wet. Now I add perlite, which makes a well-drained mixture that is adequate for most plants.

Many plants, I have learned, root easily from cuttings. A cutting can be taken at any time, especially once the burst of fresh growth slows. Stems of some plants like begonias and coleuses never harden completely, so they are easy to root at almost anytime. Next easiest to root are tender cuttings of hardy herbaceous plants (plants with soft tissue, such as a hardy perennial that gets killed to the ground in winter but returns in spring) taken in midspring. Cuttings can also be taken in midsummer. As a matter of fact, cuttings can be successfully taken at almost any time. Many of my cuttings are taken in late fall or early winter before the first killing frost.

Cuttings taken from deciduous plants are handled differently. The degree of hardness of the cutting determines whether it is a softwood or hardwood cutting. Cuttings taken from young growth of deciduous woody plants are called "softwood" cuttings. As soon as new growth can remain turgid after being cut, a softwood cutting can be taken. A good test is to snap the stem like a stringbean. If it snaps easily, it is a suitable cutting. Later, when the shrub's new growth stops growing and the bark toughens, cuttings are considered "semihardwood." Most broadleaf evergreen shrubs like azalea or holly are rooted from semihardwood cuttings. Still later, as wood becomes mature, cuttings are called "hardwood." Hardwood cuttings of evergreens have leaves on them, of course, and are treated differently, but the deciduous broadleaf shrubs are usually completely dormant and leafless when hardwood cuttings are taken.

Extensive information and descriptions of all the different kinds of cuttings and techniques for rooting them are described in several reliable sources. Among my favorite references is *Making More Plants: The Science, Art, and Joy of Propagation* by Ken Druse. Consult a good reference for more detailed information about propagating plants.

I don't get so scientific about it, but I have started hundreds of pots of perennial plants in spring when they are growing vigorously. It's too easy! Just take cuttings with several nodes and stick them into the soil. Five or six cuttings per pot make a nice, bushy plant in a short time. Then put these pots in a protected place and keep watered. The cuttings strike roots almost without fail.

Several plants respond well to this type of cutting. Pentas, Philippine violets, firespike, shrimp plants, plectranthus, amaranthus, and most salvias root easily. Turk's cap, angel's trumpets, vines of various kinds, as well as many herbs root in a snap. Ornamental sweet potato vines are readily rooted in soil or in water. Begonias, coleus, impatiens, and other fleshy-stemmed annuals are surefire winners. Purple heart roots from stems broken off and put into soil.

Most directions that I read say to cover a newly struck cutting with plastic or glass. That probably does help with some hard-to-root species, but it is not necessary for the aforementioned. Just stick most cuttings in soil, put them in a shady place until new growth begins, and then fertilize with a weak solution of a complete fertilizer every couple of weeks or until they are transplanted or sold at the next plant sale.

Hardwood cuttings taken from deciduous plants offer another easy means of propagation. Cuttings are taken any time after a plant's leaves have dropped, but before buds begin to swell in spring. Simply take cuttings that have several nodes, and discard the terminal tip. Mark the earth end of the twig. I often do this by cutting a slanted cut at the top of each stem and a straight cut on the bottom. Then I bind the cuttings together with string and dip the end with the straight cut in rooting hormone. These prepared cuttings are placed in a box and covered with damp sand and put in a cool place (perhaps a refrigerator) until spring. When I open the box, I expect to see calluses that have formed on the basal ends. Potted up in well-drained soil, these cuttings will develop roots and shoots quite rapidly.

Of course, there are many other ways to propagate plants. Leaf cuttings can be taken from certain plants like sansevieria, African violet, and begonia. Root cuttings are successful with some plants. Naturally, we gardeners are avid seed collectors, and starting plants from seed is particularly satisfying.

This is a situation that benefits everyone. Plants are sold and beautiful things happen. The buyer gets a splendid plant that grows well in this area, and the seller gets money to donate to good causes.

A MEAL OF TURNIP GREENS

November is a special time for us Bullock girls. My sisters and I have a reunion—just us girls. The fellows are not invited. Each year we meet at a different place and plan a weekend of visiting and sharing confidences that only sisters can divulge.

One year we decided to gather at Amiable Spouse's and my fishing place on Black Creek in Freeport, Florida. We got there at about dark on the second Friday evening of November.

Although we talked into the wee hours, we got up early Saturday morning and made plans for the day. We decided to take a tour of Seaside and Eden State Park. Of course, since we were so near the Gourd Garden, we had to stop by there. Everyone found something special for their gardens. After a light lunch we headed back to camp.

Then the real fun began. Jan, my youngest sister, brought turnip and mustard greens that she had grown in her Mississippi garden. We planned to have them for dinner. At the fish camp we were a bit cooking-challenged, but we made do. Out came the gas cooker and the extra large pot that are sometimes used for boiling shrimp and crabs. We filled the pot with water and put it on the cooker to boil. Turnip greens went through three washes in the ice chests, and then they were put into the boiling water to cook. We added salt and some really good pieces of ham.

While the turnips cooked, we fried bacon in the electric skillet. The bacon was removed from the pan and the fat was saved. Just a little, of course, was added to the pot of cooking turnips. We set aside just a bit for the cornbread skillet, and the rest was reserved for the salad dressing.

We also washed the fresh mustard greens and cut them up into bite-sized pieces. Into a large bowl went the chopped mustard greens, sliced fresh radishes, and pieces of small green onions—all from Jan's garden. The bacon was torn into fine bits and sprinkled atop. We were preparing our favorite wilted mustard green salad just like Mother did when we were children.

The salad dressing takes some special preparation. To the skillet in which we cooked the bacon, and in which remained a tablespoon or so of bacon fat, we added a cup of water and brought it to a boil. We scraped the bottom of the skillet to be sure that all the bacon crumbs that remained in the skillet were thoroughly incorporated. Into that concoction we poured a tablespoon or so of pepper sauce and stirred again. When we were ready to eat, we poured the hot dressing over the salad greens.

For those who don't know about pepper sauce, it is made from peppers from the summer garden. Usually cayenne peppers are used, but we Mississippi girls also like to add some mild banana peppers to the recipe. We thoroughly clean the peppers and then pack them in a bottle or jar. Then it is quick and easy to make pepper sauce. Simply boil plain white vinegar and pour the boiling liquid over the peppers. Place a lid on the jar and store it in a dark place until needed.

Made this way, the pepper sauce lasts all winter and is a necessary ingredient in turnip and mustard greens, kale, cabbage, collards, and all the wonderful green things from the winter garden. Amiable Spouse uses it on peas and beans, also.

Of course, the meal was not complete without just the right cornbread. Jan had also brought some coarse-ground yellow cornmeal from the gristmill in Foxworth, Mississippi. She gave all the sisters a bag of it, because she knew that we would need it in our cornbread dressing for Thanksgiving and Christmas.

Again we heated up the skillet. We poured a couple of cups of plain cornmeal into a bowl and then added some salt and enough water to make it stick together. We poured the mixture into a very hot skillet with just a bit of bacon grease in it. The cornbread sizzled as it touched the hot skillet, and we pressed it down firmly with our fingertips. After it browned on one side, we turned it over to brown the other side.

Finally the meal was ready, and we helped our plates to a generous serving of cooked turnip greens and pot liquor. On them we poured more of our special pepper sauce and a bit of black pepper. In our salad bowls went the wilted mustard salad with its tangy dressing, and crispy hot cornbread was served on the side. For once we all were quiet as we dug in.

It was a truly memorable meal reminiscent of our Southern heritage. We know Southern. As a matter of fact, we ARE Southern.

THE GARDEN AS A HEALING PLACE

Those of us who have gardened for a lifetime know that the garden is a healing place. I remember years ago when I was faced with the prospect of the death of a husband. He was terminally ill, and everyone knew that it was only a matter of time before his life would be over.

Those were terrible days. It was a time when personal needs were simply forgotten. As a matter of fact, they didn't even exist—not on any conscious level. After all, I was not the one facing death. Time passed, and my life progressed in a sort of suspended animation. I did everything that could be done for my ill husband. Nothing was too great a task. Personal tiredness and grief were repressed, and I continued going and doing whatever I was called upon to do without question. I just did it. I didn't complain. My problems were insignificant when compared with the prospect of death. Some time after my husband's death, I went to the doctor for a physical. It was my first realization that menopause was a thing of the past. It was all behind me, and I had not even noticed.

I remember that there were short periods of time when I was able to connect with something other than my grief. They were the times I spent in the garden. Somehow just the physical act of being out in the fresh air and pulling weeds or pruning and deadheading spent flowers allowed the stressors to fade into the background just a bit. I don't think I forgot at those times, but the burdens somehow became lighter.

One day I was in the backyard when a friend stopped by unexpectedly. She found me on my hands and knees, planting small pepper plants in the garden. Target, the cat, was on my back, and we were busy doing what cats and people do in gardens. The cat was watching each move I made with the trowel. Sometimes a worm would turn up in the soil and she would leap from my back and pounce on the hapless creature with serious intent. Afterward, she would climb on my back for a repeat performance.

Surely my friend thought that both the cat and I were crazy. She didn't know, though, that during these times I found release from the terrible burden that I carried inside me most of the time. When my time in the garden was over, I was refreshed. I was able to return to my ill husband with elevated spirits that both he and I needed to carry us through the difficult times. It was up to me to be upbeat and positive for both of us.

Sometimes I think of Amiable Spouse's experience in the classroom. He taught art to middle-school students for thirty years—in the same classroom—with no windows. Amiable Spouse loves the outdoors and nature. He has been a hunter and fisherman all his life. It's not so much because he enjoys pursuit of the game, but because of the connection with nature that he finds in the woods.

A picture of woods and snow-capped mountains hung in his classroom. Along the bottom it read, "Speak to the earth, and it will teach you." There were times, he says, when that picture kept him from falling into depression, or at least it lifted his spirits as he worked from day to day in his windowless room. By looking at the picture, he was reminded of the woods and pleasant hours that were spent there. For him, that picture was an enabler. It provided sustenance to stay the course.

Amiable Spouse must have known what researchers are now finding. Merely looking at pictures of nature has a positive effect on patients experiencing acute stress as a result of major surgery or illness. Pictures of nature scenes in intensive care units shorten the patients' length of stay and reduce their need for pain medications. According to one source, at least 12 scientific studies on both patient and nonpatient groups demonstrate that "just looking at certain types of everyday nature is quickly effective in producing a mild, open-eyed relaxation response." Anger and fear also diminish to the point of measurable improvement.

If just looking at pictures of gardens and nature offers real benefits, how much greater the benefits of actually participating in the act of gardening must be! We know that gardening is good exercise. Weeding, trimming, raking, and other light tasks burn about 300 calories an hour. Digging, hauling, and heavier work not only burn calories, but improve muscle tone and bone strength.

Regular exercise of any kind relieves depression. Gardening works better for me than walking. Once in a while I get really stern with myself and vow to walk a couple of miles every morning. I stick with the regimen for a while, but then my resolve weakens and pretty soon I find myself skipping the walking for one reason or another.

Working in the garden is a different matter. Never has there been a time when I had to make myself work in the garden. More likely, I have to discipline myself to stay inside and clean the house or cook. The call of the garden is strong, and often I long to spend more time in it than my schedule allows.

Other benefits are documented. People experience a decrease in blood pressure and muscular tension within four to six minutes after viewing a natural scene. Crime rates are less in neighborhoods with trees. Studies at the University of Arkansas found that women ages

50 and older who gardened or did yard work at least once a week had higher bone density readings than those who performed other types of exercise, including jogging, swimming, walking, and aerobics. Research has long shown that weight-bearing exercise can help women maintain healthy bones. Researchers were surprised that gardening scored so high. We gardeners could have told them if they'd asked. Those of us who lift sacks of manure, dig in gardens, haul wheelbarrows of garden debris, turn a compost pile, pull weeds, push lawnmowers, lift plants, and do the hundreds of other tasks that we do in the garden know that it is weight-bearing exercise.

Of course, horticulture therapists utilize the notion that working in gardens has a calming and sometimes curative effect on most patients. Just being outside helps the body make vitamin D, which is essential for healthy bones and may slow the progression of osteoporosis. Arthritis sufferers know that gardening uses large and small muscles, helping impaired joints function. Techniques can be modified for people whose hands, knees, or backs are stiff and painful.

Schoolteachers can also relate to the stress-relieving aspects of gardening. I don't believe there are many professions in which people are expected to do more than teachers do. Many of them deal with 150 or more students per day—one group after the other. They keep complete records and can tell you which of the children did not do their homework on any particular day, what their grade point averages are at any time, what their academic weaknesses are, and what strategies are being implemented to remediate the deficiencies. Teachers adapt their classrooms to accommodate every deficiency—hearing, vision, attention deficit, medical conditions, behavioral exceptionalities, and many others—and the adaptations are documented. Furthermore, they worry because some child does not have adequate clothing or seems distracted or unable to perform simple classroom tasks. These seemingly insurmountable problems are a part of the teaching experience. They can load you down before you realize it.

I know. I did it for thirty years. Often I came home and headed straight for the garden. There I weeded and planted, dug and mowed, and worked at a feverish clip. And as I worked, the cares of the schoolhouse began to fall from my shoulders. Time took on an entirely different meaning as I worked in the garden. The pace slowed. My mind cleared. I centered.

Charles C. Lewis, 1996 winner of the American Horticulture

Society Horticultural Therapy Award, said it like this:

> The garden is a safe place, a benevolent setting where everyone is welcome. Plants are nonjudgmental, nonthreatening, and nondiscriminating. They respond to care, not to the strengths and weaknesses of the person providing it. It does not matter whether one is black or white, has been to kindergarten or college, is poor or wealthy, healthy or ill; plants will thrive when given careful attention. What is important is that they receive the proper sunlight, soil, water and nutrients. Thus in a garden, one can take the first steps toward self-confidence.

Just being in a garden is a sensual experience. We cannot walk through a garden without becoming a part of it. All of our senses may be affected. We see and hear the birds and butterflies and the motion of grasses and limbs as they bend and sway in the breeze. We smell the fragrance of flowers and sometimes bend over to touch interesting textures. A sun-ripened tomato may be eaten on the spot, and from time to time we chew on a sprig of parsley or put a bit of sweet flower nectar on the tips of our tongues.

And as we experience our gardens, we come to the inescapable conclusion that a garden is a place of peace, a place of beauty, a place where healing can take place. I have enough sense to know that the garden does not mean the same thing to all people. Amiable Spouse came home from school every day and ran three or four miles. Others take long walks or ride bikes. To each his own. But I still recommend the garden. It's the place where I have found the most peace. Quite literally, it has been my healing place.

IV
Environmentally Friendly Gardening Through the Year

$\mathbf{M}$y garden is located in Zone 8b. In different zones, times given here may vary according to how far north or south of Zone 8b one lives. However, times do not vary enough to make the information unsuitable for other areas of the South. Remember, too, that the vegetable garden is not my favorite. Therefore, the primary emphasis on this section will be on flowers and landscape gardening rather than on vegetable gardening.

JANUARY

January is not usually as colorful as other months, but if the garden is tidy, its bones show to greatest advantage. Rake up leaves or pine straw and use them for mulch in empty beds. Cut back dead perennials—but leave any that have dried seed heads to provide food for birds and other wildlife. Consider putting out some bird feeders. They will entice brilliant splashes of color on the wing. Don't forget that birds need a source of water.

Landscape plants and lawns benefit from a deep watering about 24 hours before a freeze is expected. Moisture in the soil stores more heat during the day. Consequently, the soil stays warmer for a longer time during the night. Winter injury often occurs if plants are allowed to dry out. A good mulch of bark or pine straw and a good soaking every two or three weeks will lessen the chances of winter injury to your plants.

When planting seeds of winter annuals, be sure to plant them in beds to which organic materials have been added—especially if you garden in sandy soil or clay. Start fertilizing with water-soluble fertilizer when the tiny plants have two sets of leaves, and start thinning to the space recommended on the seed packet. When the plants reach three or four inches tall, fertilize with more long-lasting fertilizer. If you use slow-release fertilizer, you may not have to reapply for several months. Otherwise, light but frequent applications are recommended.

Don't forget to water the lawn if inadequate amounts of rain fall. In the absence of rain, apply one-half to three-quarters of an inch of water every 10 to 14 days. Turf specialists at the University of Florida report that more grass roots die during the winter from desiccation than from cold damage.

Take a soil sample for testing. Adjust soil as indicated by the test, and add organic amendments to the garden soil. Apply dormant oil to magnolia, camellia, holly, and dormant fruit trees to control scale insects if needed. Later this month or early in February, fruit trees may benefit from pruning and fertilizing.

Camellias are in glorious bloom. Sweet olives may bloom and perfume the yard if there are enough moderate days. It's bulb-planting time. Add agapanthus, amaryllis, crinum, freesia, hyacinth, gloriosa, narcissus, daffodils, and prechilled tulips and hyacinths.

Plant bare root roses, fruit trees, dormant shrubs, trees, and vines if the soil is not frozen and if it is not too wet. Plant seeds of achillea, alyssum, begonia, bachelor's button, calendula, California, Iceland, and Shirley poppies, dianthus, geranium, gaillardia, gypsophila, larkspur, lobelia, lunaria, petunia, phlox, statice, stock, sweet alyssum, sweet pea, verbena, and viola.

FEBRUARY

February is a good month to plant roses. Try some of the old garden roses. They are time tested and generally more resistant to insects and diseases than some of the modern hybrids. Consider favorites such as 'Archduke Charles', 'Old Blush', 'Mutabilis', 'Mrs. B. R. Cant', and 'Mrs. Dudley Cross'. Shrub roses should be pruned back to a few strong canes about knee-high. Prune climbing roses after flowering.

Deciduous fruit trees, grapes, and evergreen shrubs can be pruned now. In general, prune to remove dead branches and crossing stems, and to head back or reduce height. If evergreen broadleaf shrubs have outgrown their space, have been seriously damaged or neglected, or generally look ratty with most of their leaves clustered at the top with bare branches or leafless stems below, they may be renewed. Shrubs such as holly, azalea, camellia, glossy abelia, Japanese cleyera, and ligustrum can be cut to within six to twelve inches of the ground before growth begins. When new shoots emerge, pinch out the tips to encourage branching and a strong framework. Thin out some of the new shoots to make space. Do not try such procedures on needle evergreens, for they will not recover.

Crape myrtle branches may need thinning and possibly a little heading back to remove old seed heads. Resist the temptation to top crape myrtles or prune them back drastically because this will destroy the natural shape of the tree and will often result in weak top growth that will break under the weight of summer rains or windstorms.

Prune any summer- or fall-blooming shrubs if needed. These include butterfly bush, crape myrtle, glossy abelia, oleander, plumbago, Texas sage, and others. Butterfly bush, beautyberry and others that bloom on new wood can be cut nearly to the ground and expected to recover. Since flowers are produced on new wood, pruning at this time will not diminish the amount of flowers. Prune citrus.

Do not prune shrubs or trees that bloom in spring such as azaleas, saucer magnolias, gardenia, hydrangea, and dogwood unless they have dead branches. Of course, dead branches should be removed, and any suckers can be removed from the bases of the plants. Also, remove branches as needed to prevent them from rubbing together.

Now is a good time to bring some of the color inside by forcing branches of plants that bloom in early spring. Select branches with many flower buds and place them in a deep container of water. Keep them in a dimly lit, cool location, and change the water each day during the forcing period. Spray the buds a couple of times each day with water to keep them from drying. When the buds begin to show color, they can be displayed in a vase and moved to a bright room. Some plants to try are serviceberry, red maple, birch, hickory, redbud, Japanese quince, flowering cherries, dogwood, forsythia, witch hazel, beautybush, honeysuckle, apple or crabapple, mock orange, pear, willow, spiraea, and wisteria.

Dusting the plants in your home is as important as dusting the furniture. If possible, give them a lukewarm shower every two or three months. Alternatively, wipe dirty leaves with a soapy sponge, and then rinse. In addition to cleaning leaves so they get more light, these showers help combat spider mites that thrive in dry homes.

In bloom this month are camellias, loropetalum, deciduous magnolias, redbuds, red maples, native plums, forsythias, flowering quinces, Carolina jessamine, red maple, Taiwan cherries, and spireas. Bulbs to plant include gladiolus, agapanthus, amaryllis; crinum; freesia; hyacinth, and gloriosa. Plant seeds of achillea; alyssum; begonia; bachelor's button; calendula; California, Iceland, and Shirley poppies; dianthus; geranium; gaillardia; gypsophila; larkspur; lobelia; lunaria; nasturtium; petunia; phlox; statice; stock; sweet alyssum; verbena; and viola.

MARCH

Along about mid-March, spring fever afflicts most gardeners. We're just itching to start planting flowers for spring and summer color. Wait, though, until after the last average frost date for your area. Even then, be prepared to protect new plants from an unexpected cold snap. Take the edge off the fever by planting a few hanging baskets or other containers that can be moved to protected places when a freeze is expected.

When they have finished blooming, fertilize and prune azaleas, camellias, and other spring-flowering shrubs if needed. Most plants are stimulated to grow as weather gets warmer and the sun rises higher. Fertilize all those showing new growth if needed, including plants inside and outside. Replenish mulch around flowers and shrubs to keep moisture levels even and to help control weeds.

Mow liriope or mondo grass with the mower on its highest setting to remove dead foliage. Prune ornamental grasses to about 6 to 12 inches above the ground. Summer and fall flowering perennials may be divided as new growth starts.

The world is awash with color as perennials such as coreopsis, gaillardia, gerbera, Louisiana phlox, stokesia, verbena, and amaryllis bloom. Shrubs and trees such as azaleas, dogwood, forsythia, Indian hawthorn, spiraea, banana shrub, philadelphus, rose, guava, elaeagnus, hawthorn, silver-bell, fringe tree, Confederate jasmine, clematis, and honeysuckle sparkle in their corners.

Plant bulbs of amaryllis, calla, canna, crocosmia, Eucharis, gladiolus, gloriosa lily, haemanthus, zephyranthes, and iris. Seeds to plant include abelmoschus, ageratum, amaranth, balsam, begonia, celosia, cosmos, gomphrena, hibiscus, impatiens, marigold, thunbergia, vinca, and zinnia.

APRIL

April is an exciting month for gardeners in the South. Many irises bloom. Roses are on their best behavior. Beautiful shades of green and gold from newly emerging leaves cause us to pause and try to absorb the beauty of it all. Honeysuckle, banana shrub, sweet shrub, amaryllis, and many other flowers bloom in April.

As soon as the lawn is completely green, it may be fertilized with slow-release fertilizer such as 16-4-8 at the rate of one pound nitrogen per 1,000 square feet. See the chapter about lawns for more complete information.

Spruce up the yard with some colorful annuals. Though it is not too late to plant seeds, most of these plants can be purchased ready for transplanting into the landscape. Choose ageratum, balsam, begonias, coleus, caladiums, celosia, impatiens, melampodium, portulaca, vinca, and others. Plant seeds of annual vines such as moonflower, hyacinth bean vine, Malabar spinach, and love-in-a-puff. Soak seeds overnight or until they have swollen and absorbed water. Germination will be quick, and they may be planted in containers or directly in the ground. For yourself, hummingbirds, and butterflies, plant a bed of zinnias, pentas, lantana, and salvia.

Many reseeding annuals begin coming up at this time. Pot up or transplant ornamental peppers, cosmos, perilla, button flower, and others that have sprung up by the hundreds around last year's plants. Continue to add canna, daylily, gloriosa lily, lycoris, gladiolus, and caladium.

Azaleas, wisteria, and other spring-blooming shrubs and vines may be pruned when they have finished blooming.

MAY

When May arrives, we know for certain that spring is here. Most plants are actively growing, and many flowers come into bloom. Cannas grow tall and put on their first blooms, and agapanthus are in heavy bud. Lilies such as Easter lilies, tiger lilies, Oriental lilies, species lilies, and others add immeasurably to the landscape. Ginger lilies have come up, and some of the *Curcumas* have sent up spikes of their substantial bracts. Society garlic and certain species of black-eyed Susans come into full bloom. Purple coneflowers sport their first blooms of the season, and daylilies, gaillardia, hibiscus, lantana, summer phlox, rudbeckia, blue salvia, stokesia, verbena, and others accompany them.

Persicaria 'Red Dragon' and purple plectranthus (*P. hybrida*) promise delicate blooms and colorful foliage. *Cupheas* of several kinds are beginning their show. Purple heart and four-o'clocks are full-grown and doing their thing. Gauras were at their best in April, but they begin to bloom out in May. Aphids line up on the stems and tiny birds fly from the area each time I venture near. Soon I'll be cutting them back for another flush of blooms. In shady areas, hostas and ferns sport tender new leaves, and the achimenes begin to send up tiny sprouts. Amaryllis seeds may be harvested and planted in trays as soon as the pods split.

Tender perennials that gardeners in the South usually treat as annuals are all abloom. Porterweed, blue daze, pentas, fanflower, and many others color the landscape. It is not too late to add more of these long-blooming plants.

Caladiums that may have been planted earlier continue to unfold their colorful leaves. It is not too late to plant more caladiums in beds or in containers. They need soil at least 70°F before they will begin to grow. Planting them in cold soil often causes them to rot.

The herb garden is resplendent with blossoms and fragrant foliage of poliomintha, toothache plant, savory, chives, cardoon, borage, self heal, and scented geraniums. Rosemary, oregano, Cuban oregano, basil, lemon balm, mints, bay, stevia, bouncing bet, perilla, pineapple sage—and too many to mention are growing vigorously.

Bromeliads are showy on their cypress knee summer homes. Last fall they were removed from the cypress knees, potted up, and placed in the greenhouse. As soon as frost danger was over, they were removed from their containers. Their roots were wrapped in sphagnum moss, and they were tucked into crevices and knotholes in the cypress pieces.

Shrubs in their full glory are hydrangeas and gardenias. Butterfly bush (*Buddleia davidii*) is beginning its first flush of blooms, and chaste tree (*Vitex agnus-castus*) has begun to bloom.

In containers and relishing their place outdoors free from the confines of the greenhouse are calliandra, abutilon, angelwing begonias, and tender plants of all descriptions. Hanging baskets of firecracker plant and hoya are blooming. Wandering Jew, Tahitian bridal veil, creeping Charlie, and other hanging baskets are growing vigorously.

Heat-tolerant annuals lighting up the scene are ageratum, amaranthus, coleus, cosmos, gomphrena, impatiens, nicotiana, portulaca, purslane, salvia, torenia, and vinca. Begonias are filling out their space in containers and in the landscape. Ornamental peppers, yellow cosmos, perilla, and other reseeders come up so fast that one is kept busy potting up the extras or transplanting them to other areas of the garden.

Start rooting cuttings of coleus, basil, scented geraniums, shrimp plant, blue salvia, angel's trumpets, *Clerodendrum ugandense* (blue butterfly bush), *Clerodendrum thomsoniae* (bleeding heart vine) and other glory bowers, pineapple sage, and other shrubs and perennials.

JUNE

I have given the matter much thought and have decided without a doubt that June is the most beautiful month of the year. Deciduous trees have brand-new dresses of fully leafed-out green. The lawn is at its best. The world is all new and the worst of summer's heat is not yet here. The landscape is decorated with blossoms of altheas, hydrangeas, oleanders, vitex, magnolias, and such vines as honeysuckle, allamanda, mandevilla, passionflower, morning glory, and thunbergias such as sky vine and black-eyed Susan vine. Bulbs awaken and such wonders as agapanthus, calla, canna, hymenocallis, Philippine lily, gladiolus, rain lily, and crinum send up glorious blooms.

Crape myrtles are coming into bloom now. When selecting cultivars for your landscape, consider differing growth habits. If you want a low-growing shrub, select a low-growing cultivar. Shrubs can be had that mature from 18 inches to about 35 feet tall. Select one that will mature at the desired height rather than cutting the top out of the crape myrtle. For instance, if a white crape myrtle is wanted, consider just how tall you'd like it. A bit of research will reveal that 'Acoma' grows to about 10 feet, while 'Natchez' matures at 25 feet tall. Big difference!

Plant a colorful tropical for a splash of color all summer. Consider Chinese hibiscus, copper plants, croton, mandevilla, ixora, pentas, bougainvillea, or allamanda. Plant one of these in the ground or in a large container. They will bloom all summer if watered and fertilized regularly.

Prune azaleas before the month is over if you have not already done so. In July they will begin setting flower buds for next year's growth.

Check large trees in the landscape. Remove dead limbs for hurricane protection. Avoid cutting new limbs, however. Cuts stimulate new growth, which is easily damaged in high winds. Enjoy this, the most beautiful of all months!

JULY

Do your plants and the environment a favor by using grass clippings and leaves or pine needles in your landscape instead of sending them to the landfill. Use these beneficial materials around shrubs and trees. Mulch moderates soil temperature, blocks weed growth, retains moisture, and adds nutrients to the soil as it breaks down. Mulch can be the

lifeline for plants as they struggle through the hottest part of the summer.

After crape myrtles finish blooming, remove flowering heads if you can reach them. This may encourage another bloom before the end of summer.

Keep an eye out for fungus and insects such as chinch bugs and mole crickets in the lawn. If you see signs of damage, call the extension agency for treatment recommendations. Make sure that lawns receive at least an inch of water per week. Water on an as-needed basis instead of with a timer set on automatic, if possible. Keep lawn-mower blades sharp. Avoid fertilizing when it is hot and humid, as it often encourages brown patch. Consider replacing some of the lawn with drought-tolerant ground covers such as Asiatic jasmine. For shady areas choose liriope, ferns, aspidistra, selaginella, or low-growing, shade-tolerant shrubs.

Annuals that have grown leggy may be cut back now so that they will be full in the fall. Trim impatiens, begonias, narrow-leaf zinnias, and annual salvias back by one-third. They will grow back more rapidly if some foliage is left on the plants. Water and fertilize with a slow-release, granular fertilizer. Reapply mulch if needed.

Prune hydrangeas to dry for winter bouquets. Cut when the flowers are slightly aged. Strip off all leaves, and hang the stalks upside down in a cool, dry place.

Keep a lookout for butterflies in the garden. Plant plenty of lantana, pentas, or butterfly bush as a nectar source, and be sure that the garden includes plenty of plants for larvae such as milkweed, parsley, or fennel. Butterflies love mud puddles. One can be made in the garden by digging a hole, lining it with plastic, and filling with dirt. Be sure to keep it wet.

Late June or early July is a good time to root camellia, gardenia, azalea, aucuba, and other woody shrubs, as the wood is now just beginning to harden, but it is still in the growing mode. Root by stripping the lower leaves from four- to six-inch cuttings and sticking them in moist, well-drained soil. Keep moist.

Many plants dress up the border in deep summer. Ageratum, begonia, blue daze, celosia, cleome, coleus, dusty miller, fanflower, gomphrena, impatiens, Madagascar periwinkle, melampodium, narrow-leaf zinnia, pentas, purslane, portulaca, vinca, and several other annuals add long-lasting color. Shrubs such as crape myrtle, althea, and hibiscus add to the show. Ornamental grasses are beginning to bloom and sway with the breezes.

AUGUST

Groom the garden by removing old flowers on annuals and perennials. Continue to cut back leggy, straggly plants and fertilize them to encourage a new flush of growth and bloom. Set out tomato plants for a fall crop. Try heat-tolerant varieties such as Solar Set or Heat Wave. Watch crape myrtles for aphids. A telltale sign is sooty mold, which causes a heavy film on the leaves. Use insecticidal soap for control.

Soil solarization has been used to reduce damage caused by a wide range of soil-borne fungi, weed seeds, and nematodes. July is an excellent time to start this process. Prepare the bed for planting, and dampen the soil thoroughly. Cover with a clear polyethylene tarp. Secure the edges, and let bake for four to six weeks. Avoid disturbing the soil when the tarp is removed. Plant directly into this prepared bed.

Spread grass clippings on mulched areas if they are not left on the lawn. Leaves work well if mixed with other materials. Maintain a two and one-half- to three-inch layer of mulch on the soil surface beneath plants, but be sure to pull it away from the base of plants to prevent crown rot. As organic mulches decompose, they enrich the soil, lessening the need for chemical fertilizers. Most well-established shrubs and trees that have been supplied with a good layer of organic mulch usually do not need additional fertilizer. Mulch can provide a design element in the landscape by adding a contrast of color and texture that complements plantings.

Evaluate your landscape periodically and remove plants that are not growing well because they are not adapted to the site or are doing poorly because of the ravages of pests or diseases. Take a hint from Mother Nature. If plants begin to die, replace them with hardy, pest-resistant plants that are better suited to our climate.

Sow seeds of summer annuals to replace those that burn out in the heat. Try threadleaf zinnia, 'Profusion' zinnia, portulaca, melampodium, globe amaranth, and ornamental peppers. These flowers will add color until frost cuts them down if they are started now. Pinch back annuals such as impatiens and marigolds that have gotten too leggy. A light pruning of begonias, perennial salvias, artemisias, and coleus can rejuvenate them for the fall season. Remove spent flowers and weak stems; then shorten stems by about one-third. Do not, however, prune too heavily because plants may be severely damaged or even killed. Annuals may benefit from a light application of fertilizer or sprinkling of compost.

Pay attention to fall-blooming perennials such as purple coneflower, butterfly weed, black-eyed Susan, *Salvia guaranitica*, pineapple sage, Mexican sage, autumn sage, Philippine violet, firespike, firebush, cigar plant, ginger lilies, and others. Plan to add some of these to your landscape this fall or next spring.

Pull out fast-fading summer vegetable crops and add humus to the soil. Buy seeds for broccoli, cabbage, beets, cauliflower, mustard, turnips, carrots, collards, kale, and lettuce, and get ready to plant them when the weather cools a bit.

Angel's trumpets, Turk's cap, azalea, camellia, hydrangea, salvias, and other woody shrubs root readily from cuttings of established plants. Now's a good time, although they will continue to root until frost cuts them down.

Get ready to spruce up the herb garden. Purchase seeds for parsley, sage, thyme, coriander, dill, fennel, and rosemary. Plant in late September.

SEPTEMBER

Order cool-weather vegetable and flower seeds so that you will be ready to plant when the weather moderates. You may wish to order such reliables as bachelor's button, sweet pea, calendula, nigella, can-
dytuft, alyssum, mustard, turnip, spinach, lettuces, cabbage, dill, broccoli, cauliflower, and numerous others.

Divide amaryllises if they bloomed poorly last spring. Carefully dig and separate the bulbs. Add organic matter to the soil in the entire bed. Dig holes eight to ten inches apart and sprinkle a tablespoon of slow-release bulb food into each planting hole. Replant in the prepared holes. Leave the foliage intact—it will die down naturally. Daylilies, crinums, Easter lilies, irises, and other spring- and summer-blooming perennials and bulbs may also benefit from separation or division.

Many perennials are now at their best. Summer phlox continues to bloom if spent blossoms are cut off as they fade. *Gaura* is putting on a flush of flowers after last month's pruning. Butterfly weed, cigar plant, and purple shield continue to decorate the border.

Other perennials for seasonal color include Mexican bush sage, Philippine violet, cigar plant firespike, chrysanthemum, goldenrod, and Mexican mint marigold.

Blue plumbago and society garlic add their cool colors. 'Indigo Spires' salvia and shrimp plant create an interesting contrast in color and form. Forsythia sage stretches up in preparation for a fall show. The beautiful princess flower has spent all summer gaining strength and stature and now unfurls its passionately purple flowers.

Shrubby perennials such as firebush, golden dewdrop, and Turk's cap light up their corner. Adding to the splendor are the motion and color of butterflies and hummingbirds as they fly from flower to flower.

If your garden suffered from the late summer blahs, consider adding some of these flowers to your border next year. Perennials and shrubs can be planted when the weather moderates.

OCTOBER

Dig caladium tubers and store in dry peat or sand in a frost-free place for the winter. Fertilize lycoris and other cool-weather bulbs and annuals during their first days of growth. Continue planting seeds of sweet peas, California poppy, bachelor's button, larkspur, sweet alyssum, dianthus, petunias, and candytuft. Pay attention! Some, such as sweet alyssum, require light to germinate. Covering the seeds will result in no flowers!

Set out pansies, snapdragons, ornamental cabbage and kale, and calendulas as soon as the weather moderates. These winter annuals are in plentiful supply at local garden centers. Plant in amended beds. Feed lightly with granular fertilizer.

Plant bulbs such as amaryllis, iris, leucojum, Easter lily, lycoris, narcissus, sprekelia, and tigridia. Refrigerate tulip and hyacinth bulbs. If refrigerated now and planted in January, they will have met their chill requirement.

Continue planting English peas, snap peas, turnips, radishes, beets, spinach, carrots, and other cool season veggies. Plant transplants of broccoli, cabbage, onions, collards, and Brussels sprouts. Be sure to thin vegetables when they reach between two and three inches high.

Now is an ideal time to shop for winter annuals at the garden centers. Before heading out for your purchases, however, be sure that the beds are prepared so that plants will not be held in their tiny cell packs or containers any longer than necessary. Beds should be in a sunny place and a two- or three-inch layer of organic matter should be incorporated into the soil. Peat, manure, compost, or well-decomposed pine bark can be used for this purpose. Usually, beds need to be dug or tilled thoroughly to a depth of at least six inches.

Fertilizer can also be mixed into the planting bed. One to two pounds of balanced garden fertilizer per 100 square feet of bed area is about right. A light sprinkling of fertilizer every four to six weeks will keep your plants growing vigorously.

Plants should be spaced in the beds so that they are not crowded. The top of the root ball should be even with the top of the ground when the planting job is finished. Mulch will prove beneficial, as always.

Water thoroughly after the plants are set out. This is necessary to settle the soil around the roots and to drive out air pockets within the soil. Water daily until the plants are established, and then water only as needed. Pinch or prune spent flowers as they fade. This will keep them blooming all winter and spring.

Use lawn clippings and vacuumed leaves and pine needles to mulch tender plants and bulbs. Sow annual rye grass at the first of the month if you want a green lawn this winter. Fertilize with a complete fertilizer after you have mowed a few times.

Remember that plants in the landscape usually look better in masses of one kind of plant than in mixed combinations. Too many kinds of plants can be confusing and detract from the appearance of your landscape. Consider limiting your choice of winter bedding plants to one or two kinds if your planting space is limited. Plant in wide swaths or large groups for greatest impact.

NOVEMBER

Oh, exquisite relief! Finally heat and humidity so thick and heavy that you can hardly pierce it with a trowel gives way to cooler days that make thrusting the trowel into the earth particularly delightful. Many plants enjoy these cooler days, too, and the earth seems to breathe easier. Plants slow down, colors begin to show in deciduous trees and shrubs, and leaves flutter to the ground with the slightest breeze.

Seeds of winter vegetables recently sown begin to sprout. A frilly green haze floats just above the enriched soil of the garden as the tiny leaves push up and reach toward the light. New pine needles carpet the ground under the pine trees, and homeowners frequently take their pickup trucks and rakes to the park to gather more.

It's no doubt the gardener's second-favorite gardening season—after spring, of course. Tasks wait to be completed as the gardener scurries around much like the squirrels as they prepare for winter.

November is a good time to walk around the garden and evaluate the successes and failures of the past year. We find many things that went well in the garden, but it is the failures from which we learn the most.

As we walk around, we notice that many of the plants are now little more than dead stalks. Some of the stalks such as sunflowers, salvias, and purple coneflowers have seed heads. Other plants will be killed by the first frost. Many gardeners are unsure whether or not to remove all of the dead plants. Should we, or shouldn't we? Actually, there is no succinct answer. It all depends.

The standard answer in favor of removing spent stalks is that by removing them, any remaining energy is returned to the plant for root formation instead of being spent on forming seeds. Also, neat freak gardeners have trouble tolerating the dead stalks in their gardens.

There are also arguments in favor of leaving stalks in place. Certain seed heads add interest to the winter garden. Seeds that are left on sunflower stalks, grasses, and some perennials and annuals provide winter cover and food for wildlife. If we cut them down, we deny birds and other wildlife a tasty meal. Also, many butterflies overwinter in plant material that is left in the garden.

Removal of some plants needs no justification. Plants that show obvious signs of disease or insect infestation should be removed and destroyed. Damaged branches of trees and shrubs should be removed. Of course, weeds should be pulled before they set seed in order to avoid an infestation next year.

If annual plants self-sow, the gardener needs to take that into consideration. Some, like garlic chives, may become so numerous that they overtake a bed if they are allowed to go to seed. Others, such as cosmos and zinnias, may be desirable in next year's garden. When pulling these plants, shred the desirable seed heads in place. Next spring you'll be rewarded with a fresh crop of colorful flowers.

Continue to add fallen leaves and pine needles to mulch around shrubs, trees, and tender plants. Do not use more than two or three inches, however, and never make a mulch "volcano" around plants. Clear mulch a few inches away from the stems of plants.

It's time to fool the tulips into thinking they spent winter up north. Purchase bulbs now and store them in the refrigerator for at least six weeks before planting out. They will bloom in early spring before the weather turns hot. After bloom, throw them in the compost bin. Tulips are annuals in the South.

Dependable bulbs that will last for years may be added now. Some to try are alstroemeria, amaryllis, iris (Dutch and native), leucojum, Easter lily, narcissus, and tiger lilies.

Much confusion exists about what to fertilize in the fall. Do not, under any circumstances, even think about winterizing your lawn—or any dormant plants, especially with fertilizers that contain nitrogen. Doing so at this time of year could cause more harm than good by forcing new growth that will be damaged by the season's first freeze. On the other hand, plants that grow in winter, such as our winter bedding plants; lycoris, whose growing season is winter; and seasonal vegetables, need fertilizer to keep them growing vigorously.

Camellias will be hitting their stride as winter progresses. Both *Camellia japonica* and *C. sasanqua* are long-lived, dependable shrubs for our gardens. Both can be depended on to bloom and add color at a time when little color is seen. Choose camellias for the landscape while they are in bloom. Visit parks, garden centers, and other places to learn which cultivars you like best. Plant camellias in light shade in acidic, well-drained soil. Mulch well and water regularly until established. If tea scale appears on the underside of camellia leaves, spray with Ultrafine Horticultural Oil as directed.

Continue to plant winter vegetables. You'll particularly enjoy holiday salads. Even a few tender leaves of various lettuces, mesclun mix, green onions, sorrel, chives, dill, parsley, and other seasonal greens added to iceberg lettuce make a dramatic difference. If you do not have a vegetable garden, many of these are pretty enough for the flowerbed or to grow in a container. Be prepared to spray your new vegetables with Bt (*Bacillus thuringiensis*) or insecticidal soap if worms or aphids decide to share your crop.

Tuck more winter-blooming annuals into the landscape. Edge beds with sweet alyssum. Count on pansy, dianthus, and calendula for color near the front of beds. Plant seeds of stock, nigella, bachelor's button, larkspur, candytuft, and other hardy annuals for welcome color in the early spring. Now is the time to plant seeds of such hardy wildflowers as coreopsis, phlox, black-eyed Susans, and gaillardia.

If any tender plants are still outside, it's high time to move them to protected places. Before taking them inside, however, try to dislodge any insects that may be hiding. I fill a large plastic garbage can full of water. Then I submerge each plant, pot and all, under water for about five minutes. Most critters in residence inside the plant or container rush to the top of the water where I can handily dip them out before bringing the plants inside. This procedure has saved many little frogs and lizards. Also it has kept some less-desirable creatures such as ants and roaches out of my house.

One of my favorite things to do during this season is to collect magnolia cones, sweet-gum fruits, fallen hickory nuts, acorns, and other local dried materials for use in arrangements or for seasonal decorations. Grape vines twisted into a wreath make a wonderful place to display your finds. A walk in the woods will yield many treasures.

As keen observers of nature, gardeners do not fail to notice the migratory birds that pass through at this time of year. They put out feeders of various kinds and try to attract them to their yards for a closer look. Bird baths and water features provide them a handy place to drink and splash. It is for these avian creatures that many of our plants are chosen. If we have chosen well, we are sure to see them visiting seed heads of annuals and perennials still standing as well as berrying and fruiting shrubs and trees.

Continue to plant cool-weather ornamentals listed for October.

Consider edging your flowerbeds with parsley. Its bright green is a treat for the eyes in winter. Keep on dividing and transplanting spring- and summer-blooming perennials. Pot up your extras for friends or contribute them to a plant sale. Just be sure to put pots in a protected place to prevent winter freezing.

Gardeners who want fresh onions next spring should set them out this month. Be sure to choose "short day" onions such as Grano, Granex, Texas Grano, Excel, or Tropicana Red. Plant them four to five inches apart in rows that are one to two feet apart. Fertilize lightly every four to six weeks throughout the season. Late next April or early in May you will enjoy fresh, bulbing onions.

Strawberries should also be planted now. They are very cold-hardy and will produce fruit during early spring. Use "short day" strawberry varieties such as Chandler, Sweet Charlie, Dover, Selva, Oso Grande, Florida Belle, and Florida 90.

Other crops to plant for winter include broccoli, cauliflower, collards, turnips, beets, Brussels sprouts, cabbage, carrots, endive, escarole, kale, kohlrabi, leek, lettuce, mustard, parsley, and radish. For many Southern gardeners, growing vegetables during the fall and winter is far more rewarding than trying to grow them during the summer.

Many flowers will last throughout the winter if they can be kept from freezing. Petunias, for instance, love the cool weather but cannot withstand freezing temperatures. Consider planting some petunias in a container that can be moved to a protected place during extremely cold weather. Lobelia is another choice for similar treatment.

Plant a few herbs to enjoy during the winter. Parsley, dill, cilantro, fennel, rosemary, lavender, and all of the thymes love the cooler winter weather.

As leaves and pine needles fall, use them to mulch flowerbeds, shrubs, and trees. If you have too many, consider starting a compost bin or pile. Rotted leaves make an excellent soil amendment.

Sister Bonnie and I keep close track of the weather at this time of year. We know that a killing frost is sure to come, so we take many cuttings. Jars line our kitchen counters waiting until we have enough time to stick all of the cuttings that have been taken. Our favorites are begonias, allamanda, angel's trumpets, coleuses, cupheas, firebush, firespike, glory bowers, impatiens, mandevilla, pentas,

Philippine violet, salvias of all kinds, shrimp plant, tibouchina, Turk's cap,—and as I think about it, almost any perennial or tender shrub that gets killed by frost can be propagated at this time if cuttings are taken before the frost damages them. Most will root if stuck in damp potting soil and kept in a greenhouse or other protected place. They will root during the winter months and we will have a head start for the spring garden.

DECEMBER

I often think that December is a good month for Christmas and all of its glitter and tinsel. Somehow it seems to make up for the dormant landscape.

If you have not already done so, it is not too late to add some winter color to your landscape with colorful pansies, ornamental cabbage or kale, dianthus, sweet alyssum, or other cool-weather annuals. Plant a few near the entry, perhaps in a beautiful container, to lift the spirits of all who enter. Don't forget the beautiful gourmet lettuces and red giant mustard greens. They not only add color to a flowerbed, herb garden, vegetable or container garden—they also add spice to the salad bowl and beautiful garnishes for holiday meals.

Prune hollies, nandinas, pyracanthas, and junipers for holiday decorations. Consider planting a holly to provide decorations for next year, as well as berries relished by many of our birds. Think twice, however, before planting berrying nandina (*Nandina domestica*) and coral ardisia (*Ardisia crenata*), as they are on the list of invasive species in some Southern states.

Keep holiday amaryllis bulbs after they finish flowering. Next spring they can be planted in the garden, for they are perfectly hardy in the South.

Many people enjoy having a live Christmas tree each year, and choosing just the perfect one is a rite of the season. Of course, we want to keep them in good condition as long as possible. The best way to get a fresh tree is to cut your own. If that is not possible, many fine trees can be purchased from retail lots. Watch for new shipments and purchase one as soon as it is unloaded. When you get the tree home and ready to set up, cut off an inch or so from the bottom of the trunk and place the tree in water immediately. If you are not ready to decorate, leave it outside in a cool, shady place.

Never let the water level go below the cut surface. When that happens, a seal of dried sap forms over the cut stump in four to six hours and the tree is no longer able to absorb water. If this happens, make another fresh cut to the base of the tree's stump.

Be sure to check the water level frequently. A tree can absorb as much as a gallon of water in the first 24 hours plus one or more quarts each day during the first week. As long as the tree is taking up water, it is relatively fire resistant.

Disregard all those fancy recipes or products that are supposed to prolong the life of your tree. Research shows that plain water is the best preservative for Christmas trees.

To be sure that your poinsettia will last through the holidays, choose a healthy plant that has been cared for properly before you purchase it. After you get it home, avoid placing it near hot or cold drafts. An optimum temperature would be 60°F to 68°F; temperatures above 75°F can cause them to decline. Overwatering kills the roots of poinsettias. Either remove decorative foil wrappers or punch holes in them so that excess water can drain away. Water when dry, and place near a bright window but not in direct sun.

Be careful of these poisonous holiday plants: azalea, mistletoe, Jerusalem cherry, and Christmas holly berries. Avoid using them where children can gain access to them. Fortunately, the poinsettia is not at all toxic. Researchers at Ohio State University indicated that a child could eat 500 to 600 poinsettia leaves and not show any signs of poisoning.

Enjoy eating turnip and mustard greens, collards, and other leafy greens from the garden. Even if you have not grown your own, they are in plentiful supply at supermarkets and vegetable stands. Consider purchasing an assortment of gourmet lettuces to add to the garden now. They add color, interest, and good taste to herb, vegetable, and container gardens as well as to flowerbeds.

Manipulate the color of next summer's hydrangeas now. Add lime if pink is desired and aluminum sulfate if you want next year's flowers to be blue. Follow directions. Too much of anything will influence the ability of your plants to absorb nutrients. Moderation is advised.

Most trees and shrubs will fare well if planted in winter. Plants set out now will grow roots out into the surrounding soil over the winter and have a head start over plants set out in spring. Summer's heat stresses hardy plants more than winter's cold.

Use our glorious magnolia leaves, grapevines, and other native plant materials to make beautiful wreaths and swags. Prune hollies, pyracanthas, podocarpus, and junipers. In fact, with our wealth of evergreen material, there is no need to look beyond the garden or the woods for holiday decorations.

If a freeze is predicted, water your landscape thoroughly. Move plants in containers into protective structures. Mulch around outdoor plants to protect the roots. If plants must be covered for protection, be sure to remove the covering as soon as temperatures are above freezing. Avoid using plastic covering, especially if it touches the leaves of plants. It can do more harm than good. Plastic is a poor insulator, but it holds heat well. When the sun comes up the following day, your plants may bake under the plastic covering.

We gardeners float along and do our gardening tasks in due season. Each one is unique and different, and we revel in the opportunities and delights offered by all of them. Enjoy the holiday season and a bit of rest from gardening. Soon spring will be upon us and we'll find plenty of reasons to garden then.

INDEX

Illustration {in braces}   Color Pictures [in brackets]

B

Bachelor's Button (also Cornflower), (*Centaurea cyanus*), 118-19, [33]

Bacillus thuringiensis (Bt), 126, 155, 156, 222

Bald Cypress (*Taxodium distichum*), 35, {35}

Barnard, Ed, 71

Barroom Plant (*Aspidistra elatior*), 10-12

Bat-Faced Cuphea (*Cuphea llavea*), 106, [27]

Beautyberry (*Callicarpa americana*), 103

Beefsteak Plant (also Shiso, Wild Basil), (*Perilla frutescens*), 100-101

Begonia, 76-78
    grandis (Hardy Begonia), 78
    x *rex-cultorum* (also Rex Begonia), 77
    x *semperflorens-cultorum* (Wax Begonia), 76-77, [9]
    x *tuberhybrida* (Tuberous Begonia), 77

Begoniaceae (Begonia family), 76

Beneficial Insects, 153-54, {148}, {153}, {155}

Berberidaceae (Barberry family), 57

Biological Controls, 154-56

Black Alder (*Ilex verticillata*), 42

Black, Bob, 176

Blackgum (*Nyssa sylvatica*), 38, {38}

Black Swallowtail, Larvae, 192, {192}

Blue Agave (*Agave tequilana*), 45

Blue Butterfly Bush (also Blue Glory Bower), (*Clerodendron myricoides* 'Ugandense'), 107, [28]

Blue Daze (*Evolvulus glomeratus*), 78-79, [10]

Blue Glory Bower (also Blue Butterfly Bush), (*Clerodendron myricoides* 'Ugandense'), 107

Border grass (*Liriope* spp.), 9-10, [1]

Botanical Controls, 158-60

Brassica oleracea (Ornamental Cabbage and Kale), 125-26

Brassicaceae (Mustard family), 119, 125, 131, 135, [37]

Broomsedge Bluestem (*Andropogon virginicus*), 23

Bt (*Bacillus thuringiensis*), 126, 155, 156, 222

Burr, Betty, 7-8

Bush Allamanda (*Allamanda schottii*), 75

Butter Daisy, 91, [16]

Buttonflower (*Centratherum intermedium*), 80-81, [11]

C

Caladium, 212-13, 218, {212}

Calathea louisae (Emerald Feather Calathea), 12-14, {12}

Calendula officinalis (Pot Marigold), 136

Callicarpa americana (Beautyberry), 103

Camellia, 221

Camphor Tree, (*Cinnamomum camphora*), 172-73

Candytuft (*Iberis umbellata*), 119-20, [34]

Cape Jasmine (also Gardenia), (*Gardenia jasminoides*), 52-53, {52}

Caprifoliaceae (Honeysuckle family), 39

Capsicum annuum (Ornamental Pepper), 95-96, [18]

Cardinal Spear (also Cherokee Bean, Coral Bean), (*Erythrina herbacea*), 49-51, {49}

Carex morrowii (Japanese Sedge), 16-17, [3]

Cashmere Bouquet (*Clerodendron bungei*), 146-47, [42]

Cast Iron Plant (*Aspidistra elatior*), 10-12, {11}

Cat's Claw Vine (*Macfadyena unguis-cati*), 174

Category I Exotic Invasives, 161

Category II Exotic Invasives, 161

Centaurea cyanus (also Bachelor's Button, Cornflower), 118-19, [33]

Centratherum intermedium (Buttonflower), 80-81, [11]

Century Plant (*Agave americana*), 43-45, {43}

Chaste Tree (*Vitex agnus-castus*), 45-46, {45}

Cherokee Bean (also Cardinal Spear, Coral Bean), (*Erythrina herbacea*), 49-51, {49}

Chinaberry Tree (*Melia azedarach*), 165, {165}

Chinese Juniper (*Juniperus chinensis*), 26

Chinese Privet (*Ligustrum sinense*), 166-67

Chinese Wisteria (*Wisteria sinensis*), 173

Christmas Fern (*Polystichum acrostichoides*), 19

Christmas Tree, 224-25

Chrysanthemum cinerariifolium, 160

Cigar Plant (*Cuphea ignea*), 106, {106}, [26]

Cinnamomum camphora (Camphor Tree), 172-73

Cinnamon Fern (*Osmunda cinnamomea*), 19

Clerodendron bungei (Cashmere Bouquet), 146-47, [42]

myricoides 'Ugandense' (also Blue Butterfly Bush, Blue Glory Bower), 107, [28]

Club moss (*Selaginella* spp.), 6

Cogongrass (*Imperata cylindrica*), 174

Coleus (*Solenostemon scutellarioides*), 81-83, [12]

Colocasia esculenta (Elephant Ears), 167-68, {167}

Common Buckeye Butterfly, 130

Common Lantana (*Lantana camara*), 172

Common Persimmon (also American Persimmon), (*Diospyros virginiana*), 47-48, {47}

Common Zinnia (*Zinnia elegans*), 111

Consolida ambigua (Larkspur), 134-35

Container Gardening, 112-15, [32]

Convolvulaceae (Morning Glory family), 78, 97

Coral Ardisia (*Ardisia crenata*), 173, 224

Coral Bean (also Cherokee Bean, Cardinal Spear), (*Erythrina herbacea*), 49-51, {49}

Coral Tree (also Crybaby Tree, Christ's Tears), (*Erythrina crista-galli*), 51

Cornbread, 199

Cornflower (also Bachelor's Button), (*Centaurea cyanus*), 118-19

Crape Myrtle, 209, 214, 215

Ryania, 159

Woody Huckleberry (also
  Sparkleberry, Farkleberry),
    (*Vaccinium arboreum*), 67-
    68, {67}

Y
Yaupon Holly (*Ilex vomitoria*), 42

Z
Zing, Zap, Zest, Adding, 185-87,
  {186}

Zingiber zerumbet (Pine Cone
  Ginger), 104, {104}
Zingiberaceae (Ginger family), 104
Zinnia 'Profusion Orange', 110, [31]
Zinnia spp. 110-11
    angustifolia (linearis) Narrow-
      leafed Zinnia
    elegans (Common Zinnia), 111
    Profusion (*Zinnia interspecific*),
      110, 111

Here are some other books from Pineapple Press on related topics. For a complete catalog, write to Pineapple Press, P.O. Box 3889, Sarasota, Florida 34230-3889, or call (800) 746-3275. Or visit our website at www.pineapplepress.com.

Gardening in the Coastal South by Marie Harrison. A Master Gardener discusses coastal gardening considerations such as salt tolerance; environmental issues such as pesticide use, beneficial insects, and exotic invasives; and specific issues such as gardening for butterflies and birds. Color photos and charming pen-and-ink illustrations round out the text, which covers perennials, herbs, shrubs and small trees, vines, and edible flowers. ISBN 1-56164-274-6 (pb)

The Art of South Florida Gardening by Harold Songdahl and Coralee Leon. Gardening advice specifically written for the unique conditions of south Florida. This practical, comprehensive guide, written with humor and know-how, will teach you how to outsmart the soil, protect against pests and weather, and select the right trees and shrubs for Florida's climate. ISBN 1-56164-088-3 (pb)

Exotic Foods: A Kitchen and Garden Guide by Marian Van Atta. Take advantage of year-round warm weather and grow fruit trees, exotic vegetables, and rare delights such as Surinam cherry. Discover tips to keep your garden free of pests and producing for years. Includes a wealth of delicious and nutritious recipes for drinks, main courses, desserts, relishes, jams, and jellies. ISBN 1-56164-215-0 (pb)

Flowering Trees of Florida by Mark Stebbins. If you just can't get enough of majestic trees, brightly colored flowers, and anything that grows from the ground up, you'll love this book. Written for both the seasoned arborist and the weekend gardener alike, this comprehensive guide offers 74 outstanding tropical flowering trees that will grow in Florida's subtropical climate. Full-color photos throughout. ISBN 1-56164-173-1 (pb)

The Ferns of Florida by Gil Nelson. The first field guide in 25 years to treat Florida's amazing variety of ferns. Includes color plates with more than 200 images, notes on each species' growth form and habit, general remarks about its botanical and common names, unique characteristics, garden use, and history in Florida. ISBN 1-56164-193-6 (hb); 1-56164-197-9 (pb)

Guide to the Gardens of Florida by Lilly Pinkas. This comprehensive guide to Florida's gardens includes detailed information about featured species and garden facilities as well as directions, hours of operation, and admission fees. Learn the history and unique offerings of each garden, what plants to see and the best time of year to see them. Traveling outside of Florida? Check out *Guide to the Gardens of Georgia* and *Guide to the Gardens of South Carolina* by the same author. Florida ISBN 1-56164-169-3 (pb); Georgia ISBN 1-56164-198-7 (pb); South Carolina ISBN 1-56164-251-7 (pb)

Landscaping in Florida by Mac Perry. A photo idea book packed with irresistible ideas for inviting entryways, patios, pools, walkways, and more. Over 200 photos and eight pages of color photos, plus charts of plant materials by region, condition of soil and sunlight, and purpose. ISBN 1-56164-057-3 (pb)

The Mongo Mango Cookbook by Cynthia Thuma. Much more than a book of easy-to-make recipes, *The Mongo Mango Cookbook* is also a compendium of mango history, legend, literature, and lore. It traces the fragrant fruit's genesis and its proliferation throughout the world's warm climates. It also explains why the mango's versatility and palate-pleasing flavor make it a favorite among the world's most creative chefs. Extensive appendices include lists of current cultivars and mango-growing countries as well as information on nurseries and garden clubs around Florida. ISBN 1-56164-239-8 (pb)

Ornamental Tropical Shrubs by Amanda Jarrett. Stunning color photos and full information profile for 83 shrubs including country of origin, drought and salt tolerance, growth rate and suitable soils, preferred sun exposure, mature size and form, flowers and fruits, potential insect and disease problems, and more. ISBN 1-56164-289-4 (hb); 1-56164-275-4 (pb)

Poisonous Plants and Animals of Florida and the Caribbean by David W. Nellis. An illustrated guide to the characteristics, symptoms, and treatments for over 300 species of poisonous plants and toxic animals. ISBN 1-56164-111-1 (hb)

Priceless Florida by Ellie Whitney, Bruce Means, and Anne Rudloe. An extensive, full-color guide to the incomparable ecological riches of this unique region in a way that will appeal to young and old, laypersons and scientists. A cornucopia of colorful illustrations and exquisite photos makes you feel you're there. The comprehensive text enlightens with facts and brims with intriguing curiosities while bridging multiple fields in a crisp, readable style. ISBN 1-56164-309-2 (hb); 1-56164-308-4 (pb)

Seashore Plants of South Florida and the Caribbean by David W. Nellis. A full-color guide to the flora of nearshore environments, including complete characteristics of each plant as well as ornamental, medicinal, ecological, and other aspects. Suitable for backyard gardeners and serious naturalists. ISBN 1-56164-056-5 (pb)

The Trees of Florida by Gil Nelson. The first comprehensive guide to Florida's amazing variety of tree species, this book serves as both a reference and a field guide. ISBN 1-56164-053-0 (hb); 1-56164-055-7 (pb)